PLOTTING

PEACE

THE OWL'S REPLY TO HAWKS AND DOVES

Some say a cavalry corps,
  some infantry, some again
will maintain that the swift oars
  of our fleet are the finest
sight on dark earth; but I say
  that whatever one loves, is.

SAPPHO
610-580 BC

PLOTTING

PEACE
THE OWL'S REPLY TO HAWKS AND DOVES
Ronald Higgins

BRASSEY'S (UK)
(Member of the Maxwell Pergamon Publishing Corporation)
LONDON * OXFORD * WASHINGTON * NEW YORK * BEIJING
FRANKFURT * SÃO PAULO * SYDNEY * TOKYO * TORONTO

HICKSVILLE PUBLIC LIBRARY
169 JERUSALEM AVE.
HICKSVILLE N Y

First edition 1990

UK editorial offices: Brassey's, 24 Gray's Inn Road, London WC1X 8HR
orders: Brassey's, Headington Hill Hall, Oxford OX3 0BW

USA editorial offices: Brassey's, 8000 Westpark Drive, Fourth Floor, McLean, Virginia 22102
orders: Brassey's/Macmillan, Front and Brown Streets, Riverside, NJ 08075

Distributed in North America by the Macmillan Publishing Company, N.Y., N.Y.

Library of Congress Cataloging in Publication Data.
Higgins Ronald.
Plotting peace: the owl's reply to hawks and doves/Ronald Higgins.—1st ed.
p.   cm.
Includes bibliographical references.

1. Peace.   2. International relations.   3. Security, International.
4. Nuclear arms control.   I. Title.
JX1952.H52 1990 327.1'72—dc20 89-22270

British Library Cataloguing in Publication Data
Higgins, Ronald
Plotting peace: the owl's reply to hawks and doves.
1. International security
I. Title
327.1'16

ISBN–0–08–033618–3

Printed in Great Britain by BPCC Wheatons Ltd, Exeter

TO LIBBY

Contents

Contents

Preface

OVER the last 10 years I have been privileged to discuss the manifold problems of international security with hundreds of experts, commentators, officials, activists and others, of all perspectives and views, at *Dunamis*, the open forum based at St James's Church, Piccadilly, in Central London. I am grateful to them, to it and to the many so-called ordinary people who have shared their fears, hopes and ideas. Like every writer on these issues, I am also indebted to countless authors, some mentioned, many not, and to the publishers of works from which I have quoted.

Dunamis, of which I am the Director, listens more than it speaks: it never campaigns. What follows therefore is my own personal struggle through the host of arguments put up by hawks and doves about this awesome subject. I have tried to stay in touch with the views and feelings of both sides throughout. Where I finally part, about equally, from the views of some new peace movement friends and some old Foreign Office colleagues, I trust I shall be forgiven. Indeed my central conclusion is that, in addressing the changing problems of a new era, it is vital for us to escape the obsessive toils of the old dualisms, partly by radically enlarging our concept of security and partly by reappraising what we can, and cannot, reasonably expect from the rough old trade of politics. Instead, I believe we need to construct a new coalition of 'owls' who are at once deeply alert to the many global dangers and cannily pragmatic as to the best means of reducing them.

I am especially grateful, for help and encouragement well beyond the calls of friendship, to Malcolm Dando, Geoffrey Goodwin, Hugh Hanning, Oliver Ramsbotham, Patrick Rivers and Victor de Waal. Sue Prior's help with the manuscript has been invaluable. Above all, I thank my remarkably patient wife, Elizabeth Bryan, who now breathes again. Responsibility for errors and misjudgements — and opinions — is of course solely my own.

Preface

Finally I thank Donald Reeves, Jenifer Wates and the whole *Dunamis* team, present and past, including the late Neil Wates, whose passionate commitment to peace, yet honest doubts about how to get it, still best define the task of all of us.

November, 1989   RONALD HIGGINS

Introduction

Map me no maps, sir, my head is a map, a map of the whole
world,

Henry Fielding (1702–1754), *Rape upon Rape*

IN A strong glass case only a dozen miles down the valley from our
hill-top house lives the *Mappa Mundi*, the unique mediaeval map
and masterpiece that was made by Richard de Bello, a clergyman,
around 1300 AD. Hereford Cathedral's proudest possession has
miraculously survived seven centuries of natural deterioration, riot,
effigy-burning and war to remind us of humanity's perennial
concern to understand not only its physical home but itself.

Map-makers like Richard de Bello were cosmologists as well as
cartographers: they sought to explain the world as well as describe
it. The world of the mediaeval pilgrims who flocked to Hereford's
shrine of the Bishop Cantilupe was one of largely unexplored lands
and menacing waters, of dark forests and grotesque beasts. It was
a cosmos of mysterious powers, of evil spirits and angelic ones, of
unpredictable events, of sinister threats not just to life but to the
soul.

Most modern maps attempt to summarise only a few selected
aspects of physical or human geography. By contrast, there was
nothing intellectually modest or scientifically neutral about the
mediaeval map-maker. He was not only cartographer but theologian, philosopher, historian, mythologist, naturalist and encyclo-
paedist. Hereford's *Mappa Mundi* presents a world view in both
senses, geographical and metaphysical, combined within an elaborate Christian symbolism. Jerusalem and Calvary are of course at
the very centre of a flat world; Asia, the East, is on top; Europe is
to the right; Africa to the left. There are Old Testament sketches
of Adam and Eve; images of Noah's Ark and of Moses on Mount
Sinai; sketches from moralising bestiaries and, finally, Richard de
Bello's personal plea for our prayers.

Surrounding his flat earth is an uncrossable ocean. Some think the *Mappa Mundi* was a defence of orthodoxy against the pagan heretics who were already daring to suggest that the world was spherical and that there were inhabited lands across that ocean. This reminds us that maps are too often treated as pure Truth rather than inevitably distorted approximations. After all, Truth does sometimes change, and change so radically that the old Truth may be almost wholly superceded.

Modern maps are generally thought to be as free of bias as are their makers of superstition. Yet for centuries we have unquestioningly accepted the common Mercator projection which shows the Equator two-thirds down the map and thereby hugely inflates the land masses occupied by Earth's northern peoples (mostly rich and white) relative to those of the southern peoples (mostly poor and non-white). It took Dr Arno Peters's projection, with its own half-way Equator and genuinely proportionate land areas, to demonstrate how misleadingly Eurocentric and intrinsically prejudiced and unjust our view of the world had been.

Current maps as well as mediaeval ones therefore remind us that selection and distortion are inevitable in any description of reality. Maps tell us much but must never be confused with the landscape itself. We must remain fully conscious of the kinds of selection and projection we are employing. What we call bias and philosophers call value judgements are inescapable to anyone who draws or writes or says anything. The remedy for distortion and prejudice lies less in avoidance, which is finally impossible, than in awareness.

The mediaeval pilgrim sought not only a view of the world but a world view — a philosophy, religion or cosmology with which to comprehend an otherwise baffling and frightening existence. Our own world is very different but no less baffling and frightening. We, too, are driven to interpret it and for us, too, the geography is not enough. If we are to make meaning out of apparent chaos we need not only a broad grasp of the main facts of international life — and planetary life in general — but ideas, concepts and values with which to fashion them into a reasonably civilised and coherent picture and then into adequate recipes for constructive action.

Any book aiming to interpret the contemporary world scene is bound to deal not only with many contentious issues of fact (just what is the East-West military balance?) but controversial issues of moral values (just what are the proper limits to violence?). Such a study must show awareness of the spiritual aspects of humanity's current dilemmas and of what the barbaric century of Auschwitz and Hiroshima has reminded us — the sometimes savage psychic forces for which the mediaeval map-makers employed the language of myth and legend.

A map is in essence a simple (if fallible) instrument for taking bearings in a complex world and that is what this book seeks to be. The reader might like a preliminary sketch of how it came to be written.

A Diplomat at Large

My first attempt to make sense of the contemporary world situation — an absurdly ambitious but necessary task — was in a book called *The Seventh Enemy: the Human Factor in the Global Crisis*[1] first published in 1978. In it, I argued that there were six immense, impersonal threats to the human future — over-population, famine, resource shortage, environmental degradation, technology racing beyond human control and the most singular example of that threat, nuclear abuse. These six impersonal challenges were intensified by the human factor, the Seventh Enemy: the frightening inertia and myopia of our political institutions combined with our own obstinate blindness, as individuals, to late twentieth century realities. I tried to end on a note of cautious hope. Some said it was so cautious they did not see it.

In making this mostly grim assessment I had been strongly influenced by a sense of the sheer intractability of the main international problems that I had acquired in 13 years in the British Diplomatic Service. I had served both at home in the Foreign Office and abroad in the Middle East, Western Europe and South-East Asia. I had also been fortunate enough to serve for two-and-a-half globe-trotting years on Mr Edward Heath's personal staff when he was in charge of Britain's first attempt to negotiate entry to the European Community.

That was not the only instructive failure with which I was involved over the years. My frequent, no doubt entirely fortuitous, coincidence with disaster started in 1956 with the Anglo-French conspiracy with Israel to occupy the Suez Canal and topple President Nasser — a massive and blood-stained deception, a last fitful spasm of British imperialism which ended in retreat and humiliation. Later there were crises involving Jordan and the Lebanon, in which Britain played far worthier roles, before I was moved to Copenhagen for a period of cosy quiet except for a sort of North Sea 'Cod War' amongst friends. I was so bored that I volunteered for the war-torn Congo of Lumumba and Tshombe. The Foreign Office replied that the cod needed me.

My period with Mr Heath, then Lord Privy Seal and the Foreign Office spokesman in the House of Commons, was over-shadowed by Britain's first European negotiation. We worked all hours, travelled extensively, bargained patiently. Much of my understanding of the capacities and limits of international statecraft at the highest levels derives from this time. In the end, our application for entry was cynically vetoed by the imperious President de Gaulle. It felt like two years' work down the drain.

Then I served for nearly three years as Resident Clerk, the Foreign Office duty officer who runs the operations room every night and each weekend. While others sleep or mow their lawns, his job, in sometimes chilling isolation, is to grapple with a stream of messages arising from the sudden events of a turbulent world — a threatened invasion or terrorist kidnapping in the Middle East, a crisis in Cyprus, a revolt of army units in East Africa, a typhoon in Bangladesh, the threatened failure of a trade negotiation in Tokyo or a tricky border incident in Berlin.

A Resident Clerk is far too junior to take important decisions himself (except as to which are important) but he does get thoroughly involved in the decision-making process. He sees all the telegrams and intelligence reports and directly witnesses the way Under-Secretaries and Ministers reach their often hasty conclusions. As they, too, are temporarily isolated, perhaps sitting up in bed in the small hours and bereft of other advisers, the Resident Clerk himself is often asked for his view. (Rule One for the ambitious: avoid or postpone decision if at all possible; masterly inaction sounds wise beyond your years and often sees a crisis subside. Rule Two: if you must make a decision, decide to do nothing. This is far easier to justify than an initiative that goes wrong. Most Ministers seem also to prefer it.)

After three years of all that — and occupying the busy 'Egypt desk' during the weekdays — I was posted as Head of Chancery, chief of the political section, at our Jakarta Embassy. This was

1966 when British and Malaysian forces were fighting President Sukarno's Indonesians in the 'Confrontation' War in Borneo. The RAF flew me to Borneo to meet our General Officer Commanding and talk to his staff, to get some sense of the infernal complications of making war in the jungle, before I went on to Jakarta. There we were in a peculiar relationship of 'no war — no peace' and, because the Embassy offices had been burned down by a mob, we worked in a bungalow behind barbed wire in the Ambassador's garden. It was a curious and sometimes frightening situation. However, a year or so after I got there, a combination of worldwide diplomatic action and strong but always calculated military pressure in Borneo (including many secret and totally denied British cross-border raids in 'Operation Claret') eventually persuaded Sukarno to stop his campaign. It seemed an occasional success was possible, even with me around.

After I left the Diplomatic Service in 1968, I worked for eight stimulating years at *The Observer*. In that less hidebound atmosphere, surrounded by often radically-minded commentators, I got much closer to the real world and gradually became aware of the tragic if understandable shortsightedness, parochialism and apathy of most ordinary citizens. And I saw in turn how this reinforced the inertia and the myopia of governments in confronting problems that called for courage and sacrifice.

A year or two after finishing *The Seventh Enemy*, my wife and I began a new life on our small hill-top homestead in Herefordshire and, as a freelance writer and lecturer, I was able to become more involved in various groups concerned with international, defence and ecological issues. I helped to found *Dunamis*, an open forum on security issues based at St. James's Church in Central London and, later, *Defence Information Groups*, a briefing service to parliamentarians and the media, now succeeded by the *International Security Information Service*.

These activities brought me into close contact with leading members of both the strategic community, civilian and military, and the various peace movements. It became clear to me that, unless we could find ways of defusing East-West tension and its nuclear perils, there could be no serious prospect of humanity devoting enough time, energy and resources to coping with the more fundamental and longer term threats from Third World poverty and environmental deterioration which had up to then been my main preoccupations.

Introduction

Humanity's Triple Crisis

I came to see that humanity is faced, in essence, with a triple crisis and a dual problem. The triple crisis is made up of:

▷ a short-term waning, but potentially cataclysmic crisis between East and West. (Despite recent improvements in their relations, there may be only a decade or two to find reliable ways of avoiding incineration by accident or miscalculation.)

▷ a medium-term crisis between the world's rich North, capitalist and Communist, and the human majority in the Poor South. (We have perhaps 50 years to prevent global injustice fuelling some sort of global civil war and perhaps worse.)

▷ a long-term crisis between Man and Nature, a profound, perhaps perennial, conflict between human appetites and the planet's finite resources.

The dual problem immediately facing humanity is: how to devise the right sort of policies for a sustainable human future of relative peace, plenty and social justice; and how to persuade governments to adopt and co-operate in these policies and the public to support them.

This last point is vital. Right policies are not automatically persuasive. An 'ideal' policy that cannot be sold is useless or worse. We need to devote much more attention not just to the 'issues' but to the political process, its serious limitations and its opportunities.

This book argues that we need a radical re-definition of national and international security to take account of all three of the human crises. It sees the East-West conflict as the most urgent of these but the dogmas of doves and hawks, like their shared obsession with weapons, as equally unhelpful.

I see no reason why we must choose between the doves' total renunciation of nuclear weapons and the hawks' grateful acceptance of them. Having spent some years on both sides of the nuclear fence, I have come to a different view from either of these, to a kind of lateral thinking that has less to do with formulae (though these play a part) than with the gradual changing of agendas, the practice of step-by-step co-operation, the slow building of limited confidence, the development of a more creative diplomacy and the eventual transformation of the remaining nuclear weapons into the almost ritualised role of 'weapons of last resort'.

Of one conclusion I am entirely confident: long-term stability between East and West will hinge far less on the two Superpowers driving hard bargains on arms than on the careful cultivation of constructive political processes leading to mutual reassurance.

The Course to Peace

We must in effect learn to plot peace stage by stage rather than persist in the belief, common to many doves *and* hawks, that we can eventually discover the one great formula that will enable us finally to engineer its achievement. We need to plot peace in the sense of navigating towards safer waters, like a mariner plots his course in careful consciousness of rocks and eddies and constantly shifting conditions of tide and wind. We need to plot our course despite the frequent unreliability of our charts and persist, despite the limited competence of our officers and the often irrational behaviour of a divided and sometimes rebellious crew.

We have to recognise that our voyage has no limit of length or duration and no precise or permanent destination. Some may call it a voyage towards a land of peace, justice and stability but we should realise that we shall never finally reach such a place. We shall, I pray, come unsteadily closer to much calmer and kinder waters but new squalls and tempests are always likely to re-emerge.

Even though plotting peace already seems treacherously difficult for a single ship of state, we must also fully recognise that we sail a sea crowded with suspicious rivals under other flags. We are all in danger of collision, damage or destruction *en route* and some ships of state are especially hard to persuade to navigate in the same general direction.

But there is another resonance in the notion of 'plotting' peace that I cannot exclude even if it affronts those who seek total purity of heart and action. I mean the 'plotting' involved in secret diplomacy, back-room deals, and even international arm-twisting. Idealists see such manoeuvrings as intrinsically corrupting and entirely dispensable. Few of us find them exactly appealing and they can in truth be corrupting. They are also often unavoidable, sometimes essential. Innocence itself can be corrupting if it distorts one's perceptions of an often cruel world. In any case, peace and a modicum of justice are prizes for which it is worth spending a little virtue.

It might also be objected that 'plotting' peace sounds rather like the sometimes cynical pragmatism traditionally practised by statesmen and diplomats of the past. There is something in this: the moralistic propaganda and megaphone diplomacy of the nuclear and televisual age would have appalled Talleyrand with his sensible motto of '*Pas trop de zèle*'. The past still offers useful lessons.

Yet traditional statecraft and diplomacy have one great drawback: while highly suited to preserving the *status quo*, for which they were after all largely developed, they are inadequate by themselves where large and urgent changes are required, not least in the policies of the most powerful states. Traditional thinking about international security must therefore be amplified, enriched and energised if we are not only to transform relations between the Superpowers but find the breathing space — and the energy — with which to tackle the wider problems of human deprivation and environmental depletion.

Only when East and West can work out ways of not dying together may humanity at large work out ways of living together, and in harmony with the limits of its finite planet. As this book finally goes to press in November 1989, the Berlin Wall has crumbled and the political revolution that had begun in the Soviet Union, Poland and Hungary has spread to East Germany and Czechoslovakia, and even, tentatively, into Bulgaria. Talk of the end of the Cold War, of a reunited Germany and of the dissolution of the military blocs has suddenly become common and further immense changes are certainly now on their way. Yet terrible shocks and reverses are also still possible so, although there can be larger hopes of a secure peace, there must also be anxiety about a phase of inevitable instability.

The splintering of Cold War barriers and old certainties makes the radical philosophy of the co-operative security articulated in this book not only more necessary than ever but more achievable.

Hectic excitement at the progress of freedom can now give way to cool, practical thought about how to build the mutual reassurance vital to the various power groupings collaborating in meeting the shared global challenges.

PART I

Diagnosis

1

Looking Life in the Eyes

We have talked our extermination to death.
Robert Lowell, poet, 1917–77

FOR MOST of the time since the atomic bomb crashed unmercifully into human consciousness in the summer of 1945 we have remained obsessed by the problem of international security but have been talking at each other or past each other, not with each other. Whether between radical and conservative, hawk and dove, or East and West, the debate has been fervent, the arguments often fierce, the loquacity undeniable and the listening poor. The result has been the vulgarisation of most public and media discussion of the issues and a descent into arid slogan-swopping.

When listening is poor, so is the learning and hence also the chance of creative thinking and the prospects for compromise and constructive movement. Indeed, compromise itself has acquired for many — on both sides of the various divides — the smell of weakness, even depravity; of a willingness to bargain with evil. All sorts of extreme positions have prospered. Absolute principles and absolute condemnations have flourished. Pragmatic approaches have attracted less interest and little commitment.

In recent years, there has been some real dialogue and hence learning among specialists in the universities, in parts of the media and in some corners of the political world. Very remarkable groups of young strategic thinkers have also emerged. Broadly speaking, however, people have tended to identify themselves early and firmly on one side or other and have neither conversed nor budged. Even after President Gorbachev's electrifying speech at the United Nations in December 1988, there were some voices immediately warning of 'an attack with an olive branch', and some heralding a

3

secular Messiah. It may, of course, be right sometimes to caution against complacency or to applaud vision but we must all beware knee-jerk stereotyped responses of whatever kind.

Most newspapers, like most political parties, have stuck rigidly to one basic line. Most publishers will frankly say they are only interested in extreme (or clearly defined) views and genuinely believe they reflect the public appetite, while reinforcing its primitive over-simplifications. Most books on defence and security issues are readily identifiable from the outset as essentially committed either to a total rejection or to a ready acceptance of nuclear arms. To me, it is odd that so many people can reach a view on an issue bearing so closely on the fate of freedom and the fate of the earth, while showing so little sign of hesitation, pain or doubt.

Yet perhaps the contrivance of monstrously destructive capacities in a world of strong ideological differences was bound to give rise to extreme positions and Utopian hopes. It may not be remarkable that visions of absolute destruction should foster demands for absolute moral virtue, an unqualified rejection of violence or a spiritual transformation of which this rejection would be a corollary. It is equally no wonder that the invention of absolute danger should create demands for absolute safety and hence allegedly total solutions, whether through overwhelming military superiority, total disarmament or total defence.

We not only have horrendous weapons; we know — or should know — that we are quite capable of using them. Over the last 75 years or so, mankind has learned to be deeply frightened of itself. A progressive blunting of human sensitivity has produced a curiously impersonal hatred of The Enemy. Its effects can be traced from the atrocities of the American Civil War to the blind slaughters of the Somme; from Mussolini's gas warfare against the Abyssinians to the ruination of Guernica; from the German destruction of Rotterdam and Coventry to the British incineration of Dresden; from the seige of Leningrad to the razing of Warsaw; from the industrialised slaughter of Auschwitz to the instantaneous obliteration of Hiroshima and Nagasaki; from the carnage of a hundred postwar conflicts to the high-tech torture and terrorism that is now spreading world wide.

This daunting backcloth to our times inevitably adds to our absurd hunger for the all-saving formula, the panacea for all international ills. And so, perhaps, may another peculiar feature of our period — an historically unprecedented confidence (some would call it *hubris*) in human 'can do' capabilities. Moreover, one of its by-products, the relative affluence of the world's developed nations, capitalist and Communist, also encourages a shallow optimism. Perhaps no human generation has ever had to find its bearings in more schizophrenic conditions: a combination of arbitrary good fortune, unprecedented vulnerability, technological optimism, uneasy conscience and underlying foreboding. What are we to make of all this?

Looking Life in the Eyes

To be deeply fearful for the human future is not now unusual. The mushroom cloud, the devastated city, the scorched fields and the desperate victims, whether of war or terrorism, of repression or torture, of neglect or famine, are common images of contemporary foreboding and the nightmares of children. As the Russian saying has it, we must look life in the eyes. Television news bulletins daily bring us vivid images of unreason, violence and deprivation. Our popular films constantly explore the myriad plots and repercussions of disaster. Much of literature, popular and highbrow, rehearses apocalyptic themes. So does much of the music of our young people, as they struggle to live within the affluent world's contradictions; of restless hopes and awful fears; of lavish entertainment alongside African starvation; of wealth without limits alongside lives without work and poverty without measure. There are of course what are vulgarly called 'merchants of doom and gloom' in every generation but the arts are the seismograph of their time. Before 1914, poets of all European nationalities were predicting a great war even though most people were comfortably optimistic. It is as if an inner self may sense what our conscious minds often resist or dismiss.

We are having to understand and deal with a new world of still accelerating change in which startling technologies seem already capable of saving life miraculously or destroying it comprehensively. As the American Catholic Bishops have put it,[1] 'we are the first generation since Genesis with the capacity to destroy God's creation'. Despite the distracting comforts and discomforts of what we call ordinary life and the insular distractions of our narrowly national politics, most of us recognise in some part of ourselves that the fundamental question of our time is simply whether humanity can survive.

Take the matter of our weaponry. Since early 1945 the high explosive equivalent of our largest bombs has climbed from 10 tons at Dresden, to 13,000 tons at Hiroshima, to 1,000,000 tons, a megaton, in the early 1950s. At Bikini Atoll in 1954 an unbelievable 15 megatons went up in one detonation and in October 1961 the Soviet Union released a test explosion of some 57 megatons — a prodigiously stupid exercise, militarily and politically as well as environmentally.

We have now lived for many years in an age of overkill in which either Superpower has had sufficient weaponry to destroy the entire human race. The world's nuclear stockpile today is about 18 billion tons of high explosive equivalent — 6,000 times the total firepower used in the Second World War. How can one understand such a capacity either mathematically or humanly?

Not content with this capacity, the strange logic of threat, counter-threat, pre-emptive threat and so on has prompted lavish investment on improving the accuracy, sophistication and 'survivability' of nuclear weapon systems and, indeed, of huge arrays of remarkable conventional weaponry and instruments for chemical and biological warfare. We have created immense submarines which can each launch 400 city-destroying warheads; terrain-hugging cruise missiles capable of flying thousands of miles before landing only a few metres from their target; nuclear sea mines, shells and torpedoes galore; nuclear landmines capable of incinerating huge tracts of the ground we are seeking to defend; nuclear back-pack munitions capable of erasing a small city; killer satellites capable of tearing out the 'eyes' of the opponent in outer space and enhanced radiation weapons ('neutron-bombs') capable of killing people while preserving property or, as others put it, 'while greatly reducing collateral damage'.

Following the immolation of Hiroshima, Arthur Koestler called 6 August 1945 'the most important date in the history of the human race'. After that date, he said, man had to live with the prospect of his death not just as an individual but as an entire species. Yet even this formula may be too neat and cool to encapsulate what has happened. We have to reckon with the extinction not just of our species but of all the beauty and wisdom that men and women have created, recorded and celebrated throughout the ages. The very possibility of extinction is like a cynical retrospective comment on the finest strivings of everyone who ever lived, and would leave only what has been called a scorched republic of insects and grass.

Responding at Depth

Nor would even the insects and grass necessarily survive. For if the recent scientific assessments of potential 'nuclear winter' are no more than broadly reliable, our new powers could threaten not only genocide and sociocide, the death of peoples and culture, but ecocide, the death of nature itself.

The psychic burdens of all this are heavier than we recognise. Perhaps we are all in some way what the Japanese call *hibakushu* or 'explosion affected persons'. Psychologists like Robert Jay Lifton[2] have suggested that we may have fallen under a 'death spell' in which there are various elements — deadened feelings, a kind of impaired mourning, elements of paranoia and the guilt both of surviving and of somehow having contributed to the disaster. As Jim Garrison[3] has said: 'All of us, whether immediately present at the blast or a half-a-world away, have participated in the death immersion Hiroshima signifies . . . Hiroshima replaced the natural order of living and dying with a macabre and unnatural order of death-dominated life'. These perceptions, and some of those so movingly articulated by Jonathan Schell[4] demand of us that we try to respond to the crisis at the painful depth that it calls for. As has often been remarked, we need the courage to despair and the strength not to despair.

To see dreadful possibilities for what they are and yet retain the will and power to struggle against them is a huge and sometimes stressful task. Through habit and social expectation we run reasonably equable lives, do our work, pursue our hobbies, fill our time with family and friends. We suffer personal pain, loss and disappointment but rarely allow ourselves really to fear for our world.

Yet is not Armageddon now a permanent possibility? Is the arms race not a reality? Do we not spend millions a day on arms despite the World Bank telling us there are still hundreds of millions of the 'absolute poor'? Opinion polls reveal that substantial majorities in the West at least expect a nuclear war in their own lifetime. Why then do so many accept this passively and leave the argument to others? And why do the rest of us so often translate the stuff of global dilemma and high decision into the petty cash of factional controversy and party political advantage?

In our wiser moments we know, with Martin Luther King, that the critical issue is very large and very simple: we can live together as men or die together as fools. We know also that twentieth century man has proved capable of much worse than foolishness. No one who has made the desolating pilgrimage to the pitiless camp sites at Auschwitz, as my wife and I did in 1984, needs further persuasion of the dark, irrational yet clinical savagery of which even the most civilised nations — and individuals — are capable.

A Positive Side to the Equation

Most people do not think about the human outlook in such large and gloomy terms. Some are too modest, some just live for the present. Others speak of the extraordinary adaptability of man, of our duty to hope and our capacity to love, or insist that God will provide. Others, more prosaically, argue that international society is probably more stable than it looks and that anyway no one could want a nuclear war. For myself I have increasing doubts whether such generalisations, pessimistic or optimistic, can be at all useful.

We should not, however, deny that our time has had its achievements. Since 1945, we have witnessed the liberation from colonial rule of about one hundred countries. Between us we have created a materially secure life for a substantial fraction of a much-enlarged humanity. We have facilitated a rapid, if still inadequate, spread of public health, education, transport and communications to the newly-independent nations. We have increased the number of nations in which democratic values more-or-less apply. We have had well over 40 years without world war (albeit with one hundred smaller ones). We have probably acquired the wealth, capabilities and expertise — granted global co-ordination and much political will (and assuming that the natural world can take the strain) — to contrive the basis for a decent and sustainable life for all nations within the next century or so. Not least significant, our best minds have become aware of the profound interconnection between such issues as peace, poverty, human rights and environmental needs. Global interdependence has never been more clearly understood, if only, still, by a small minority.

We therefore live in a consciousness of immense human potential yet also of grotesque human failure; a litany of continuing wars, millions dying of starvation across sub-Sahelian Africa, irreplaceable Brazilian rain forests falling in ruin, tribal peoples facing extinction, massive pollutions of air, land and water, accumulating threats to the entire web of life from greed, neglect, ignorance and stupid short-sightedness. We are ravishing the earth in the accumulation of a kind of wealth that for many is now going sour and for the human majority in the Third World is simply not available, or even perhaps possible.

Guilt, then, has to be carried along with the pride, and nowhere so poignantly as over our unleashing of the power of the atom. Here our split-mindedness reaches a peak; extreme hopes of unlimited energy and hence prosperity, and extreme forebodings about a capacity for 'omnicide'.

The Appetite for Complete Solutions

The proportions of these threats to human continuity have encouraged a profoundly dangerous appetite for complete solutions. Political and strategic theories, positions and commitments abound. It is as if no respectable citizen should be found without his or her set of clearly labelled convictions.

The media constantly juxtapose pairs of over-simplified rival positions, encouraging the highly prevalent and foolish notion that human affairs must be discussed in terms of black or white, yes or no, either, or. Media people tell us they have neither time or space for light and dark greys. They have little patience with 'perhaps' and 'partly'.

Dualistic thinking, with all its spurious certainties, seems to be especially prevalent in what we arrogantly call the developed or advanced world and has acquired extra prestige from its association with the noble, if flawed, intellectual revolution that underlay the rise of science and technology. Dualism certainly has its intellectual strengths and practical uses but its rigid categories and 'either, ors' are nearly as inadequate to the complexities of political life as they are to the subtleties of personal life.

Genuinely all-inclusive theories and all-saving remedies are impossible. If our technological wizardry has brought mankind both benefits and curses, one of the most menacing of the curses is the naive belief that solutions, in any strict sense, are ever possible in human affairs. Total solutions are only to be enjoyed in such disciplines as mathematics, pure logic and chess. In human affairs we can salve but never solve, improve but never wholly cure. One of our main problems may be the way we frame our problems — as if there is bound to be a complete answer if we only think hard enough.

What in the real world we can hope and work for are improvements in the prospects of peace, substantial help to the world's poor and reduced threats to our shared environment. All these are possible, indeed essential. What is not possible, either in theory or in practice, is the single formula that resolves all the dilemmas. Human affairs inevitably involve conflicting interests, conflicting values and warring priorities. Human desires and appetites are infinite, our means are finite; choices are inescapable.

There is no escape from the permanent human need, individually and collectively, to choose between evils. There is always a price. In my wife's profession of medicine it is acknowledged that every drug is also a poison, every act of surgery is also to some degree a mutilation. What matters is the balance of gain and loss or of potential benefit and risk. As in medicine, so in politics: our need is the well-balanced course of treatment rather than the magic elixir, sovereign formula, arcane spell or ritual chant.

No abstract blueprint will save us. Neither the cynic's plan for world hegemony by one Superpower nor the idealist's plan for world government are likely to produce a peaceful world. Nor unfortunately, as we shall see, is any academic formula for a world without nuclear weapons likely to prove practical.

Nor again, sadly, can we place hope in grandiloquent utterances like that of Willis Harman[5] that the 'true solution' will lie in a 'non-violent cultural change which is so deep that we overcome the programming that leads us to violence'. There is some value in that sort of thought but I believe there are no 'true solutions' in human affairs, whether philosophical, moral, spiritual, psychological, technological, legal or political. All these dimensions can make valuable contributions. All, indeed, may be vital. None of them is sufficient by itself. Our way can be neither simple nor easy.

2

Humanity's Triple Crisis

Short of thermonuclear war itself, population growth is the
gravest issue the world faces over the decades immediately
ahead.

Robert McNamara,[1] *Foreign Affairs*, Summer 1984

Perhaps I have been in danger of sounding like the grandmother of
the aviation pioneer, Eddie Rickenbacker, who begged him always
to fly very slowly and close to the ground. Pragmatic caution is
necessary but without momentum and direction it becomes yet
another recipe for disaster, a rationalisation for inertia, apathy and
passivity. Humanity's problems have become so huge that the
management of the world now plainly demands energetic analysis
and action.

I have said that humanity has to cope with three simultaneous
and interlocking crises of which the first, the East-West conflict, is
only the most obvious because it could be humanity's last. The two
Superpower alliances comprise only a small fraction of the world's
population yet their hostile rivalry is being witnessed by the human
majority with a largely powerless apprehension.

Humanity's second crisis lies in the increasing tensions between
the Rich North, with about one billion inhabitants, and the Third
World, now commonly called the Poor South, with about four
billion souls. This North-South conflict is deeper seated, more
complex and in the long run potentially more significant and
dangerous than the conflict between East and West. To put the
point at its most elemental, East and West only have to learn how
not to incinerate each other, an objective they might gradually
be persuaded to agree upon. North and South have to learn to
share their drastically unequal resources, a far more testing task.

11

Self-interest alone could bring a stable peace; justice will require much more. And without some measure of global justice, no sort of peace is likely to be long assured.

Both the East-West and the North-South divides are essentially of man against man, human group versus human group; they are conflicts over human values, needs and fears. Yet precisely this man-centredness has led us into the third and perhaps most enduring crisis, that of Man versus Nature. Anyone with the slightest sense of the prodigious acceleration in the growth of human populations, and of the destructive environmental impacts and insults of our galloping technologies, will recognise that our fragile biosphere cannot permanently survive the pace of recent change, whatever labels of nationality, race or doctrine are worn by its various exploiters. As Mrs Thatcher suddenly said at her party conference in October 1988, 'It is possible that . . . we have unwittingly begun a massive experiment with the system of the planet itself'.

The problem is no longer one of just conserving attractive landscape and decorative species but of meeting a gathering crisis for Nature's life support systems by land, air and water. It is also, therefore, a crisis for Man's values. The biosphere could endure happily without Man. Only such creatures as the tapeworm, the flea and the rat would particularly miss him. But Man cannot live without the biosphere. In the tropical forests alone we may well lose half-a-million species by the century's end, and another half million elsewhere.

The Pace of Change

The most neglected feature of our period is not change itself but its stupendous pace. It is only about nine millenia since our species moved beyond hunter-gathering to settled agriculture. The first large scale civilisations, including the Christian era itself, are still very recent in the human story. But change has continued to accelerate. Our century has seen changes from horse transport, through the motor car, to the moon buggy. In the last 40 years or so, we have seen the United Nations grow from 50 to over 160 sovereign states and the rise of powerful trans-national corporations whose annual sales have long exceeded the total national income of the Third World — itself a post-war concept and coinage.

A century ago only four cities exceeded a million souls. By 1960 there were 141 and now there are over 200. Mexico City has already reached 20 million. Along with mass-cities have come mass consumption, mass transport, mass education, mass media, mass politics. Along with mass communication and mass entertainment have come new social movements from welfarism and youth culture to permissiveness and the counter-culture. There are sharp new tensions, as between a revived materialistic individualism and a new alternative politics emphasising consumerism, participation, environmentalism, foreign aid, feminism and peace. The orthodox political structures have really not yet caught up with any of these ideas.

In an age of such complex change, not only in our material conditions but in our ideas, we are often taken by surprise whether by a Suez, a Cuban missile crisis, the fall of a Shah or a Marcos, the rise of a Thatcher, Gorbachev or a Benazir Bhutto, a massive oil price hike, a disaster like Chernobyl, a great financial crash like that of 1987, a political counter-revolution like China's since Mao, or the sudden crumbling of the East German Communist regime in the autumn of 1989 and of the Berlin wall along with it. We are even taken aback by more gradual processes like the rise of Islamic fundamentalism or the immense economic growth of Japan. We tend to be preoccupied by the here-and-now and neglect the longer view; we are obsessed by events and disregard trends, perhaps especially the immense, quiet ones, like population growth, resource exhaustion and environmental degradation.

Far too little thought is being given to assessing the various regional and global development options over the next few decades and their implications for all of us. Predictions are dangerous but systematic speculation as to the various plausible alternative futures can help us weigh up risks, come up with fresh thinking, test policy options and make more rational choices. Commerce and industry often employ 'future studies' as a necessary part of their equipment for strategic planning; indeed lead times for the design and making of new products, services and systems enforce it. However, most governments, except notably some American administrations, have sadly failed to follow their example. Democratic governments rarely look beyond the next election and tend to regard any official speculation, let alone forecasts, as perilous hostages to malicious leak, political scandal and electoral disaster. Edward Heath's Think Tank, the Central Policy Review Staff, was sensibly intended to examine the long-term problems with which Ministers were precisely *not* concerned. It was first emasculated, then extinguished, by his successors. (Nor has Britain had a single Royal Commission, the next best thing, for over 10 years.)

International institutions — except, very creditably, the Organisation for Economic Co-operation and Development (OECD) — have not done much either. Even the universities, mostly devoted to narrow specialisms, have largely failed to take up the challenge of 'thinking big'. From the media, preoccupied with 'topicality', even less can be hoped.

Against this rather bleak background it was heartening in this respect to be in Beijing in September 1988 to watch the Chinese Government's almost gluttonous response to the outpouring of ideas at the tenth International Conference of the World Futures Studies Federation. Two hundred scholars from all over the world were joined by as many Chinese Ministers, officials, researchers and professionals to explore both likely and possible developments in areas as apparently diverse as international security, urban and rural development, the future of educational and health provision and the status of women. Too few governments are showing the same intelligent openness to alternative futures. (The savagery of the hard-liners' response to the student demonstrations of May, 1989 tragically evidenced quite the opposite attitude towards democratic change.)

The Underlying Dynamics of Global Change:

Although 'futures' theorists will take different views about policy, nowadays they almost all agree on the main underlying dynamics of current global change. My own analysis of these fundamentals, given in *The Seventh Enemy*, was that there were basically six impersonal forces, each of which could threaten the human future; those concerning population, food, other resources, the environment, the technological drive in general, and the nuclear dimension in particular. Clearly, all these factors will play critical parts in the unravelling drama we are now living through.

The First Threat: Population Explosion

It took all of history until about 1800 for the world's population to reach one billion. It took only 130 years, until 1930, to produce the second billion. Assisted by modern sanitation, scientific medicine, improved nutrition and so on, the next doubling took only 45 years. At the present rate — 90 million more mouths a year — mankind will double again even more quickly. Within the last dozen years alone, we have added another billion, and so passed five billion. Most forecasts have the human total at least doubling to over 10 billion some time in the coming century, before levelling off.

Whether so vast a total population could long be sustained on a finite planet must be seriously doubted. As we shall see, the natural world has already taken an immense beating, resources are limited and in some regions hunger is already endemic. Some human geographers doubt whether even a population of two or three billion is sustainable at recent rates of consumption. They may be wrong but it is a thought staggering enough to counteract the nuclear and East-West obsessions of our time.

Of the billion or so people to be added to the world population by the end of this century, over half will be born in very poor countries with GNP *per capita* of under $400. Already today, well over half of humanity is Asian. India's population, now nearly 800 million, could well double in the next 30 years, making the country even more populous than China. Many Asian, African and Latin American countries are growing faster. Few realise that if birth rates were miraculously slashed to about two children per couple, the world's numbers would still rise for 40 or more years. Contraception alone cannot prevent the next doubling because the Third World populations are generally so young. In some of them nearly half the people are under 15 years old. The mothers of the next generation are already alive, and in prodigious numbers.

Birth control should, of course, be part of any plan for Southern economic development, and indeed global survival, but even where it is widely available, as in India, successes have been very patchy. The poor want children for that security in old-age which their governments cannot or will not provide. Any serious hope of voluntary curbing of family size hinges not only on birth control advice and materials but on higher incomes and education, especially for women. In most of Black Africa, living standards have at best stagnated in the last decade. Literally thousands of children are dying each day of measles and whooping cough alone. In Brazil only 32 per cent of the population are of productive age; the rest are too young, too old or too sick. One third of the

South's adults are illiterate. One third of its children have no school.

Drastic action is possible on the Chinese model — late marriage, compulsory family limitation, communal social security provision and the insistent propaganda of national discipline — but the political (and moral) price is high and no other Third World country has yet followed suit. Somehow or other, the world's political and economic arrangements will have to be adapted to further immense increases in sheer numbers, or chaos will ensue for all.

The Second Threat: Food Shortage

The real significance of population increase hinges on its relation not to space but to supply, distribution and sharing of resources, especially food. Where there is a food surplus, the poor often lack the means to buy it. Already half the people of the South are under-nourished. By World Bank standards, a quarter live in 'absolute poverty'. The infant mortality rates are horrifying. Tens of millions of children suffer irreversible brain damage through want of protein. Can we stop it all getting worse?

Until the early 1970s the prospect looked quite hopeful; food supplies were growing faster than population. Then disastrous weather cut production, the rise in oil prices slowed economic growth and new Right-wing Western governments were much less responsive to Southern needs. Food prices rose; world grain reserves sank to their lowest since 1945; food aid was halved; the fish catch fell; monsoons were late, floods hit some areas, and drought devastated others. Hundreds of thousands died in the sub-Saharan Sahel, Ethiopia, Bangladesh. Many died outside stores of grain from which they could not afford to buy. This last decade's toll alone has been millions.

With the North, capitalist and Communist, continuing to eat more meat and dairy produce — a nutritionally very costly diet — the world's food supplies must rise by an average of three to four per cent a year, even though world population growth is only half that. Bigger crops will depend mainly on more intensive cultivation of existing land with equipment, irrigation and fertilisers which are far beyond the pockets of the poor. It is they, of course, who are also the immediate victims of crop failure, plant disease, locusts and rats, bad monsoons and drought.

16

The Green Revolution's high-yield tropical cereals have produced gains — not least in India — but hopes of transformation have been chilled. Africa's food production per person has fallen since 1970 and some agronomists have called the outlook 'almost a nightmare'. If black Africa and parts of South Asia could be cast adrift and sunk — some people do talk in terms of 'life boat ethics' — the rich world could safely turn its back. In the real world a crisis in one continent could easily precipitate a crisis for all.

The Third Threat: Resource Scarcity

In recent decades the rich North has also been consuming prodigious quantities of the natural resources on which industry and affluence depend. Its energy consumption has been doubling every 15–20 years. The Age of Oil began with the century but we are already within range — 50–150 years — of exhausting all substantial deposits of oil and natural gas. A 150-year period is nothing, yet almost no one seems to care a damn. Even British coal, which is relatively abundant, is unlikely to last more than another couple of centuries. We can build more and more nuclear power stations but only at a high cost in money, energy itself and nuclear risk. Thermonuclear fusion is at best a long way off. On any rational long-term view, rather than an essentially short-term market force analysis, we are also running short of such basic materials as forest products, tin, zinc and lead.

Plainly we could be much less extravagant. We can conserve the irreplaceable, recycle waste, produce substitutes. But how long can we go on extracting or recycling at low enough cost to allow large-scale industry and consumerism to endure, let alone grow, and be spread to the South?

Narrow, nationalistic and short-term thinking has obscured some unpalatable facts for those who still believe in the exploitative cowboy economics of the frontier rather than the truly conserving economics we need for a finite spaceship — Earth. A resumption of full-scale, materials-crunching economic growth in the North will sooner or later seriously exacerbate the competitive tensions over strategic resources already evident in Southern Africa. As William Gutteridge[2], then Secretary of the British Pugwash Group, has rightly warned: 'The world today is facing a situation in which a growing scarcity of various essential commodities is likely to lead to increased competition for access to them'.

Furthermore, the Group of 77, an association of Third World countries pressing for economic reform, has demanded at least 25 per cent of world manufacturing capacity by the end of the century, compared with the present miserable 10 per cent. On recent trends, this is bound to take very much longer. Sooner or later, however, the annual demands on world resources will be several times what they are now and the likely duration of supply will be correspondingly even shorter. Politicians, some very senior, with whom I have taken this up, have said this is no more than speculation, that science may come up with miracles and that anyway we cannot be fussed about generations beyond our own. This is an extraordinary attitude, combining reckless optimism with an astonishing indifference towards succeeding generations. Can we simply consume the inheritance of our great grandchildren and go giggling into the dark? Apparently the answer is, 'quite easily'.

The Fourth Threat: Environmental Degradation

In tearing up the planet's surface and pouring out various forms of waste, we are also depleting or harming other more fundamental resources: the land, the air and our natural water systems. Much fertile land is being lost to towns, tarmac, soil exhaustion, salination and erosion. Many forms of pollution and destruction are assaulting our various ecosystems. There is anxiety about many rivers, lakes and seas in Europe, including the North Sea. Southern rivers are being throttled by aquatic weeds thriving on sewage and fertiliser run-off. Tropical rain forest is being lost at a rate of 50–100 acres a minute. Meanwhile the annual loss of top soil from the world's croplands has been estimated at 23 billion tons and the processes of erosion are likely to accelerate as cultivation is forced into ever more marginal areas. Increasing soil erosion must eventually lead to higher food prices and greater risks of famine, not least in Africa and the Indian sub-continent.

Noise, smoke, congestion, overcrowding and the other stresses of industrial life are well recognised. So, at last, are the hostile effects of acid rain, which were so long denied. Less noticed, though now rapidly growing in public consciousness, are the threats of damaging disturbance to our climate, regionally and potentially worldwide, from industrial dust, concentrations of carbon dioxide and other gases such as the chloro-fluoro carbons, to say nothing of the multiplying emissions of man-made heat. These climatic dangers (including a threatening rise in sea-levels) are coming close; yet for the most part of our industrial system still bustles on as if they were science fiction.

The Fifth Threat: Uncontrolled Technologies

There is something of the same wilful optimism about the way we allow science and technology to rush ahead without adequate social or moral control. The technological imperative is immensely strong and rarely questioned. Power is intoxicating, publication of results is treated as nearly sacred and application is allegedly unstoppable. Apart from the persistent hunt for new weapons and delivery systems, our century has seen staggering advances not only in medicine, transport, communications, the media, industry and agriculture but in relatively unfamiliar directions like computing, robotics, genetic engineering and lasers. These new sciences and technologies already hint at extraordinary future possibilities including the Big Brother society, the worker-drone economy, the fatal escape of an artificial microbe, the militarisation of space and other quite new dimensions in peace and war.

The benefits of technology have been huge. So have the 'disbenefits' whether in social or environmental terms. The miscalculations, abuses, accidents and unintended consequences have been nearly as prolific as the prizes. Not the least index of our failure of control is the savage disproportion between the resources allocated to arms and those to constructive purposes. Barely five per cent of total world research is devoted to the particular needs of the Poor South in, for instance, semi-tropical agriculture and medicine. We of the rich world lavishly experiment with new cosmetics, car stylings and organ transplants while much of the human majority lacks even elementary medicine, clean water, sanitation and one square meal a day. Meanwhile, we are suffering what Alvin Toffler[3] calls 'future shock' and are perhaps threatened with adaptional breakdown, psychologically and politically.

Technophobia is no more rational than technomania but we must be on our guard against the reckless hubris implicit in the common faith in the technological fix. Fantasising about feeding the masses on plankton or exporting human surpluses to the planets, or finding an all-powerful defensive shield, distracts us not only from the fallibility of all technologies but of all human beings and societies. The problems, like the remedies, lie less with our instruments than ourselves.

The Sixth Threat: Misuse of Nuclear Capacities

The nuclear threat provides the most spectacular example of technology running beyond control but since much of the book is about this I need only summarise here. Potential dangers of civil nuclear power includes the accidental release of radioactive materials, catastrophic accident such as a reactor meltdown, disastrous leakage resulting from sabotage, the loss or theft of fissile material and the further spread of nuclear weapons. The potential dangers from military misuses range from the obvious ultimate of total obliteration to every scale and variety of destruction from blast, fire and radiation, including that of virtually permanent radioactive pollution of parts of the earth and genetic damage to its inhabitants.

These, however, are only the ultimate physical dangers of nuclear misuse. We also must weigh the politico-military challenge of nuclear terrorism, probably just around the corner; of nuclear conflict between Third World countries like, say, Iran and Iraq; of nuclear threat or action by a Western client-state such as Israel, as well as that of direct nuclear conflict between the superpowers.

There are also many questions concerning the special psychological, and hence political, impacts of rival weaponries so demonic that no means can seem too evil to counter them. The combination of nuclear peril with viciously fast and accurate delivery systems is probably ideal fuel for mutual hatred, fear and paranoia. This also plainly intensifies pre-existing international and ideological tensions and distracts public attention from other global problems as well as subtracting from the resources available to deal with them.

When the stakes are so high, and hence also the potential cost of an accident, theft or security breach, the state's concern with nuclear secrecy and public security becomes so intense that liberty and legitimate dissent are sacrificed. French protesters have long spoken of 'electro-fascism'; whether the 'plutonium society' could also be a democratic one is at best doubtful.

From Vicious to Virtuous Circles?

All these six threats to the human future are profoundly interconnected and mutually reinforcing. For example, increasing population clearly puts new demands of food supply and this creates new pressures on arable land, on the wider environment, on fertiliser supplies and on fossil fuels. The enlarged demands on fuels, added to those from industry, tend to increase the demand for nuclear energy and hence for nuclear technology, and with that the risk of nuclear weapons proliferation. Human greed, especially in the Rich North, alone accounts for a large share of mankind's escalating demand for nutritionally wasteful animal foodstuffs and for what remains of the irreplaceable chemically-rich oil deposits which current generations are burning up as mere fuel.

The interconnection between the threats does, however, present opportunities as well as dangers. Policies which deliberately restrained the kinds of growth that depend on high use of material resources and energy would, for example, much diminish pressures not only on mineral and fuel resources but on arable soils and the environment in general. Granted far-sightedness, vicious circles can be transformed into virtuous circles. Yet that means drastic changes in national and international policies. Such changes would require a radically-revised appreciation of the six threats, which are still dismissed by most governments — especially the rich and powerful ones — as little more than worthy subjects for high-minded United Nations conferences.

The Global Arena

The political as well as the economic repercussions of the six threats could be momentous. They are converging within a highly unstable global arena in which the human majority of the Poor South already suffers a cruel cycle of deprivation: ill health, illiteracy, under-employment, insecurity and poverty. The gap between rich and poor is large and, for many, still growing; and to the injury of present suffering is added the memory of colonial humiliation and the awareness of continued powerlessness. We tend to assume things are getting better; in parts of Africa and Asia they are getting worse.

The nations of the Rich North still control about three-quarters of the world's wealth and dictate the rules of world trade and finance in (as they see it) their own interests. They control or heavily influence most prices, most terms of trade, most investments. They possess or control well over three-quarters of the world's science and technology, its heavy and light industry, its transport, communication and media systems and, of course, its armaments. The Group of 77, now comprising 110 less-developed countries (LDCs), want not just a new deal but a new order — the New International Economic Order. The famous *Brandt Report*[4] which so emphatically called for this, has sadly faded from public awareness but its basic contentions remain as valid as ever.

Tension and conflict between the rich and the poor is at once as old as the hills, and freshly and painfully raw. It is centuries since Cervantes said there were 'only two families in the world — the Haves and the Have-Nots'. It is only in the two or three decades of instantaneous global communication that consciousness of a savage gap in terms of wealth and power has become a central focus of international politics. To an age-old injustice has been added a brand new awareness and anger.

Tragically, the North-South division of the world is also racial and, as the almost inevitable tensions grow, the world's white races will need to pay heed. The Rich North is overwhelmingly white, the Poor South is overwhelmingly black, brown or yellow. The coincidence of privilege with a white skin is of course the more infuriating to people of other colours because of memories of white imperial rule and patronising insult. Moreover, the Poor South often feels it has shaken off political subjugation only to fall under a more crudely economic sway and more subtle cultural thrall.

Most of the rich world still looks at all this with a basic indifference. Capitalists say 'the present economic system has served the world well' (I quote Henry Kissinger) and claim that, with whole-hearted acceptance of the free market mechanism, poverty would disappear. Soviet Communists have, until recently, attributed Third World poverty to Western imperial exploitation alone and indignantly denied that Communist wealth and power are also relevant. When it comes to action rather than rhetoric, what the Brandt Report called ' the great social challenge of our age' is still largely ignored.

Meanwhile the huge accumulation of Third World debt, eccentric currency movements and the failure to harmonise economic policies have threatened to cause a recession, to multiply protectionist pressures and open up possibilities of a financial crash far worse than we saw in 1987. The rich world complains because its growth has flattened out while the poor world receives provocative images of a materialistic paradise on its tinpot communal television sets. Not nearly enough free market wealth has been 'trickling down' to those who have mined the copper, felled the timber, humped the loads or spread the questionable insecticides of the agri-business corporations.

My Foreign Office colleagues were always cautious about accepting generalised assertions about Third World deprivation and rightly pointed out huge differences between the situation of, say, the OPEC oil-producing countries and the drought-afflicted countries of the Sahel, or between that of the prosperous Pacific rim and a teeming, troubled country like Bangladesh. They could also point at much mismanagement, corruption, political oppression and financial exploitation of their own people by Third World élites.

Such qualifications to the usual emotive and over-simplified 'Poor South' portrait are well made. Nevertheless the deep involvement of West and East in the economic exploitation of the South and their own quite disproportionate wealth and power make Northern responsibilities clear. Nor could Northern peace and prosperity long survive alongside growing instability in the Poor South. Self-interest alone demands saving action.

Some Westerners fantasise about casting the whole Poor South adrift and make it paddle its own ill-provisioned canoe. The opposite face of this coin is a Western dream of self-sufficiency. Both 'lifeboat ethics' and autarchy are nonsense on stilts; even a Fortress America would still depend for half its oil on the Gulf and for more than half its other raw materials on Third World sources. Not only is the Rich North economically and financially dependent on the Third World but is also strategically deeply involved in it.

A New Challenge

The involvement is also environmental: no national boundaries will keep pollution and degradation at bay. The 'greenhouse effect', the ozone layer and maritime pollution have to be a common concern. Environmental degradations that were once thought of as incidental problems of industrial wealth are now seen as survival issues for the developing nations and a potential threat to all.

This was quite rightly one of the key starting points for the 1987 so-called Brundtland Report[5] to the United Nations in which the World Commision on Environment and Development pointed to 'a decade and a half of a standstill or even deterioration in global co-operation' and articulated strategies for substainable development. It refused equally to see economic development as merely making poor nations materially richer or to see environmental issues as separate and somehow subsidiary. It also lamented that 'we have amassed weapons arsenals capable of . . . creating a planet our ancestors would not recognise' and demanded, in essence, an integrated and interdisciplinary approach to global concerns and our common future. In doing so, it became perhaps the first internationally authoritative report to recognise in effect that all three global crises, over security, development and the environment, are profoundly linked.

Collision Course?

Mrs Brundtland's report, although unanimous, made less public impact than Chancellor Brandt's and even less in political terms. There was no return to the great hopes of the 1960s. The retreat from social and humanitarian concerns continued. The preoccupation with crude and short-term economic benefit has not lessened amongst the rich nations. Within a decade or two, the aggrieved nations of the Poor South may gradually combine to extract from the North by pressure what they have failed to secure by persuasion. North and South could well be set on a collision course. It is not easy to see what shape this will take. Whether Southern producers of raw materials could combine like the OPEC oil powers in a supply boycott against the rich nations is open to doubt but they might well attempt selective trade boycotts, the renunciation of debts, punitive nationalisations and, eventually, covert terrorism.

The Rich North looks immensely strong on paper, especially in military and economic terms. It is therefore salutary to note how the United States failed to impose its will on a tiny North Vietnam and the Soviet Union, likewise, on 'feudal' Afghanistan. Moreover, the great industrial powers are singularly vulnerable to selective sabotage: they are, for example, highly dependent on unified electricity and water supply systems in which one 'fuse' can rupture all. Ideas of great power vulnerability looked wildly improbable until recent years. Now, after a surge of terrorism and kidnapping, we are no longer so sure. Moreover, the rich white world will represent barely one-fifth of world population within a decade, and by 2050 only one seventh. In psychological and political terms this is a quite staggering prognosis which the Superpower alliances amongst others have as yet scarcely begun to contemplate.

The Human Future

The North–South division demands not only an intelligent accommodation but material sacrifices which the privileged simply refuse to make. East and West are still too obsessed with each other and too preoccupied by the competing claims of military spending, domestic consumption and their own social welfare to take wider and longer term dangers, economic and environmental, really seriously. Where acknowledged at all, these are mostly dismissed as 'hypothetical'. Governments have even failed to appreciate that, despite real improvements in East–West relations, the dangers of nuclear war are themselves far from 'hypothetical'. We must now further widen our diagnosis by looking at them.

3

The Effects and Chances of Nuclear War

> ... after a nuclear exchange the ashes of Communism will be indistinguishable from the ashes of capitalism, even by the most perceptive ideologist.
>
> Professor J. K. Galbraith,[1] *The New Yorker*,
> 3 September 1984

An experienced American scientist has suggested that the world's political and military leaders should witness an atmospheric nuclear explosion every five years, dressed only in their underwear. What most impresses is the heat. A senior Foreign Office official was bolder: he told me we needed an accidental nuclear explosion to drive home the dangers.

It is far too easy to declare nuclear weapons unusable. They have been used. They are being threatened. They do go off. We must not confuse the ethically 'impossible' with the practically impossible. British Prime Ministers among others hold regular exercises in crisis management of which simulated nuclear 'release' is part. Someone like Mrs Thatcher does not suddenly cast her character aside. Hawks and doves alike should be very clear what 'release' could mean in practice and what could precipitate it.

The Effects of Nuclear War

A Single Nuclear Explosion

Nuclear warheads range in power from the West's man-portable nuclear demolition charges to the Soviet Union's SS-10 intercontinental ballistic missiles (ICBM) at 20 megatons. Andrew Wilson[2],

26

amongst others, has given a well-documented account of their variety and effects. The estimated toll from a one megaton air-burst over Detroit, as calculated by the United States of Technical Assessment[3], is half-a-million deaths and as many again injured, within the first hour alone. Radiation, and especially any firestorm, would greatly increase these figures. Dr H. Jack Geiger[4], who has closely analysed them, says:

> Even the conservative estimates are beyond anything in all recorded human experience. Never have more than a million people with profound and incapacitating injuries been located in one place at one time — injuries, furthermore, that require the most complex and technologically sophisticated medical care for effective treatment. Third degree burns cases alone would probably exceed 200,000 — 100 times more than all the intensive care burn beds in the United States.

Despite such careful analysis there will always be idiots who will not face the facts, some of them in high positions. A former United States Army General[5] has said: 'All you need to do to escape the effects of a one megaton bomb is to walk for an hour and hide behind a bush'. Thomas K. Jones, then President Reagan's Deputy Under-Secretary of Defence told Robert Scheer[6], that nuclear war would not be nearly as devastating as we had been led to believe: 'If there are enough shovels to go round, everybody is going to make it'. The shovels were for digging holes and throwing the soil on the improvised roofs. 'It is the dirt that does it', said Mr Jones.

A Massive Nuclear Attack

Death tolls depend not only on the number and size of the warheads but on whether most of the weapons are ground-burst to maximise radioactive fallout, on whether the population is in the streets or hiding deep in shelters, and on the luck of the prevailing winds. An official American scenario[7] foresaw a reprisal attack hitting Moscow with 60 warheads equivalent to 1,400 Hiroshima bombs. Talk about over-kill! The same report concluded that in a general nuclear war each side would lose 25 million – 100 million dead and have 65 – 90 per cent of its industry destroyed, along with its 200 largest cities.

Such statistics obscure the realities, even for the survivors. Thousands of corpses littering streets filled with collapsed buildings, thousands trapped in the wreckage; people with appalling injuries screaming helplessly out of blackened faces, the blinded stumbling through smoking rubble. Any intact fire and rescue vehicles are mostly immobilised. Fires are raging from broken gas mains, water mains are flooding, power lines are down, bridges have fallen and most hospitals have been destroyed. Oil refineries explode and nuclear power reactors are turned into devastating radiological weapons. We are speaking of a scale of calamity that would make the Armenian earthquake of 1988 look trivial and its surviving medical resources lavish.

Many strategies, including NATO's, involve not only targeting the enemy's forces but also his 'war recovery capability'. We must therefore contemplate extremely widespread destruction, a smashed infrastructure, gross shortages, debilitating epidemics and a virtual absence of outside help, combined with a profound psychic shock. All confidence in traditional values would go and social anarchy would almost certainly follow with aggressive bands rampaging for scarce resources. To suggest that democratic freedoms or capitalism or socialism or even basic social order could survive in such chaos is plainly absurd. Yet worse could follow.

Nuclear Winter

All flesh is grass: cold and dark kill the grass. This is the essence of a now famous American study[8], which calculated the likely results of the huge quantities of smoke, soot and dust that the fires of nuclear war would release into the upper atmosphere. By savagely reducing the sunlight reaching the earth, they would cause disastrous world-wide climatic and environmental changes. This 'nuclear winter' would in turn freeze crops, disrupt agriculture far beyond the regions of battle and starve vast numbers of those humans and animals which did not die of exposure. A drop of only two degrees Centigrade over a growing season could ruin the entire Canadian wheat crop.

No less awesome are estimates that within two weeks the huge dust veil would begin to drift into the southern hemisphere where it could essentially eliminate the monsoon circulation underpinning all sub-tropical ecosystems and agriculture. Large areas of Africa, India, South-East Asia, China, Japan and Australasia would then suffer prolonged periods of low temperatures and drought. Major oceanic currents could also be disrupted.

Nuclear winter is a journalistic phrase covering various phenomena and some scientists are sceptical about the Southern hemisphere being severely affected. Yet only one year's climatic disruption in the North alone would lead to widespread hunger. These awesome possibilities are still not part of our general understanding of nuclear war: it means that on this account alone, leaving aside wind-carried radio activity and so on, a major first strike could also become an act of national suicide *even if the enemy had not struck back*. This is the sort of consideration with which the traditional military mind (now more common amongst politicians than the military) has scarcely come to terms.

The Chances of Nuclear War

No policy can be risk-free, but even very small risks must be taken very seriously if the risk is of catastrophe. Whatever our own views, we all therefore need to weigh up the many various ways in which nuclear conflict might be precipitated.

Possible Precipitants of Nuclear War

It is very easy for statesmen to come out with propositions like President Reagan's 'A nuclear war cannot be won and must never be fought'. Unfortunately history shows wars are as often slithered into as decided upon. The current thaw in the Cold War gives us no immunity to sudden crisis or false moves. Great powers sometimes feel they must choose between surrender and confrontation and it is the resulting escalation of threat and counter-threat in an atmosphere of gathering fear and suspicion that most usually produces open conflict. At least seven factors could sufficiently destabilise our shaky international system to precipitate a nuclear war: the size and growth of nuclear arsenals, the proliferation of nuclear weapons states, accident, miscalculation, destabilising weapon developments, destabilising strategies, and failures of command and control.

1. THE SIZE AND GROWTH OF THE NUCLEAR ARSENALS

Despite some peace movement rhetoric, increases in armament do not always or necessarily increase instability. Not only may undue weakness invite aggression; it may also induce the weaker nation itself to make a pre-emptive strike to exploit surprise to stop a bad situation becoming worse. Nevertheless, the huge postwar increases in the arsenals of East and West, not least in the past decade, have plainly been unnecessary. No more than 1,000 warheads, probably far fewer, would suffice to destroy all the major cities on either side, yet both the United States and the Soviet Union have over 20 times this capability. The world now has over 50,000 warheads, of which a high proportion are at least 100 times more powerful than the Hiroshima bomb. This is a condition about which Lord Carver[9], a distinguished former Chief of the British Defence Staff, has said 'one is driven to the conclusion that the world has gone mad'.

We should try to translate all these reciprocal fears into the psychology of individuals. 'The ghastly proportions of what you seem prepared to do to me is bound to convince me of the evil in you. It will probably also amplify my hatred of what you stand for, and reinforce my determination to give as good as I get. Perhaps, in a crisis, I ought even to hit you first. After all, I am no sucker; nice guys finish last, and God is on my side.'

The significance of modern arsenals lies less in the arithmetic of missiles than in the way they are perceived on either side. It is fingers that press buttons; minds and emotions that instruct fingers.

The term 'arms race' can be misleading. The United States authorities claim that they have 8,000 fewer warheads than in the 1960s and only a quarter of the megatonnage. Yet this attempted reassurance can itself be misleading. The 'race' has become more technological than numerical. Warheads are smaller but with greater range, accuracy and capacity for penetration and hence of effective destructive capacity.

The competition is tautened by the remarkably short warning time provided by modern missiles. An American President would have at most 14 minutes to decide on retaliation (while also evacuating the White House, with or without spouse). This pressure has amplified military demands for introducing launch-on-warning (LOW) systems whereby part of the missile armoury is fired off automatically on electronic indications of an enemy attack. The dreadful logic and psychology of 'use them or lose them' could then come into play.

2. WAR THROUGH HORIZONTAL PROLIFERATION

Probably 35 or more countries now have enough plutonium, knowledge and skills to develop nuclear weaponry of some sort within a year or two of so deciding. Most industrialised countries could do it quite easily and, as a crude delivery system, any airliner, tramp steamer or motor boat will serve. Although it lacks teeth, the Non-Proliferation Treaty (NPT) of 1968 has certainly inhibited the horizontal spread of nuclear weapons but its continuation beyond the critical 1995 review is doubtful unless the Superpowers fulfil their side of the original bargain by themselves carrying out considerable arms reductions. Even so-called minor nuclear powers like Britain, France, and China have acquired historically unprecedented destructive capacities.

In addition to Israel, India and Pakistan, a number of other states including South Africa, Iraq, Libya, Taiwan, South Korea, Argentina and Brazil may be within reach of nuclear weaponry. Cliché or not, it *is* disturbing to think of the finger of an Ayatollah, a Pol Pot or a Colonel Gaddafi on a nuclear trigger. Moreover, the necessary safeguards against the spread of fissile materials have been badly neglected and the rot could spread quickly, not least as Third World countries build or buy ballistic missiles, as have Iran, Iraq, Israel and Saudi Arabia (from China) amongst others. There could well be 10 or more new nuclear powers within the next decade.

Sooner or later, nuclear devices will certainly be put together by terrorists: there have already been substantive reports of a plutonium black market in Khartoum and warhead designs appear in the open literature. Nuclear weapons could also be obtained by theft, hijacking or the ambush of military transport. Serving officers could themselves seize and wield nuclear weapons for their own political purposes. France got close to a military rebellion in de Gaulle's time; so could South Korea, where United States forces have hundreds of nuclear weapons. A small power could hardly simulate a superpower attack, but in a time of tension a wild action by, say, Syria or Israel could well trigger a chain of events leading to nuclear catastrophe.

3. ACCIDENT

Similar arguments apply in the case of an unintended launch of a nuclear weapon or some equivalent unauthorised explosion. Nearly two dozen United States aircraft carrying nuclear bombs crashed in the 1950s and 1960s and five out of six interlocking devices on a massive 24-megaton bomb were set off when a B-52 had to jettison it near Goldsboro, North Carolina in 1961. In September 1980, a Titan II ICBM exploded at a base near Little Rock, Arkansas throwing a 9-megaton warhead over 900 feet from the silo. In 1960 the United States submarine Scorpion, carrying anti-submarine torpedoes with nuclear warheads, sank in the Eastern Atlantic. At least six accidents have been reported of Soviet submarines carrying similar weapons, including the sinking of one in the West Atlantic in 1986 and the loss of another off the North Cape of Norway in 1989.

Early warning systems have often been accidentally triggered by meteors or flights of geese. In 1980 the failure of a 46-cent computer chip at NORAD Headquarters led to the alert of United States forces, including 100 B-52 bombers and the President's airborne command post. After such incidents, corrective measures are always taken. No one, West or East, is casual in such matters. The world survived some 1,500 false alarms in 1970 alone and today's systems are certainly less vulnerable.

Whether this is sufficiently reassuring is another matter. Similar things are said about today's chemical plants, jumbo jets, nuclear reactors, bridges, dams, ferries and tankers. They still explode, crash, collide, leak, fall or sink. Bhopal burns, the American space shuttle Challenger blows up, Chernobyl erupts or a Basle chemical plant poisons the Upper Rhine. Intuitively none of us is surprised. We know Murphy's Law: 'If something can go wrong it will'.

In a highly stressed situation, with some forces already on high alert, the quality and balance of military commanders and personnel is crucial yet high levels of psychological disorder, drug abuse and alcoholism in American nuclear units, including strategic missile bases, is officially acknowledged. Other nations are no doubt equally prone but less frank. (*Glasnost* has not got that far yet.) Most nuclear weapon systems are designed with Permissive Action Links (PALs) which necessitates their being operated by two persons at once, rather than one person alone. Whether this system is safe enough must be doubted, especially once warheads are distributed during a crisis. Moreover, American submarine-based warheads lack PALs and so could be launched without express authority, or even despite it. This relative freedom was allowed to submarine commanders to deter the Soviet Union from launching a 'decapitation' strike against the United States which, by destroying the command system, might otherwise prevent retaliation. Former Secretary McNamara apparently now regrets allowing it.

Aberrant behaviour is not hard to imagine. Take two young officers isolated in their underground launch control capsule day after day, in a schizoid situation combining cataclysmic destructive power with utter boredom. One told Jonathan Steele[10] at a Titan missile site at Omaha, Nebraska: 'We have two tasks. The first is not to let people go off their rockers. That is the negative side. The positive one is to ensure that people act without moral compunction!'

The need for fastidious procedural as well as mechanical safeguards is obvious but each new system of authentication inevitably reduces reaction time to any genuine attack. Moreover the missiles from a single hostile submarine might destroy most of a nation's bomber force. One Trident could wipe out all the major Soviet cities. This extraordinary vulnerability creates an inescapable tension between nuclear safety and preparedness, where the latter is most likely to win.

4. WAR THROUGH MISCALCULATION

Many historians believe that the First World War was not intended by any of its protagonists. Most of them had miscalculated the intentions and capabilities not only of their adversaries but of their allies. Suspicion, fear and inadvertently interlocked 'contingency plans' can bring about just what is most feared. When everyone prepares for war to avert war, the preparations may precipitate the war. This is a fundamental point in understanding the contemporary situation despite improvements in East–West relations..

War by miscalculation is plainly brought closer when nuclear threats are used not as a defensive last resort but as a means of pressure over less desperate issues. President Eisenhower believed the threat of atomic war brought about the armistice in Korea in 1950. He also used nuclear threats in 1955 and 1958 in crises with Mao over the Nationalist-held offshore islands of Quemoy and Matsu. At that time, however, the Americans had a nuclear monopoly. Since Moscow caught up, both superpowers have been very wary of offering nuclear threats against third parties. But they have sometimes talked very toughly to each other while placing their nuclear forces on high alert, as they did over the missile crisis in Cuba in 1962. President Kennedy later spoke of a one-in-three chance of that crisis having provoked thermonuclear war. Dean Rusk said: 'We looked into the mouth of the cannon; the Russians flinched'. General Curtis Le May's urgent advice to President Kennedy even *after* the Soviet ships had U-turned away from Cuba was said to be to assail the Soviet Union 'in any case'.

The seemingly permanent dangers along the Inner German Border (IGB) are so obvious that special efforts are made to avoid provocation. During the Soviet invasion of Czechoslovakia in 1968, perfectly legitimate Western reconnaisance flights over West German territory were stopped. Quietly reassuring noises also came out of NATO during the Polish Solidarity crisis of 1980, even while the West's political campaign against Soviet intervention was, quite rightly, going at full blast.

NATO Headquarters rates the chances of deliberate planned Soviet invasion as very low. More plausible would be a trail of military repercussions arising from instability in Eastern Europe, say, or, probably more likely, from Soviet or United States military support of a client state in the Middle East or the Gulf. President Carter declared that Gulf oil was important enough to America for him to be prepared to use 'any means' of assuring its supply (an amazing piece of unconscious superpower greed and self-importance). If the United States did in fact threaten to intervene there with its Rapid Deployment Force, the Soviet Union could easily react to this threat in its immediate backyard by reinforcing the Inner German Border so as to strain American capabilities and resolve. Only a small miscalculation could then precipitate fighting. Another scenario could begin with an Israeli nuclear threat to Damascus (over, say, renewed conflict on the Golan Heights) precipitating first a Soviet nuclear guarantee to Syria and then a counter-threat from Washington.

A further complication is the likelihood of local air, land or naval commanders using their initiative by coming to a higher state of alert than had actually been ordered. Some United States naval units did this during the Cuban missile crisis; they probably thought they were doing a grand job. We often forget, too, the volatility of great affairs. President Nixon pressed aid and arms on the Shah of Iran as a strong dependable Western 'prefect' in the Middle East but then suddenly the Shah fell. Red China was refused diplomatic recognition by the United States for years but by 1985 she was receiving American arms supplies and naval visits. Until 1973, the British Foreign Office totally discounted the possibility of dramatic rises in Arab oil prices, yet these were soon to transform the global economic scene.

Moreover, few rulers are consistently calm, clinical and cautious in decision-making. They vary profoundly in knowledge, experience and emotional stability. Account must also be taken of the ill health of an Eden, the proud parochialism of a de Gaulle, the defiant dogmatism of a Mao. Nor has the general calibre been high. Recent Soviet leaders include the erratic Krushchev, the cautious Brezhnev, a fragile Andropov who died without ever visiting the West and a sick Chernenko who died almost as soon as he settled in. On contemplating the list of recent incumbents of the White House from Nixon and Ford to Carter and Reagan, a contemporary historian has remarked that even the arbitrariness of British royal inheritance has rarely produced a line so lacking in distinction.

5. DESTABILISING WEAPON SYSTEMS

Not only new weapon systems but new methods of defence or weapon protection are liable to increase fears of surprise attack and hence the dangers of crisis instability or war. For example, an ICBM with a single warhead can at best destroy one opposing ICBM but a force of ICBMs which have been MIRVed (when each missile has three, four, five or more separately targetable warheads) can destroy an equal or larger force, whether or not that force is MIRVed. All it has to do is get in there first. Moreover such missiles look the same from the outside, say from a satellite, as does a missile with a single (or a conventional) warhead.

Also highly destabilising is the world's first counter-silo missile system, the Minuteman III. Such systems inevitably encourage the other side to adopt pre-programmed missile responses either of launch-on-warning (LOW) or launch-under-attack (LUA). Equivalent dangers are now arising from submarine-launched systems like Trident II which are also accurate enough for selective and hence first strike use, not just for blanket retribution.

Submarines, being hidden, have so far been the most secure and therefore 'crisis stable' nuclear delivery system. In the curious logic of the nuclear era, the relative invulnerability of submarines can be seen as a reciprocal (if limited) safeguard against pre-emptive attack. They would be the safest vehicles for a minimum nuclear deterrent, should we get down to that stage. It would therefore be very worrying if there were large advances in submarine tracking and anti-submarine warfare. Unfortunately the United States (at least) is working hard on the various relevant technologies such as the Sound Surveillance System (SOSUS), the elaborate passive hydrophone systems now installed off the East and West coasts of America, and on mobile acoustic systems using helicopter-based dipping sonars, sonars buoys and guided torpedoes. This is a technological race that neither side can safely win: safety demands a permanent stand-off.

6. DESTABILISING STRATEGIES

'War fighting' strategies which envisage taking so gigantic a first strike at the enemy that any nuclear response ('only 20 million dead') would be small enough to be 'survivable' are plainly destabilising, even though some people still support them. So, I think, are strategies involving a high dependence on the use of nuclear weapons in response to a purely conventional attack, as in NATO's current doctrine of Flexible Response. (This complex issue will be discussed later). Traditional, though now changing, Soviet doctrine has also made far too little distinction between nuclear and conventional arms, notwithstanding the Soviet Union's declaration that it would not use nuclear weapons first. As we shall see later, another destabilising strategy is the Strategic Defence Initiative (SDI), despite its ostensibly defensive intent.

Failures of Command and Control

Once any fighting at all had begun, the first need would be to prevent it spreading, intensifying or becoming nuclear. Even a one-off 'demonstration' bomb could easily provoke a devastating 'general nuclear response', the official euphemism for all-out war.

The political and military systems required for the very selective control of military operations, whether to protect vital interests, to foreclose enemy options, to deter escalation or to induce negotiation, are described as Command, Control and Communication (C_3), or more commonly C_3I which includes Intelligence, a clearly vital input throughout. To be effective and survivable, much redundant C_3I capacity is built in. The Americans employ over 40 communication systems including satellites and have the 494-L Emergency Rocket Communication System which allows at least one last message to be transmitted to United States strategic forces.

It would presumably say either 'Fire everything' or 'Cease fire'. The Soviet C_3I system is probably similar.

When time is short and information patchy, much depends on the previous contingency planning, and especially on how 'hair trigger' the launch policies are. The close integration of conventional and nuclear forces within the same units and the number of dual-capable weaponries has increased the dangers. The decision whether to use any of the thousands of tactical nuclear weapons in Europe (some equivalent to only 100 tons of TNT) rather than, say, large fuel air explosives, would have to be delegated in practice to individual military commanders, despite the flat denials of governments. In consequence, the psychological and moral power of the nuclear threshold could depend somewhat more than we would wish on the sophistication of an infuriated Colonel.

Other anxieties, for both doves and hawks, are the physical vulnerability of strategic communications and the absence in either superpower country of a sufficiently coherent and flexible yet sensitive decision-making structure. Military thinkers have long worried about errors arising from the confusion and malcommunication they call the 'fog of war' and this would be hugely intensified with the first nuclear use. Fifty warheads could destroy a national command system. According to Desmond Ball[11], the electromagnetic pulse (EMP) resulting from only a few nuclear explosions might disrupt high frequency communications and impair electronic and electrical systems at great distances from the actual points of impact. With such factors in mind the distinguished strategist John Steinbrunner[12] has urged that, 'regardless of the flexibility embodied in the individual force components, the precariousness of command channels probably means that nuclear war would be uncontrollable, as a practical matter, shortly after the first tens of weapons are launched'.

Conclusions

There are plainly immense uncertainties to discourage anyone from initiating nuclear strikes, no matter how limited the other options. On Desmond Ball's[13] view, the use of nuclear weapons for controlled escalation (as in NATO's Flexible Response) is as difficult to envisage as their use for massive retaliation. But if controlled and limited nuclear war fighting is a chimera then, as he says, more attention must be paid to the conditions of conventional deterrence.

The big question, however, remains: how likely is a superpower war in the forseeable future? Most specialists would say the chances are very small. They call the present system 'robust'. Yet there are really no experts in this field. Moreover the professionals may have an unconscious interest in minimising the dangers. They tend to be conservatives who accept the ruling strategic orthodoxies (however changeable) and largely depend, as sources and 'market', on military and political people who themselves have a high investment in public confidence. After all, the one-in-a-thousand chance of cataclysm can come up tomorrow, not just lie in wait for years.

There are other reasons for caution. About half the general public seems to believe nuclear war is likely before the end of the century and public instinct may be more perceptive than academic calculation. People doubt whether mighty arsenals will gather dust for ever. It has rarely happened before. It is perhaps intrinsically unlikely that another world war is intrinsically unlikely!

I have, myself, seen too much anger, impetuosity, bloody-mindedness, idiocy and sheer chance in international politics to be reassured by either pundits or pure calculation. Pre-war pundits thought a Hitlerian holocaust inconceivable in theory, impossible in practice. Whether we shall descend into Armageddon is up to us. It depends on decisions yet to be made, consciously or unconsciously. We must therefore sustain a definite if measured anxiety. President Gorbachev's striking initiatives certainly give promise of a more secure peace. But both superpowers have a very long way to go and there is some danger of a savage rebound of hostile emotion if the Soviet (or Western) response to some new crisis looked like a reversion to the Old Adam.

Nevertheless, the multifarious facts of nuclear danger are not by themselves proof that nuclear deterrence is either wrong or irrational. Or that it will be easily dispensable. Furthermore, the equation includes the fate of freedom. The key question is *how* to prevent nuclear war. To think clearly about this, we must avoid strapping ourselves into primitive polarisations, whether as hawks or doves. Or so I shall now argue.

4

Hawks versus Doves: A Sterile Debate

The greatest derangement of the human mind is to believe in
something because one wishes it to be so,
Louis Pasteur, Scientist, 1822–95

Not very long ago I found myself crouched up cold, deafened and
somewhat frightened in one of a stream of British Army Lynx
helicopters flying very low some miles south-east of Hanover in
West Germany. As some sort of reward for having lectured to staff
officers on the global outlook (a modest little subject), I was being
allowed to witness an Army Air Corps 'Hellarm' exercise simu-
lating a massed air-to-ground missile counter-attack on 'enemy'
armour.

To avoid being seen by hostile eye or radar we approached the
target area through a wooded valley and once in the open flew
'tactically'—hugging the ground, roaring low between trees and
under the power cables. Then, hovering behind a copse and a
village church, we aimed and 'fired' our TOW high explosive
missiles at the group of target army vehicles not far beyond an
autobahn. The commuters driving home to supper hardly seemed
to notice us.

Moments later, all six helicopters suddenly wheeled away,
screaming over the fields and a twisting river. Again we flew
'under the wire' dipping between the pylons. Birds rose in pan-
icked flocks into the mist and hares dashed for cover. Again my
nerve faltered. Just below us a canoeist did not even look up. Like
the commuters, and much of mankind in the last few decades, he
had become used to living alongside the extraordinary, even the
unimaginable.

Betraying Principle?

I had been the house guest of an old friend, a General commanding a crack British division. Returning home a few days later, I mentioned the visit to some Peace Movement friends in the pub further up the Golden Valley. Largely sedentary freelance writers cannot waste such few adventures as they have to tell.

My friends were not amused. They were shocked. As they saw it, I had forgotten that any contact with the Armed Forces was intrinsically compromising, even polluting. The military were, by definition, militarist. Willingness to use any weapon in any circumstances was at once wicked and stupid. Perhaps some wars in the past had been just wars; now any threat of violence could ignite the fuse to nuclear catastrophe. Mankind had to choose between force and persuasion, war and peace. They had chosen peace. I, who had once seemed an ally, had betrayed the cause.

After a week spent amongst sophisticated senior soldiers, I could and did respond by arguing with some conviction that they seemed well-disposed to the keeping of peace and to the saving of lives, not excluding their own. British or NATO policies might be right or wrong but at least the motives of these people appeared honourable. Some of them were also keen to reduce NATO's dependence on nuclear weapons. That indeed had been precisely the point of our nerve-shaking 'Hellarm' exercise: far better use precision-guided high explosive missiles than nuclear warheads that could destroy an entire battlefield and everyone on it. Of course the longer I went on in this vein the more suspicious my friends became. I had clearly been brainwashed by charm, hospitality and flattery; I had sold out to the warmongers, abandoned principle.

The irony was that amongst one group of the army officers in Germany I had been generating an opposite suspicion. These officers had heard, quite correctly, that I had recently organised a weekend conference of Sovietologists, academic peace theorists and others on the potential for East–West co-operation. Did not such talk weaken Western resolve, some of them had asked? Was it not a sell-out to the pacifists and neutralists? If not, indeed, to the Communists? I mentioned that some of the participants were Foreign Office officials. This cut no ice at all: wets or worse to a man, they had muttered. The sort that abandons principle.

Polarisation Rampant

Public life has reached a sorry state when otherwise sane and serious people can instantly associate the opposite side of a crucial policy debate with some kind of unforgivable betrayal whether of country, democracy, party or morality. When rival factions start appealing to their invariably vague and lofty 'principles' you may fairly doubt the quality of their argument, or at least their confidence in it. When they appeal to their 'sincerity' or your 'loyalty' you may be even more suspicious. It should remind one of the passionate Latin American delegate at the United Nations who, having left his speaking notes behind on the rostrum, was discovered to have side-lined one crucial passage 'Weak point: shout here'.

The extreme polarisation of hawk and dove and their shared dislike for 'compromisers' of the centre is bad for civility and for the quality of debate and the resulting policies. The literary critic Lionel Trilling long ago pointed out how every party or faction profoundly depends on the quality of its opposition to test and sharpen its own thinking. Polarisation means predictability and, hence, boredom and irritation. It offers no incentive to learning if the argument can be conducted by 10 slogans on either side.

Over-polarisation is also inimical to the building of the public consensus on which durable policies (and alliances) finally depend. It could even threaten democracy itself. Governments sometimes mutter that defence issues cannot be determined by popular whim; Nanny knows best. Nanny is then tempted to cut all sorts of corners in terms of secrecy, surveillance, censorship, illicit propaganda, lying and other manipulation. (Those who believe they could be justified in pressing the button, can easily come to believe they are entitled to bug a few telephones in roughly the same cause.) Needless to say, however, the erosion of freedom also erodes what we would be supposed to be fighting for.

Predictable Packages

Crow's Law says 'Do not think what you want to think until you know what you want to know'. Yet most people, including opinion-formers and decision-makers, appear to adopt their defence policy positions on the basis of their general political outlook, rather than on relevant information and their own reasoning. We too easily identify ourselves in pre-packaged groups whether as 'unilateralists' or 'multilateralists', peaceniks or NATO loyalists, rather than gradually draw our own assorted conclusions — and retain our own sort of honest doubts.

The defence debate has mostly been primitive, over-emotional and crippled by stereotypes and set positions. Many doves have cried out in understandable horror or pain at the arrival of the nuclear dimension, but without helping to find practical policies to cope with it. Many hawks have furiously denied that nuclear arms have changed the world's essential problems and insist on 'strong' defence without re-examining what that means. The stark polarisation in Parliament, the popular Press and the public bars would surprise no one experienced in public life. Yet it is mostly the same in the quality Press and what used to be called polite society; express doubts in the wrong company about either of the standard positions and people are apt to look at you sideways. Apparently there are only two kinds of people, our lot and their lot.

The hyperbole often seems to come from totally alien worlds. In his Introduction to *Ethics, Deterrence and National Security*, J. E. Dougherty said of the then current debate about Pershing and cruise missiles that it 'is not really about nuclear war. It is a political struggle for the soul of the Europeans, especially the Germans, and the future political fate of the Continent'. This is stirring stuff for an issue safely buttoned up only three years later in the INF Treaty. Yet from out of the other world Robert Jay Lifton and Richard Falk, both distinguished academics of liberal persuasion, write in *Indefensible Weapons*[2] with equal confidence and fluency of 'powerful, vicious, mystifying and self-mystifying social forces tied up with the reign of nuclearism'. They then, incidentally, speak of this as a disease, an especially emotive and question-begging metaphor (which also appears to imply that reason is helpless against it).

Few would deny that a fully human response to late 20th century possibilities, including both apocalypse and totalitarianism, must include much anguish and anger. But the forceful expression of powerful emotions can make constructive dialogue almost impossible. 'Peace people' too often accuse NATO traditionalists of unfeeling blindness to the potentials of nuclear devastation: NATO protagonists too often caricature their opponents as foolishly idealistic, if not positively unpatriotic. Mutual accusations are fed by underlying contempt. The cries of 'militarist!', 'appeaser!' have sometimes brought me close to despair.

I do not deny that some of the debate has suffered from too little emotion. The cold calculations of some strategists smack of

Chess, even Poker. Yet there is sometimes a similar cool glibness, a parallel split between abstract argument and human consequences, in some pacifists. Moral Law may or may not dictate absolute non-violence; historical experience shows it often entails not only sacrifice of self but immense suffering for others: not to recognise this is to betray both intelligence and honesty. *Every* position has its dilemmas; we should all admit it.

Neither Left nor Right

The primitiveness of the discussion is magnified by ignorance. Take the, all too rare, defence debates in Parliament. Between 1983 and 1987, when I was closely in touch with the scene as chairman of a defence information service, we reckoned only about 30 Members knew much about the subject. Moreover almost all Members' positions, on Trident for example, were strongly correlated with Left – Right affiliation. (The few exceptions kept their heads down: one Tory explained to me that he did not wish to be 'misunderstood' by his constituents, colleagues or leader.) The same sort of rough Left – Right correlation is common throughout the West. Provided the party line makes the politically appropriate noises (pro-strength, anti-war or whatever) politicians will 'loyally' follow, out of a mixture of obedience, idleness and self-interest. Few on the Right would risk being thought 'soft' on defence or 'anti-American'. Few on the Left would risk being thought hawkish or positively pro-American.

Except for a few consenting adults in private, the greatest questions of our day are not seriously discussed by British legislators. Their constituents' main concerns are jobs, homes, health, schooling. A former Minister told me the effort of learning up a whole extra subject was just not worth the candle, 'unless you happen to be interested in that kind of thing'.

People are sometimes defined as 'Left' or 'Right' according to their views on defence but the argument then becomes circular. There is actually no logical connection between defence policy positions and Left- or Right-wing attitudes on, say, private enterprise or public ownership. Can there really be a 'socialist' case against chemical warfare or a 'capitalist' case in favour of Flexible Response? Is the Right to be thought pro-nuclear because the Left is so often called anti-nuclear? In accusing the Left of being 'disarmers', is the Right declaring itself against disarmament? As

43

John Biffen[3], a former Tory Cabinet Minister, has rightly said; 'It would be foolish for Conservatives to suppose a non-nuclear defence policy was the monopoly of the ultra-Left'.

Sources of Belief

Doves do tend to be questioners of the *status quo* and hence more radical, just as hawks tend to be more accepting of existing conditions and of hierarchies of authority. It is also true that it is about as rare to hear a member of the Campaign for Nuclear Disarmament (CND) applaud Conservative economic policies as it is to hear a Conservative criticise NATO. But this is to re-state the problem, not to justify black and white polarisations.

The hawk – dove and Right – Left divisions seem to be related to general dispositions like the dry and the wet, the carnivore and the herbivore, the soft-centred and hard-centred or, as one journalist put it, the smooth and the hairy. At all events our opinions certainly cluster in shamefully predictable patterns. Give us some-one's view on capital punishment or foreign aid or pornography or public ownership and we can probably predict their views on the other subjects, and on nuclear arms as well. What logical connections are there between opinions on the noose, the nude and the nuke? For the sources of these belief patterns we may have to go back to personality types — the tough and the tender-minded or the authoritarian and anti-authoritarian personality.

Caricatures and Dispositions

The hawk of caricature is the tough anti-Communist who sees himself fighting for Good against Evil and is out to liberate Eastern Europe if not the Soviet bear's own lair. He may even be prepared to risk nuclear war in the process. For many in the American Bible Belt, Apocalypse is anyway in the foreordained script.

The caricature dove might be the near-pacifist, seeing much good in wicked people, extremely averse to making any threat of force and willing to make large 'appeasing' concessions in the conviction that conciliation is always both possible and effective.

Such a hawk – dove distinction is clearly too crude to be useful. There are some tough-minded pacifists and some tender-minded believers in nuclear deterrence. There are a few who are a mixture — 'tough' about the need for nuclear parity but 'tender' in the pursuit of détente. In this looser sense there are hawks and doves on the Left and the Right in both Washington and Moscow. In this broader context, hawk and dove are relative, not absolute, descriptions. Greenham Common protesters raising placards 'Against Power, For Life' would no doubt brand as hawks both Richard Perle, former United States Assistant Secretary of Defence, and Sir Geoffrey Howe, the British Cabinet Minister. But when Richard Perle described Sir Geoffrey's careful questions on SDI as 'shallow and ignorant' he was hardly regarding him as a suitably robust partner in Western defence. Howe's views on Perle remain unknown.

Miniature Portraits

There are many intermediate hawk and dove positions that are neither red in tooth and claw at one extreme nor pure as the driven snow at the other. The hawk typically reckons the primary cause of war to be weakness and, within the NATO context at least, will warn about the dangers of Munich-style appeasement of totalitarian dictatorships. His policy is one of diplomatic firmness based on military strength, ideally, perhaps, superiority. He will think a nation's commitments and interests should be spelt out clearly and the would-be antagonist met promptly with whatever level and kind of force the threat requires.

The dove typically holds that wars are caused by arms races and warns that excessive military strength can easily become provocative. (Some scholars say the Japanese attack on Pearl Harbour was to pre-empt growing United States strength in the Pacific — quite the opposite of the classic 'appeasement' theory in relation to Hitler.) The dove may strongly disapprove of a hostile power but is inclined to give its intentions and deployments the benefit of the doubt. His own policy is one of conciliation and negotiated disarmament, fostered by unilateral initiatives.

Hawks and doves tend to have characteristic beliefs and attitudes about some of the ideas of groups involved in the debate. Understanding, including self-understanding, can benefit from examining some of these.

The Military

Doves, whether pacifists or not, frequently speak as if the 'military mind' is bound to be 'militaristic'. They insinuate that soldiers are unintelligent, morally obtuse and reckless with life. They also tend to underestimate the Armed Services' respect for democratic institutions and aversion to constitutional impropriety.

Hawks tend to be more alive to the tragic choices the military must face, the discipline they show and the awful dangers to which they expose themselves, even in training. Veterans and those disabled or bereaved by war are especially sensitive to criticisms of the military. It is as if their sacrifices were not respected. Hawks often, however, show excessive respect for the 'military judgement' and tend to be over-impressed by (frequently shifting) military orthodoxies.

The Defence Industries

Doves have a predictable antipathy not only towards 'merchants of death' in the worldwide arms trade but towards the technologists who in such great numbers devise the arms, the industrialists who produce them, the commercial interests which invest in them and the trade unionists and politicians who allegedly think only of jobs and profits. They often claim that arms production is used to bolster national wealth in general though how that squares with Japan's meteoric growth (despite very low defence budgets) is not clear.

Hawks are often uncomfortable about such things as American 'pork-barrel' carve-ups of defence contracts, the combined incompetence and profiteering of some arms manufacturers and the rival Armed Services' apparently insatiable appetite for 'modernisation'. They insist however that all states need some arms and that some arms manufacture and trading is therefore morally justified; they argue for firm restraint not total condemnation and abolition.

The Politicians

Again the doves tend to be contemptuous of the politicians' self-centredness, short-sightedness and cynical exploitation of patriotism. They forget that 'national defence' is a popular democratic cause to which politicians simply must respond if they are to have hope of office and hence power to change things.

Hawks, of course, tend to be over-respectful towards figures of political authority and often irritate doves by sententious demands for a sense of responsibility, by which they seem to mean obedience.

The Nation

Doves tend to equate patriotism with nationalism. Special feeling for one's own people's ways or values is thought to be arbitrary — which it partly is — and necessarily vicious, which it is not. Doves tend to be so 'internationalist' that hawks sometimes doubt their normality.

Hawks are usually biased the other way, often suggesting that the national interest is, of itself, a moral justification. Their national pride can tip over into ethnocentrism, even chauvinism. Many British hawks unhesitatingly favour Britain's possessing a nuclear deterrent while opposing proliferation elsewhere. Why different rules apply is not clear. Hawks often fail to recognise that national security now depends on international agreements, including those between would-be enemies.

The Enemy

Doves are almost bound to play down the nastiness of the potential enemy's regime, its capabilities and its aggressiveness. They will hunt for evidence of redeeming features and wax strong against paranoia and the Cold War mentality. They can call in evidence much psychological material about projection and the macho values of patriarchal society.

Hawks show the opposite tendency, seeing any evidence that seems to qualify a dark interpretation of the Soviet Union as the result of clever propaganda, the contrivance of fellow-travellers or the flimsy sustenance of fools. They can call up much historical evidence and many contemporary denunciations by dissidents.

What neither notices is that whether a given strategy is sensible does not primarily depend on our verdict on the general nature or intentions of the opponent's regime, but on the whole complex of questions about the deployments and practical options of both sides. We also forget that a nuclear pacifist could, with impeccable consistency, be deeply worried about possible Soviet aggression while a NATO General may likewise think a Soviet invasion highly unlikely, even if necessary to safeguard against.

Diplomacy

Doves believe passionately in diplomatic persuasion and resist the case for holding sanctions in reverse, including the ultimate threat of force. Doves also invest high hopes in unilateral gestures, commercial and cultural transactions and personal contacts by 'ordinary people'. (They play down the curbs on public dissent, especially the organisation of dissent, in the Soviet Union).

Hawks tend to scepticism about diplomacy and personal contacts except where equal and verifiable bargains can be struck in terms of hard common interests or quantifiable weapon systems. Unilateral steps, however small, are construed as weakening. All negotiation must be 'from strength' and in 'the only language the Russians understand'. (What other language the West understands is not revealed.)

Human Nature

Doves tend to believe in human nature; hawks warn us about it. Doves emphasise its capacities for redemption; hawks its destructiveness. One side emphasises Man's adaptability; the other stresses his original sin and the intrinsic aggressiveness of his make-up. Arguments at this level of high generality cannot, however, compel assent to one sort of defence policy rather than another. There are fortunately also more complicated views of human nature — and of social existence.

Idealism versus Realism

Doves are certainly often 'idealistic' to the point where hawks see them as naively irresponsible. And hawks are often 'realistic' to the point where doves feel ideals have been abandoned. Doves often therefore make hawks feel they are being accused of undue pessimism, even cynicism. Hawks can equally make doves feel naive or sentimental.

You and I may believe that ideals have to be workable and therefore adapted to life in a sinful world. We may also believe that 'realism' can end in the mad rationality of the logic choppers and those who equate the most real with the most base. (About this, I too am profoundly prejudiced: right down the middle!)

Christian and Unchristian

Doves, like hawks, may or may not have a religious faith. Those who do can unwittingly cause or suffer deep embarrassment. The dove who is Christian and appeals to the Sermon on the Mount may utterly deflate his honest Christian opponent. Yet he may himself be deflated by the counter-appeal that we are called to live in a permanent crucifixion between the opposites of loving aspiration and fallen reality.

A dove may be asked if choice between evils no longer applies in a nuclear world. A hawk may be asked what Christianity is uniquely saying if his moral arguments are indistinguishable from those of the secular world and his actions could lead to the immolation of millions.

An Unholy Mess

Doves and hawks hold tight to opposite clusters of deeply held beliefs which tend if anything to reinforce the convictions of their opponents. The nonsense A talks, as it were, only demonstrates how very right B has been all along. So long as A and B persist with the ludicrous assumption that there are really only two sets of views to choose between, their own seems all the more obviously right.

As we have seen, this primitive polarisation suits alike the interests of simple-minded politicians, lazy citizens, cliché-ridden journalists and cynical party managers. Self-righteous condemnation is thoroughly enjoyed by most, and only a few recognise the need to graft away at devising safer policies. In the British context, much of the Labour Party has seen Conservative (and past Labour) defence policy as chauvinistic nuclearism, while many Tories have seen 'Left-wing' Labour defence views as craven crypto-neutralism. Convinced of the sheer lunacy of the other side, each has ignored the intellectual difficulties of its own position.

This was especially evident during the 1987 British General Election which ended with a Conservative poster showing a British soldier holding his hands up, with the caption 'Labour's Defence Policy'; with the Labour Party counter-lampooning Tories as nuke-loving warmongers. Note for example the replies of Labour's then defence spokesman and of the then Conservative Defence Secretary to a battery of questions on global, NATO and British policy assembled by Oliver Ramsbotham[4]. To all of 20 recommendations Denzil Davies said 'Yes' and to virtually all of them George Younger said 'No'. This outright polarisation over a very wide subject matter was not due to Davies being any sort of unilateralist extremist: it was, I fear, rather the result of neither man having or exposing honest doubts or even any awareness of contradiction. Neither questioned his own premise, Davies's being that nuclear weapons were unusable and Younger's that nuclear deterrence was common sensical rather than, at the least, deeply paradoxical. Both are sensible, pleasant and intelligent men but both seem to believe that the questions are simpler than they are.

New Doubt

It is time we all, not least the comfortable doves and hawks, revived our capacity to doubt some traditional assumptions. We are living in what is, for many of us, the best-ever present while confronting a possible worst-ever future. Our age of radical achievement is also one of astonishing peril and therefore of confused thoughts and feelings. Paradoxes and dilemmas abound. Ancient professions are divided; traditional responses being challenged by unaccustomed questions.

Can a Conservative statesman ever seriously threaten an obliterative war — the absolute opposite of conservation and any notion of proportionality? Can a General threaten the incineration of a whole province or city, despite all his training in the rationing of force, the safeguarding of civilians and the honouring of his armed opponents? Can a minister or a diplomat grasp that because a frightened enemy may strike pre-emptively, his enemy's security is now critical to his own? Can he see that he can himself be too strong for his own safety? Can a conservative churchman still depend on Just War doctrines to justify the threat of weapons which could expunge millions within minutes? Can a Pacifist churchman preach with the slightest political relevance to a highly armed world of many beliefs inflamed by fervour?

When nuclear defence may become nuclear suicide how should governments proceed? Can they be expected to renounce what they see as a genuinely defensive nuclear capacity? Can they respond to absolute moral principles rather than weigh the complex consequences in what may be a permanently nuclear world?

It is becoming plain that no position, whether conservative or radical, the hawk's or dove's, is now immune to severe questioning. Stock responses are no longer adequate. The arguments of both hawks and doves have strengths and the reader will have seen that each set has colonised part of me. Like many others, however, I can no longer give unqualified allegiance to either.

Wiser policies will never grow out of the party prejudices, rhetorical slogans or crusading fervour of either side, in Britain or elsewhere. The over-polarisation of debate, both nationally and internationally, is itself part of the total complex of problems now demanding treatment. But before we decide what sensible policies might be arrived at, we should try to agree about the broad nature of the political process. We shall not agree about what to do if we cannot agree about how much can reasonably be expected.

5

Politics as Process

Margaret Fuller: 'I accept the universe'.
Thomas Carlyle: 'Gad, she'd better!'
                              Thomas Carlyle, author, 1795–1881

When Harold Macmillan, the late Lord Stockton, was asked what had given him most trouble as Prime Minister he did not say the Russians, the Labour Party, nuclear weaponry, inflation or his own backbenchers. He replied with the single word 'events'. In all the convoluted arguments between rival policies, ideologies and strategies it is salutary to be reminded of the limits of government. In my university days in the early 1950s American students were apt to joke about President Eisenhower having 'delusions of adequacy'. Two years later, in the Foreign Office, I began to see adequacy as a kind of achievement.

This is not to suggest that political ideas are uninfluential but anyone with practical experience would stress the often greater influence of personality, skill, unconscious prejudice, vested interest and sheer chance. As Proudhon said: 'The fecundity of the unexpected far exceeds the statesman's prudence.'

To say these things is not to be anti-intellectual. Ideas are useful and sometimes powerful. Complex ideas are likely to be the most useful; simple ideas the most powerful, and dangerous. What happens depends much less on what statesman fondly think they have decided than on developments they did not foresee or even notice.

A chief obstacle to rational policy-making (and good government) is, therefore, a sort of managerial conceit, the almost comic notion born of ministerial self-esteem, official sycophancy and public wish-fulfilment that governments are the main agents of

52

change. In fact, most governments most of the time, including those of the Superpowers, rarely do more than adapt, rather clumsily, to events. They are mostly reactive, not pro-active. They navigate round obstacles rather than remove them.

Any radical will immediately suspect such arguments as an excuse for inaction and a classic conservative defence of the *status quo*. Yet the question of how much governments can be expected to do is plainly crucial to deciding how much we can reasonably ask of them. Differences about this basic and perennial issue underlie many of the passionate disagreements about defence policy. There are three main schools: the Utopians, the Cynics and the Improvers.

The Utopians

Many Utopians create a blueprint of the ideal society; different models punctuate the history of thought from Plato to Marx. There are also moral Utopians who offer no blueprint but assert, for instance, that the world should be organised without resort to threats of force; and the aboriginal Utopians who believe all will be well once the Enemy is vanquished.

Like other idealists, the Utopians demand bumper political crops without understanding the soil, the climate or, indeed, the plants. They have too little sense of the intractabilities of either national or international politics. The equations of choice are complex, aims conflict, powers and means are limited. Dozens of rival interests and factions press in, coalitions have to be sustained, resources and skilled people are short, unpopular priorities must be established, awkward bargains have to be struck and either justified or denied.

Even in authoritarian regimes like the Soviet Union and China, highly uncomfortable compromises have to be reached between local initiative and central control, foreign involvement and domestic development, alleged military need and transparent consumer demand. In the democracies, no great sacks of power await a new occupier of a White House, Elysée Palace or Downing Street. Apart from the legal, constitutional, parliamentary and party constraints, and those on any government's financial, economic and military resources, there is the huge matter of whether other groups, factions and governments can be persuaded to collaborate — or at least not oppose.

The time for bold moves almost never seems ripe: the United States may be approaching mid-term elections, the Japanese may be preoccupied by a scandal and the Greeks and Turks by mutual tensions while the Italian government may be on the point of resignation. And this is only to consider one's allies: most thoroughgoing reform of international power depends also on agreement with suspicious neutrals, current antagonists and potential enemies. They, too, have their priorities, schedules and difficulties.

As we have seen, almost all governments are too absorbed by current anxieties to attend to long-term or 'hypothetical' problems. A Wall Street crash, a massive oil slick, a terrorist bomb in a jumbo jet, a civil war in South Asia, will dominate the media for several days and may even be seen as reflecting deep-seated threats; in practice, however, it is mostly the immediate symptoms that are dealt with, not the long-term causes. It is far easier to hold ostentatious meetings and make the right noises on television (preferably combining reassurance with indignation) than to take far-sighted and costly action that may only benefit foreigners abroad and the government's loathed successors at home. There are not many votes in foresight and fewer in sacrifice.

It is no wonder that our leaders mostly tacitly decide to let the evils of tomorrow look after themselves. This sounds disgraceful, especially to Utopians. It is. Yet many of the intractabilities are genuine. It is therefore scarcely sensible to 'demand' a world state or the beating of swords into ploughshares without the slightest practical suggestion as to how the miracles are to be worked. We have to translate our generalised appetites for peace or justice into relevant and practical options for our particular interlocutor. Some claim rescue would be possible if only mankind rejected violence or accepted Love, or whatever. But this is to be trapped by a metaphor: mankind is an idea on the lips, not an actor on the stage. Deliberate change, for good or ill, comes from a multiplicity of specific (and often rival) sources — individuals, groups, institutions, governments. Like others I can be brought to anger and despair by vacuous demands that we somehow collectively 'renounce war'. Who in their right mind would claim the solution to murder or rape could lie in a collective renunciation of crime?

The Cynics

At the opposite extreme from the Utopians are the super-realists who would deny that morality has anything seriously to do with the workings of international society. They see the world as intrinsically anarchic; a struggle for survival among restless states of whom the fittest, not the pious, do best. For the philosopher Thomas Hobbes, the state of nature was a state of war and there was no common power to keep states in awe and hence in order. In *Leviathan*[1] he was harshly downright on the matter: notions of right and wrong, justice and injustice had no place; every man was out for all he could get and would keep it as long as he could.

This view burns through a fog of wishful thinking to recognise the greed and humbug of sovereign states, their selfish aggressiveness and grotesque self-delusions. Yet in emphasising the role of interests, selfish or not, the Cynic does also point the way to bargaining, however steely-eyed, as a more reliable basis for order than the moralistic humbug of a John Foster Dulles or the new Bible-punchers. Those who claim that an aseptic cynicism is safer than the softness of fools or the over-ambition of world saviours could be right. Fortunately we need not choose between such extremes.

The Cynics do, on my definition, include some distinguished academic followers of Hans Morgenthau, who are of entirely unaggressive temper but mainly comprise self-proclaimed 'realists' of little intellectual coherence who relish the law of the jungle, insist that morality is a marginal luxury and that nations will only respond to threats. When ex-President Truman was introduced to an audience as 'America's greatest statesman' he irreverently said: 'What's a statesman anyway? I'll tell you what he is — a politician no one is afraid of any more!'

The Cynics insist that fear is implicit in the very structure of international society. To some degree this must be so but governments are not wholly unscrupulous (nor wholly calculating). To see them so is inverted sentimentality. Over 100 governments employ torture and give foreign aid. Most governments, like the rest of us, are many-sided and muddled, good and bad. No single factor, not even cynicism, will explain all their actions. A good reputation is also a good asset. Cynics too rarely make clear whether they are describing the way the world works or recommending that it should work that way; if the latter, we have a choice. Moreover, Cynics themselves invariably slip into moral language eventually; in essence they see their position as better and safer, not just truer. They are moralists in disguise.

The Improvers

Utopians and Cynics both oversimplify the workings of the international system. Both tend to see it as an entity, however complex, whereas the Improvers see it as a constantly shifting pattern of transactions and processes which retains a general shape while changing constantly in content like a river. Or a wild garden.

The rich variety of political, economic, military, cultural and personal relations between over 160 nations constitute a sort of 'market' in which all the actor states have various interests which they try to maintain or exploit in reciprocal transactions with other actors. Many more or less persistent patterns of transactions and trade-offs are established between friends, between foes, and between both. The careful fostering of this culture of realistic, gradualist 'bargaining' may be a crucial antidote to the inflammatory moralism of our age.

But the Improver even distrusts theories seeking to encapsulate his own view! He, like the Utopian, wants radical change but insists he can do it only step by step. He, like the Cynic, is convinced of the centrality of power and self-interest in all human affairs but sees them as potential instruments for constructive use.

The Politician's Craft

The way that Utopians shudder at such compromises makes practising politicians smile. They know that anyone having his own outfit to run quickly resorts to hard-nosed dealings and less than total 'participation'. Indeed, where Utopians refuse to accept or admit compromise, the corners tend to be cut in secret and the outfit eventually becomes sick with unacknowledged and untreated internal divisions. There is perhaps an inevitable pathology affecting pressure groups, communes and other worthy institutions in which power, egoism and selfishness are denied rather than recognised, discussed and managed. (Contrary to the usual view, the Churches are often sensible about politics but bad on sin.)

Practising politicians and diplomats rightly talk a lot about 'judgement': they are expert in manoeuvring and wheeler-dealing between multitudes of interests in shifting circumstances. Their forte is negotiation. An invaluable book[2] on this is entitled *Getting to Yes* and emphasises the need to contrive 'yes-able' propositions. Politicians have a feeling for what it will take to persuade friend or

foe to do a deal and how far they can rely on that deal later. It is
a craft for people who are neither idealistic nor wholly cynical. A
few anecdotes may suggest some of the typical flavours of politics in
practice.

▷ Edward Heath, then Lord Privy Seal, to a new young
private secretary (myself) who had advocated an early
election over some issue: 'Heavens above, you don't volun-
teer for an election you are going to lose!'

▷ An academic adviser to a Labour Cabinet, discussing race:
'It really has three factions — traditional closet racists;
chauvinists worried about white jobs; and a few libertari-
ans rather bothered about the civil rights.'

▷ Harold Macmillan, as Prime Minister: 'Is he someone
you'd want to be dropped in the jungle with?'

▷ Lord Wilson, retired Prime Minister, on Denis Healey
MP: 'My thuggish friend . . . and I mean it as a compli-
ment.'

▷ A peer on an ugly party colleague: 'He is not as nice as he
looks.'

▷ An historian: 'Whenever the English solved the Irish problem the Irish changed it.'

▷ A diplomat: 'We are trying to design a ladder the opposition could climb down.'

▷ All politicians and knowing commentators: 'Can he deliver?'

The Improver's Guide to a Political Novice

My own strong preference for the Improver's position is apparent.
It is the sanest view of politics, at once pragmatic and purposeful,
but it is not easy to convey; it cannot be encapsulated in a single
formula. Some remarks the Improver might make to an apprentice
may be helpful.

▷ You can't have everything: you will have to bargain constantly. *The ally is often a rival, the antagonist is willing to trade. Both are your business associates; both can be useful, both can be dangerous.*

▷ Beware the short-term gain, it is often the enemy of long-term benefit. *President Kennedy's firmness in the Cuban missile crisis of 1962 probably reduced the long-term dangers by magnifying the immediate ones. But mutual benefit via face-saving agreement is far better than short-lived victory.*

▷ Carefully define your aims, (say over Eastern Europe) and then analyse your priorities, your available resources and the foreseeable costs, benefits and risks.

▷ Respect uncertainty. *None of us knows much. Real experts do not forget this. Be prepared to change your mind, and your tack. Be open to surprise, doubt, hesitation. It is easy to make things worse. Indeed . . . . .*

▷ *Value* uncertainty; it is perhaps the democrat's best argument against the dogmatists. *By the same token it opens the door alike to modesty, pragmatism, participation and caution.*

▷ Refuse to think in simple-minded slogans, panaceas, 'root causes' or 'principles', even if you have to use them on the hustings. *There is no 'essential' problem and the notion that there is ever 'no alternative' is ridiculous. There are more ways than one to skin a cat.*

▷ Cultivate your garden. And watch your back. *Keep most of your friends happy most of the time: otherwise you will lose the power to make them unhappy when necessary.*

▷ Never trust, or distrust, anyone completely. Even your closest ally may betray you *in extremis* — as you may him. *Even your bitterest foe may be willing to make useful, verifiable agreements.*

▷ Concentrate on events and possibilities, not grand theories or grander hopes. *Watch, listen, weigh options, talk to friends and not least to antagonists. 'Mere talk' can be a great healer; at least it buys time.*

▷ Make accidents work for you. *Keep alert to unlikely opportunities, odd twists of fate, useful coincidences, favourable chances for limited progress and confidence-building. Be ready to take advantage of a state funeral, a chance meeting at the airport, a spare evening at a United Nations conference or of the flurry around a natural disaster.*

▷ Better the right action for the wrong reason than the wrong action for the right one. *In politics, consequences matter much more than motives.*

▷ Beware managerial conceit. *Most governments have less power, less 'policy' and less competence than they pretend. They are better at tilting balances and repairing breaches than at delivering the Great Society or Peace in our Time. Beware the great claims; fulfil the clear needs. Recognise that some of the best international bridges are built by professionals swapping skills, firms making money, individuals enjoying opera or teaching each other new card tricks.*

▷ Pessimism of the intellect, optimism of the will, suggested Gramsci, the Italian Marxist philosopher. *Fear the worst and prepare against it, but keep working for the better, somehow.*

▷ Attend to manner as much as matter. *What is received is not the same as what is said: presentation can be more influential than content. The manipulation of feelings can be sickening but if you cannot do it, stay out of politics.*

▷ 'Don't fight the problem' said General George Marshall, originator of the Marshall Plan. *He meant that one should not tackle the problem head on, or as a whole, but concentrate on those elements of it that one can reasonably hope to change. The problem is not, for instance, 'Russia' but this and that particular way in which the Russians conduct themselves, some of which we can change and some we probably cannot.*

▷ 'Own the problem'. *As in psychotherapy, we need to recognise our own role in the problem, emotional as well as cerebral; only then can we encourage other individuals or governments to take responsibility for their share.*

▷ Always leave room for a second conclusion. *Distrust the knee-jerk reaction, the ideological pre-judgement and the other perils of 'conviction politics'.*

▷ Keep moving forward. *Despite all the good reasons for caution, politicians and governments need to keep pushing ahead. Passivity has its dangers too. Moreover . . .*

▷ Dare to be audacious. *There are times for totally fresh departures like de Gaulle's on Algeria, Nixon's on China, Sadat's and Begin's on Egyptian – Israeli relations, the remarkable post-Mao counter-revolution of the late 1970s, President Gorbachev's perestroika and Yassir Arafat's recent initiatives towards the Israelis.*

A Political Therapy?

Observations of this kind suggest we should play with the idea of a kind of 'political therapy'. For just as the body politic is prone to its own diseases so can its members, as citizens, suffer all sorts of disorders and disabilities, some intellectual, some more like neuroses, that may make us useless or even destructive in employing our right to influence events.

We have all heard someone stridently declaring at a public meeting that everything would be all right if only we could curb the Superpowers, abolish the multinationals, educate the racists, ban the bomb, liberate women and have love and light prevail, all within five years or so. We have also of course heard the parallel Right-wing tirades about rubbing out terrorism, neutralism, socialism, defeatism, subversion, pornography, crime and sexual diversity. Both types could benefit from help.

The political therapist's main aim would be to help people be more effective as citizens, whatever their views. His only prejudice would be hostility to prejudice. He or she is the enemy of prejudgement, dogmatism, self-deception and self-righteous moralism.

He will admit a bias towards the pragmatic 'moderate' centre but wholly concede that this position is not necessarily better than some extreme ones. However, one way or another, it very often is.

6

Six Questionable Policies

Systems die; instincts remain.
Oliver Wendell Holmes, author, 1809-94

It is, I suppose, obvious that the Utopian's view of politics is closely related to the dove's and the Cynic's to the hawk's. The dove, like the Utopian, looks for transformation. The hawk is a Cynic about the ways of the world and looks for victory. The connections are close though not of course complete. A Cynic in a weak position might adopt dovish policies out of fear. A Utopian in a strong position, like Mao, can become aggressively hawkish in pursuit of bold ambitions.

The Improver's view of politics is close to what has been called the owl's view — the position I have come to myself after periods of being a soldier, a pacifist, an orthodox diplomat, Mr Heath's 'angry young man', a quietly radical journalist, a campaigning environmentalist and a convener of defence debates.

The owl regards transformation as an impossible dream and victory as an arrogant and hazardous one. The owl instead looks first for common survival, secondly for stability and thirdly for improvement. These concerns flow from the owl's special focus on the irrational and unpredictable factors in political life and the dangers of even greater loss of control. His first concern is the threat from misperceptions, misunderstandings, mistakes and inadvertent escalation rather than from either the Arms Race (like the dove) or the Enemy (like the hawk). But before constructing the owl's policy in any detail we must critically examine the three defence policy recipes characteristically offered by doves and the three most usually offered by hawks.

Doves tend to offer either Non-Violent Resistance, Non-nuclear Defence or Neutralism. Hawks tend to offer Imperial Crusade, Military Superiority or Comprehensive Nuclear Deterrence as represented by the classic NATO 'dual track' policy of strong nuclear deterrence combined with verifiable arms control measures and political confidence-building.

Oddly enough perhaps, all these six positions have some attractions but, as I shall explain, all of them are, at least in present circumstances, seriously inadequate. Let us take the dove's offering first.

Dove's Option I: Non-Violent Resistance

Some doves claim that non-violent resistance can minimise casualties and damage while posing sufficient practical obstacles and political embarrassment to deter a would-be attacker. They point to Gandhian *satyagraha* in India (against the fairly conscientious British) and the achievements of similar methods of protest, non-co-operation and obstruction elsewhere. Passive resistance can clearly be somewhat dissuasive of attack; it cannot, however, stop an invader with a strong appetite or other motive like Hitler, or, one has to say, Israel. It may be a valuable supplement to armed resistance; it is not, I fear, a replacement, Nor, would public opinion usually accept it.

Dove's Option II: Non-Nuclear Defence

By far the majority of the United Nations' 160 members are too small, too poor, too backward, too little threatened, or are so credibly protected by other powers, even to consider acquiring nuclear weapons. The decisions of states involved in an unresolved conflict with an actual or potentially nuclear-armed neighbour are far more complex. Examples are India and Pakistan, Argentina and Brazil, Israel and the Arab states or South Africa and the black frontline states. Some of these are already nuclear powers and some are actively pursuing nuclear status. Israel has shown that even a small state can not only produce a nuclear force (with missiles) but one of the same substantial order as China's.

Obviously no government will 'go nuclear' lightly. The costs and the risks will be large, including the risk of provoking a potential enemy. There may even be moral inhibitions. Nevertheless any given state will finally decide on the basis of its own interests, not the global interest. Considering its uneasy relations with both Superpowers, it is hardly surprising that China acquired nuclear weapons. Some argue that Pakistan's acquisition of a nuclear capability to counter India's may genuinely add to the stability of the sub-continent. This is a shocking idea but we must beware applying Eurocentric double standards. It would certainly be humbug for subscribers to the NATO or Warsaw Pact orthodoxy of reciprocal nuclear deterrence (and especially perhaps the British and French) abruptly to condemn either side.

There is of course a tragic chain that operates. Pakistani renunciation would be far easier if India scrapped its own bomb but then India would feel insecure alongside China. And for China in turn to disband its nuclear forces it would plainly be necessary for the Soviet Union and the United States to do so also. These are variants of the classic 'you first' situation in which the narrowly self-interested and rational decisions of individual states may add up to what is also a condition of collective madness.

Most states would welcome an infallible scheme of nuclear abolition. The nuclear powers, however, reject the idea of disarming unilaterally and hence, as they see it, of putting themselves at the mercy of other nuclear states. Moreover they see no real possibility of nuclear weapons technology being erased from human memory. Fairly soon after the outbreak of a major conventional war, one side or the other would almost certainly construct nuclear weapons and might well use them if otherwise faced with defeat. On this analysis, the abolition of nuclear arms could never be truly permanent. And despite even massive international sanctions, a state in danger would probably make secret contingency plans to rebuild them.

Some people suggest a policy of 'let's pretend' — retaining nuclear weapons for deterrence while secretly determining never to use them. Unfortunately, however, as a credible deterrent the system has to be in full working order, with men and machines ready to go. No military apparatus is long capable of pretending to threaten while preparing to surrender. Nor could a policy easily be kept secret from either the enemy or the public, which would see it as an expensive farce.

I conclude that a non-nuclear defence policy is inevitable for most states, plainly sensible for many others, but not at all easy or obvious (I say no more at this stage) for those whose potential enemies are already nuclear-armed.

Dove's Option III: Neutralism

Neutralism is not intrinsically more virtuous, or effective, than other policies. If military defence as such can be legitimate, so can defensive alliances for mutual support as, for example, amongst South Africa's neighbours. On the other hand, neither military self-sufficiency nor political neutrality are necessarily wrong, as is witnessed by Sweden's refusal to identify itself with either super-power alliance.

Neutrality can take various forms. Finland and Austria are neutral by post-war treaty, Switzerland by historic choice and constitutional requirement, Sweden by history and choice alone. Most Third World countries are at least ostensibly neutral (or non-aligned) as between the Superpowers. Various elements are involved here: disapproval of both capitalist and Communist ideology; anti-colonialist passion; a proud nationalist demand for non-interference; fear of embroilment in superpower conflicts and a positive desire to mediate, even to create a 'third force'.

Neutralism, therefore, sounds like high principle but owes more to pragmatism. It has hard as well as soft versions: both Sweden and Switzerland maintain powerful conventional forces, strong civil defence and believable willingness to fight any invader with ferocity and in depth. Both are far more robust in their defiance and capabilities than say Denmark or Greece, both of whom are NATO members.

But could a major, middle-rank power like Britain adopt a neutralist policy? In theory certainly, but of what kind? A strenuous 'neo-Gaullist' nuclear-armed independence would be hugely expensive and is scarcely the dovish kind of 'neutralism'. But a genuinely passive non-aligment would also be difficult for a major player like Britain (or France or West Germany). Whereas Sweden and Switzerland can get a sort of free ride from it, NATO itself would probably be shattered by the defection of any of its biggest members and that in turn would change the whole security context. In practice the issues are clearly as much international as national.

Interim Conclusion on the Dove's Options

This analysis shows that each of three main dovish options, non-violent resistance, non-nuclear defence and neutralism, may be apposite for some states in some circumstances. None of them, however, is without serious problems especially for large powers. But, as we shall now see, the hawk's characteristic offerings have their own equally substantial difficulties.

Hawk's Option I: Imperial Crusade

The extreme hawk claims that his particular nation, cause or ideology has a plain right to extend its sway, even by force of arms. He (rarely she) may make two different cases for it. In the amoral version, emphasis is laid on the inevitability of conflict, the survival of the fittest and the manifest destiny of one's own cause. It is the world view of New York cops: 'Nice guys finish last' or 'When the going gets tough, the tough get going'. The argument has a hard-nosed, 'realistic' colour to it. It is, of course, amazing that serious people can so unblinkingly subscribe to it, most especially in the nuclear era.

The moral version is that of the passionately evangelistic believer in his own flag and creed and in the wickedness of the other side. He talks of rescuing the oppressed and of the sunny uplands waiting just the other side of victory.

Fortunately neither Superpower's current leadership believes it can pursue such ambitions without catastrophe. Some antediluvians on both sides may still hanker for the holy war which will finally purge the earth of the opposite ideology but Bush and Gorbachev know well that the post-war chaos would not provide quite the best foundation for a reign of peace or plenty. They also know that talking of crusade magnifies the enemy's preparedness, disturbs allies and weakens unity and resolve. The policy is morally arrogant but also — mercifully — absurd.

Hawk's Option II: Military Superiority

Some hawks seek a military superiority so marked as to make their would-be enemy come off worst in any near-confrontation (say, in the Third World). It is also ultimately a superiority which would sap its economic strength and political will. However, this policy invites an arms race and possibly pre-emptive attack. Opponents already tend to overrate each other's strength and the resulting vicious circle of fear further increases instability.

Some American officials have wanted to squeeze the Soviet lemon 'until the pips squeak'. This has frightened and antagonised most West Europeans who are apt to prefer contented fat Russians to aggressive thin ones. The argument prompted Henry Kissinger[1] to ask, 'What in the name of God is strategic superiority? What is the significance of it politically, militarily, operationally, at these levels of numbers? What do you do with it?'

Some Americans answer straight out that strategic superiority at every level would enable the United States military to 'prevail' over the Soviet state and at a cost (20 million American lives is mentioned) that would not prohibit American recovery. But if we reject this view as daft as well as wicked, what is the alternative? Would not inferiority bring both instability and defeat by making a present of domination to one's opponent? Fortunately there are many alternatives to strict numerical equality (whatever that would be) including 'equivalence', 'strategic parity' and, as I shall later commend, 'defensive sufficiency'.

Hawk's Option III: Comprehensive Nuclear Deterrence

By itself this is the least aggressive of the hawks's three options, although it is usually combined with the others as their defensive arm. Its appearance also gives us a chance to examine the vexed question of deterrence in a little detail.

As I sit here at the window in a January snowstorm, a Missel thrush is perched on our berry-laden Cotoneaster tree just outside the cottage making the grating '*churr*' of its alarm call, a sound like a comb being scraped across a piece of wood. The thrush is deterring other birds from raiding its precious food supply; and when a starling did so a moment ago, the thrush darted at him.

Four conditions of effective deterrence are being fulfilled: a defined 'territory'; a clear warning; an apparent determination to carry it through; and a capacity to inflict damage larger than the benefit the raider could reasonably expect from an incursion. This is a critical point, one that generals, let alone statesmen, have not always understood. The raider need not fear death; only a peck that is not worth a berry. And among birds even the peck is very rare; the hostile gesture is normally enough. In short, the starling fled.

This sort of deterrence is as common in human as in animal society. It is part of the foundation of law and public order — even the threat of arrest is a potential threat of graduated kinds of violence on those who do not go quietly. Different forms of deterrence have figured within and between nations throughout recorded time. Like everything else, deterrence has its dangers: too large or too public a threat can provoke counter-measures which will inhibit co-operation, magnify suspicion and may precipitate conflict; too little may aggravate the opponent without safeguarding the potential victim. Most of us would not, however, make an automatic objection to a deterrent capacity, provided it is quietly and unaggressively held. Even the smallest military force implies one. Even non-violent resistance may be seen as a threat of damage or trouble that will to some degree 'deter'.

It follows that we should never confuse deterrence in general with nuclear deterrence in particular. To treat them as essentially the same issue is, to my eyes, tragic. It makes doves look more naive than they are and hawks look more common-sensical. Nuclear deterrence with its obliterative capacities, fully deserves to be much more contentious. Each of its many different guises carries its own problems, whether of military efficacy, political persuasiveness or ethical acceptability. But for our immediate purposes, we might distinguish between Ultimate Nuclear Deterrence, a capacity in extreme circumstances to inflict massive damage, and Comprehensive Nuclear Deterrence, a capacity and willingness to respond with every kind and level of nuclear arms to any hostile action, nuclear or conventional. The reader may deeply object to this distinction but the concepts remain very different. The first is close to what is sometimes called minimum nuclear deterrence; the second is a rough summary of NATO's present philosophy.

The ultimate form is essentially a capacity to maim the aggressor as a last resort. This is a reciprocal 'existential' nuclear deterrence that is not so much a strategy as a brutal fact of life between any rival nuclear powers that do not trust each other. Most nuclear strategies, however, fall into the second comprehensive category. One example is Extended Deterrence, as when a Superpower extends a deterrent umbrella over its allies. Another is 'Counterforce', or the targeting of military objectives rather than cities and populations.

Comprehensive Nuclear Deterrence is generally claimed to have the following advantages:

> ▷ It is a 'strong' policy, leaving one's opponent in no doubt of one's resolution;

▷ Its unambiguity is expected to prevent any major war;

▷ It uses the cheapest technology in terms of 'more bangs for the buck', in place of expensive conventional forces;

▷ It is politically useful in reducing the number of troops needed (and hence any pressures for conscription) and as a strong assertion of national will;

▷ It is said to deter conventional as well as nuclear attack;

▷ It secures a seat at the top table and the capacity to 'negotiate from strength';

▷ It has 'proved', since 1945, that it works;

▷ It is fully compatible with verifiable arms control, disarmament agreements and a co-operative relationship;

▷ There is no alternative.

The arguments against a comprehensive and high dependence on nuclear weapons (as opposed to an 'ultimate' dependency) may be summarised as follows:

▷ Such doomsday devices are too powerful to be useful, sensible or moral. They could not, for example, be employed for long on the Inner German Border without killing millions of civilians on both sides;

▷ A limited nuclear war would almost certainly escalate into a total war;

▷ Such a war would damage or destroy whole regions beyond the battle zones through 'nuclear winter';

▷ High dependency on nuclear weapons fosters mutual fears bordering on paranoia, a high technology arms race and both vertical and horizontal proliferation;

▷ Comprehensive nuclear deterrence creates such acute suspicions as to spoil the prospects of any really radical measures of arms control or disarmament;

▷ The intrinsic fears of cataclysmic surprise attack generate destabilising technologies like computer-based launch-on-warning;

▷ Nuclear tensions frighten non-aligned nations, excite superpower interventions and therefore contribute to general instability;

▷ The associated demands for secrecy and internal security may weaken precisely the democratic values and institutions the strategy is meant to protect;

▷ The consequent public controversy makes consensus on defence matters increasingly hard to sustain.

One Cheer for the Doves ... And One for the Hawks too!

How does one come out from this bombardment of rival arguments? As it seems to me, all three of the dove's main options show vivid awareness of the moral obscenity of nuclear war, the fallibility of both Superpowers and the need for understanding between them. They are perhaps especially sensitive to the terrible cost of the East–West obsession in terms of the urgent needs of Third World development and environmental care. The doves clearly deserve at least one cheer.

Yet so do the hawks. All three of their main options recognise the cruel realities of international life, the prevalence of national pride, greed and short-sightedness and the pious irrelevance of policies wholly dependent on trust or goodwill.

Nevertheless doves and hawks also seem to share many serious inadequacies. Both tend to assume that most wars are started deliberately, through the conscious calculation of governments rather than through muddle, accident and miscalculation. The hawk's notion of deterrence, like the dove's faith in conciliation, tacitly assumes that governments make rational decisions on the basis of accurate information, cool logic and weighed risks. As I have argued, however, many wars begin through loss of control rather than aggressive design.

Hawks and doves also both tend to be preoccupied by weapons systems; to hawks they are the necessary tools of deterrent strength and to the doves they are the terrifying arsenal which might explode. Both arguments have some force but in an age of massive overkill, additional weapons systems do not necessarily add either to strength or, it must be said, to danger. Likewise both factions, as 'armers' and 'disarmers' respectively, see the level of arms as the decisive measure of security or insecurity. Both hawk and dove perch on the same branch albeit at opposite ends. Both, wrongly I believe, put more faith in quantifiable arms reductions than in undramatic measures of political discussion and confidence-building.

Many doves are fairly charged with reckless idealism, yet some kinds of hawk suffer from it too. A worrying idealism lies beneath the hard carapace of the crusader and a different sort of naivety in those whose immense faith in governmental competence allows them to believe that a nuclear-armed confrontation can be safely perpetuated for decade after decade.

Common Strengths

Whatever their various faults, both classic positions include perceptions and values that will be held in a creative tension in any persuasive defence policy. We might especially admire the moderate hawk's willingness to face harsh realities; his unsentimental readiness to choose between evils; his forthright robustness in the face of threat; his willingness to employ force when absolutely necessary. Yet, likewise, we may admire the dove's keenness to experiment with peaceful means of resolving conflicts; his firm belief in humanity's capacity to rise above narrow national and doctrinal interests and his unshakable recognition that a nuclear war could consort with neither virtue nor rationality.

Both extreme positions are also authentic in human terms. The warrior and the saint are equally archetypal characters and, whatever our own views, we should admire the genuine heroes of both sides — the long lines of valiant soldiers and sailors of all ranks and the heroes of non-violence like the Hungarian leader Ferenc Deak, the Brazilian Colonel Candedo Rondon, the Indian Gandhi and the Frenchman Jean Goss, whose stories have been compared by John Ferguson[2]. Both positions also take seriously international politics in general and the chances of war: they are not passive, indifferent or fatally resigned.

What most participants in the traditional defence debate have failed to see is that many of the strengths of hawk and dove are not necessarily incompatible. Much depends on how far a principle is taken or how rigidly an attitude is struck. To a surprising degree we shall discover that many of the views of the hawk and the dove can be usefully combined, even integrated, in what I am calling the owl's position.

The Owl's View

Such integration would first require us to listen carefully to our opponents and build on the common ground. Without this, no real movement will be possible. With it, the owl could become a powerful third voice in the debate. Indeed, I believe his position must gradually become the ruling consensus if we are to save our species. Secondly, we need to see that the owl's view is not just another position on military defence. As we have seen, he is very much the improver and navigator in his understanding of politics and knows that security is much more than a military matter.

The owl[3] is above all flexible and pragmatic. He is not shackled by particular visions of the human future or governed by absolute perceptions of political virtue or vice. He is clear about desirable processes and rather agnostic about ultimate destinations. He brings real honour, not merely grudging respect, to the crafts of the politician and the diplomat. Irrespective of party, the public is apt to see the owl as a self-interested creature of egoism, ambition, soft living and superficial charm who is sunk deep into back-room scheming, systematic evasion and conscienceless compromise. The owl not only acknowledges their patience and stamina in what is often a frustratingly cruel business but positively applauds those processes of give-and-take, of civilising compromise, which are vital to progress and to democracy itself. Some think of bargaining (and 'giving way') as a necessary evil. It should be celebrated as a high and virtuous craft. It is perturbing when a political leader is contemptuous of compromise and boasts of how little he or she has budged.

Thirdly, the owl tries to see the complex interactions of many factors, rather than be driven by a single pattern of ideas, the temptation alike of doves and hawks. The owl dares to unearth unspoken assumptions and settled 'convictions' of the orthodoxies. This fresh and pragmatic temper need not, however, lead to 'open-minded' passivity or dogmatism. He knows we do not know everything, that we can be wrong; and must bring others along too if change is to happen.

We are therefore right to be dissatisfied with the old thinking, the primitive dove – hawk dualism and the kinds of policy choices it has generated. To do better we must re-examine the fundamentals.

PART II

Towards Treatment

7

Peace, War and the Redefinition of Security

> There are some roads not to follow; some troops not to strike; some cities not to assault; and some ground which should not be contested.
>
> Sun Tzu, *The Art of War, circa* 500 BC

Before a conference at Kyoto in September 1986 Henry Kissinger[1] remarked to Yasuhiro Nakasone, then Japan's Prime Minister, how different the perceptions of security were in Asia than in Europe. Nakasone replied:

> The difference is the difference between European paintings and Japanese paintings. . . . In a Japanese painting it is the empty spaces which give meaning to the design and they leave a great deal therefore to the perception of the observer.

Kissinger used Nakasone's metaphor to argue that the Western debate on security had more-or-less run into the sand, to the detriment of creative policy-making. For example, despite many key differences, Asian security had been less systematically addressed than European. In contrast to Europe's clear East – West dividing line and integrated commands, Asia had no single common threat, no large alliances and no common diplomacy. There were also subtler differences like the Asians' relative indifference to weapon-counting, or arms control as such, as opposed to longer term political and global factors — the empty spaces in Nakasone's Japanese painting.

What we see here is not only a contrast between different theatres, the European and the Asian, but between different modes of perception. Each picture has its own logic, its own sort of truth. One or both may be partly distorted but each its own descriptive power. We are speaking of what political sociologists somewhat heavily call the 'assumptive worlds' of the decision-maker — the assumptions as to what is significant, connected, germane, urgent or desirable. These assumptions can be so obvious (or so disagreeable) to the decision-makers that they may be only partly conscious. We may notice how all six policies considered in the last Chapter are largely preoccupied, whether in acceptance or rejection, with violence, power and arms — the military dimension. The pacifist can be quite as obsessed by arms as a Field Marshal. Sometimes the strongest of disagreements may conceal fundamental but unexamined agreements as to the nature of the problem and hence the dimension — for instance, disarmament or rearmament — within which remedies should be sought.

An assumptive world or paradigm that is shared by antagonists is, of course, especially hard to identify and challenge. It is difficult enough for us to credit that both opposing positions may be wrong, let alone for the same reason. In this sense the two extremes are partners in an unconscious conspiracy to exclude both 'compromise' and alternative modes of thinking.

Paradigm Shift

Fortunately even the most treasured paradigms can be overturned, as when Copernicus and Galileo overthrew the view — nay, the conviction — that the sun goes round the earth, a scientific re-evaluation of staggering symbolic significance as well as scientific power. Likewise, Newton, Lavoisier, Darwin and Einstein each destroyed or transcended a previously dominant theory defended by a confidently dismissive old guard. Sometimes, of course, the old theory, like Newtonian physics, retains some crude value even though for greater accuracy and comprehensiveness we must now depend on the Einsteinian paradigm — until in turn this too is replaced.

There can also of course be profound paradigm shifts in the meanings of social and political concepts such as property, law, and freedom, although in human affairs values are also involved. You cannot study income distribution in a totally neutral way when there can be legitimate disagreements about 'life-chances' versus 'entrepreneurial incentives'. We need to notice that, traditionally, both Left and Right wings tended to want the same narrowly defined 'wealth': they simply disagreed about how to produce and share it. Now the 'Greens' are insisting that they should re-examine that old shared paradigm by taking account also of the wider social and environmental costs.

In a nuclear age there is an even more urgent need to reassess what we mean by international security and to construct a new paradigm capable of comprising more of the new realities and of gradually earning substantial support alike from hawks and doves, East and West and North and South. At the very least it should help us elaborate more sophisticated criteria — and values — than those offered by the traditional military paradigm.

Pacifism: A Tragic *Cul-de-Sac?*

What might a new paradigm of security look like? Probably the most drastic departure from current orthodoxies would be the adoption of pacifism as a political philosophy, not just as an individual moral position. I cannot go as far as that myself and I should say why.

Admiring many pacifists, and having myself been one as a young man, I frankly find this a tormenting subject. Within the Christian context, much of the pain and confusion may be due to failures to make the old distinction between the Latin *pax* and the Hebrew *shalom*. *Pax* is the usually transient peace of an ordered community, national or international, in which conflicts are restrained by negotiation, custom, law and, ultimately, by the threat of coercion. *Shalom* is the ultimate peace that passeth all understanding, the peace of God rather than the absence of conflict: a vision of justice, harmony and right relationship that Christians would associate with an idea like the Second Coming.

Pax is essentially a political concept, *shalom* a spiritual one. There are of course some connections: political peace is arguably a precondition of spiritual peace, and spiritual peace will always need to be upheld somehow as an absolute standard and vision for the political peacemaker. Nevertheless political peace and spiritual peace are not the same and what serves one does not necessarily serve the other. This is not, after all, a matter only of abstract theology but one of empirical fact measured out in the blood and tears of history.

Perhaps we need a distinction parallel to *pax* versus *shalom* between our duty as a citizen and as a spiritual being, the first requiring compromise and calculation, the second a striving for perfection as exemplified in the Sermon on the Mount. Such a splitting of our political from our personal obligations makes us feel very uncomfortable, perhaps rightly; but either way we must always be clear whether we are talking about the political practicalities of government or the spiritual requirements of a religious commitment.

There need be no argument about the evils and stupidities of war or the inspiration offered by those who self-sacrificially adopt active non-violent resistance. To describe such a pacifist as selfish, passive, cowardly, unpatriotic or dishonourable is simply foolish. But whether the absolute pacifist bases his case on divine authority, holy texts, the voice of conscience or the requirements of salvation, it is quite another matter for him to claim that non-violence would always, or even usually, produce fewer or briefer wars. This is a question of practical judgement, not moral theory. Most non-pacifists are not morally indifferent towards killing but they recognise that to cling to one absolute principle, like 'Thou shalt not kill', is often to breach another, such as 'Protect the innocent' or 'Defend freedom'. Moral 'laws' are sober guidelines, not absolute instructions; this, I take to be part of what was behind Jesus saying he brought the spirit not the law. The core of morality is to love one another; the perennial problem is how.

Beyond a certain point, abstract argument seems less powerful than practical self-questioning. Can we regret that Britain finally confronted Hitler? Or that Churchill did not surrender after Dunkirk to save life? Can we not imagine extreme circumstances in which we might ourselves take up arms in support of a beleaguered ghetto or an African refugee camp?

That worthy motives can be abused, that miscalculations can follow and that the actual results of fighting can prove disastrous, is obvious. There *is* a slippery slope but that slope is precisely where life is lived. And so it is for pacifists themselves when they face their own terrible responsibility for the lives and liberty of the innocent. One may respect the great cry of 'I can do no other' but not if there is a denial or evasion of the real cost.

In the nuclear age a new form of almost existential pacifism is emerging, for which I have some sympathy. The American poet Wendell Berry[2] says:

> It may be that ... the command to love one another is becoming an absolute
> practical necessity, such as we never dreamed it to be before, and that our choice
> is not to win or lose, but to love our enemies or die.

Such statements can be powerfully moving and one knows just
what he means. But we must recognise that we do not know how
to introduce his policy of 'no weapons' or how, in an already
armed world, to love our enemies. What sort of scenario does
Wendell Berry envisage? A burning of arms in country after
country as the revelation arrives? Who does what first? The
rhetoric is heartfelt but the fine cadences demand to be transposed
into convincing proposals for action.

The Just War

The main way in which men have sought to square the circle
between principle and practice has been the 'Just War'. Traditionally it would be fought for a just cause and by a legitimate
authority. It would be fought as a last resort but with real hope of
success and without excessive military means of disproportionate
destruction: the lives and property of the innocent would be
safeguarded, prisoners-of-war treated with respect, and the defeated with mercy.

These criteria make a powerful appeal, yet it is highly questionable whether they could be met by virtually any modern war. Our
military means are even less 'proportionate' than 'Bomber' Harris's
in his onslaught on German cities, and it is harder than ever to
safeguard, or even define, the innocent. The unselectiveness of
modern totalitarianism, as well as that of modern war, could make
us conclude that, where a war is basically just, the breach of many
traditional criteria has to be accepted. Many will argue that the
death of thousands of innocent people may be a necessary price for
the defence of millions against a tyranny. This argument plainly
treads extremely dangerous ground.

We appear to end in a moral tangle and that may be the
disturbing truth of our situation. Some moral philosophers are not
surprised, and doubt whether any satisfactorily systematic moral
theory can be constructed even where its Christian, humanist or
any other premises are taken as given. They are apt to say that the
moral life is just not like that anyway, that there is a huge gulf
between making god-like judgements and working out how to act

amidst shifting circumstances, with partial knowledge and conflicting obligations.

However, this need not mean we slide into moral chaos. It may induce some humility, discourage moral absolutism and make rational discussion easier, especially where likely consequences are accepted as the major test of policy. We may make better headway if we pay as much attention to new facts as to old bodies of moral theory, for all their inspirational value.

The Nuclear Revolution

The death knell of proportionality in war was sounded at Hiroshima. So utterly indiscriminate an act demanded a drastic reappraisal of all moral and military theories. True, some people seem to regard nuclear warheads as no more than super-high explosives but as against this grotesque simple-mindedness most of us recognise profound differences:

▷ the unprecedently immense scale of all but the smallest nuclear explosions;
▷ their instantaneity in destroying a whole city or army and therefore the virtual defencelessness of anyone in the target area;
▷ the genetic damage to succeeding generations as well as the mutilation of present ones through blast, fire and irradiation;
▷ the immense psychological impact of these death-dealing capacities;
▷ the likely impossibility of effective defence (*pace* the remaining believers in SDI);
▷ the climatic, environmental and human disaster of 'nuclear winter' to neutral states well beyond the boundaries of the warring states;
▷ the strong likelihood of any limited nuclear war escalating into total war and hence the virtual suicide of the combatants.

All this has put many key strategic concepts into grave question: 'victory' becomes virtually meaningless and 'superiority' no guarantee of survival, let alone success. The way has been opened to new ideas about the purposes of armaments and the logic of war.

The Rational War?

It is highly ironic that the Prussian philosopher of war, Karl von Clausewitz (1780–1831), second only to Machiavelli as a demon figure to the doves, produced the basis for probably the most devastating critique of current nuclear strategies. Clausewitz[3] defined war as 'an act of force to compel our enemy to do our will' and argued at great length for a concentration on efforts, once a war had begun, to destroy the enemy's forces, the source of his power, rather than to destroy the enemy in general. This relatively civilised notion is what he somewhat oddly called Absolute War. Unfortunately, however, his most quoted statement about war being 'a continuation of politics by other means' has made him widely regarded as a cynic who unscrupulously recommended the use of war when politics failed to deliver what a nation wanted.

Without painting Clausewitz as a latter-day St Francis, Field Marshal Lord Carver, amongst others, has explained that the Prussian's view was quite the opposite — that war as 'a continuation of political intercourse, with the addition of other means' signifies that the objectives and methods of any war must be judged by the same basic political criteria as governed policy before the war and will do so after it. War neither requires nor justifies resort to the law of the jungle.

As Lord Carver[4] points out, Clausewitz believed the destruction and damage caused by a war and the desire for revenge it provokes, may negate its original purpose (or justification). War is meant to result in a better state of peace, at least from one's own point of view. It is wholly irrational otherwise. For Clausewitz, it was not essential for the enemy's forces to be totally defeated; nor should a government's policy become subservient to military or strategic requirements. On the contrary, politics should govern throughout — the criteria should be reasons of state not reasons of war as such.

This fundamental principle has a number of corollaries that were already largely summed up by Sun Tzu over two millenniums ago when he told us not to forget the need to live peacefully alongside the enemy after his defeat, and to achieve victory in the shortest possible time and at least possible cost in lives, including enemy lives. War, in short, was to be limited, measured and, in its conduct, foresighted.

Tragically, of course, quite the opposite has been happening. Since Clausewitz, and certainly since the American Civil War, industrialisation, swift mass transport, easy communication, rapid weapons development, mass conscription and mass propaganda have combined to foster 'absolute wars' of quite another kind — absolute in their range, intensity and hatreds. Of such wars, and such an outlook on war, perhaps the apotheosis was 'unconditional surrender' until, that is, the arrival of the nuclear bomb.

Redefining Security: The Owl's View

In essence, the application of Clausewitz's thinking to the new era of potentially ultimate destruction makes sheer survival the supreme common interest and hence international stability more critical, to weak and strong states alike, than it has ever been. Indeed, it provides the underlying logic for the redefinition of security towards which we have been working — the view, as I see it, of the owl.

Essentially, the traditional emphasis of the hawks has been on military defence, military strength and, if war becomes necessary, military victory. The emphasis of the doves by contrast has been on non-confrontative conciliation, leading to a peace that is ideally combined with justice. The owl seeks to combine something of both views; he cannot despise or reject the military dimension nor, of course, the high aspirations of the doves. In a singularly perilous world, he applies Clausewitz's core criterion of political rationality to make the preservation of international stability, and hence the avoidance of nuclear war, his very first concern.

This concern with stability is not to be confused with preserving the *status quo* at any cost to the weak and powerless. In a fast-changing world scene, the avoidance of needless conflict, in the Middle East for example, may well demand drastic international action. Stability is not the same as either complacency or passivity.

As I see it, the basic features of the owl's view of security may be summarised like this:

▷ *Security comes before defence.* Defence almost supposes from the outset that the military dimension is the crucial one. This is rarely so: security is a broader and richer concept, even though capability for military defence is part of it.

▷ *Security is regional, even global, not just national.* Take only the dangers of epidemics or terrorism; in an interdependent world of swift communications purely national security is now impossible, whether for David or Goliath.

▷ *True security safeguards national freedoms and ways of life, not just national independence.* It is largely this broader sense of self-determination that under-writes its moral standing. Security is ultimately for people, not merely for states.

82

▷ *For this and other reasons, security is social, economic and cultural before it is diplomatic, let alone military.*

▷ *Political and military security remains crucial, however.* In my view it is essential to maintain armed forces capable of deterring or resisting any serious attack on legitimate national or allied interests. (Of course many different views can be taken of what is legitimate).

▷ *Security policies should be beneficial!* The likely benefits, including those of any actual military action, must have a very good chance of outweighing the costs. People need to feel safe in relation to their own government's policies, not just those of potential aggressors. Otherwise why should they support their government in the face of attack?

To use the language of the navigator, I would see both the hawk and the dove as believing — with unshakeable confidence — that only their way provides a safe, clear channel to peace and that the other's would lead to shipwreck. The owl sees both hawks and doves as heading for shipwreck — albeit of different kinds. He insists that there is, in fact, no 'clear channel' for anyone. There are rocks and rapids everywhere and perhaps just enough leeway to navigate to safer, if never entirely safe, waters. The owl can often be confident about what are bad routes but, conditions being as they are, he will not pretend to be able dogmatically to define a safe one himself. He knows the desirable general direction; he knows the rocks and seas (being more interested in them than in theories); he knows how ships and crews are likely to behave. He also dares to take the responsibility of being practical, of suggesting specific action. He does not just make speeches.

The Owl's View of Nuclear Weapons

Be all that as it may, where does the owl come out on nuclear weapons? Following Lord Carver, the owl says nuclear war is not war: it is not a means through which rational ends can be achieved. It could scarcely bring about a better peace than the peace preceding it, however dreadful that was. Nor could it be reasonably expected to result in conditions preferable to even the worst political oppression. Preparations for nuclear war fighting as such are, therefore, absurd: there could be no 'victory', no-one could 'prevail', there could not even be any small net benefit. The avoidance of nuclear war must therefore be a stateman's highest priority: nothing at all could be worse.

Some might say that anything is better than surrender and dishonour. This sounds very grand and is somewhat affecting. It is surely also nonsense, perhaps wicked nonsense. The highest military ethics have always insisted that surrender is right when defeat is inevitable — or victory suicidal — and no profit can come from further loss of life. Could one seriously argue that the general carnage in Central Europe of combatant and civilian alike, of friend as well as foe, would be preferable to the subjugation of Western Europe? Is it really better to be dead than red? Or capitalist blue? Such arguments are, I think, ridiculous.

They are also, surely, in some sense both spiritually and morally heretical. They are rooted in the idea that there could be no hope of redeeming, say, Communist rule: that its evil is so total that no passage of time, no exercise of the human spirit, of love indeed, could ever change it. Such a belief is, I believe, false, paranoid and absurd but it is also, finally, an expression of hopelessness. It says in effect that, under Communism anyway, there can be life *without* hope. That was not even true of Auschwitz.

The owl, therefore, says that nuclear war would be the worst conceivable evil — worse even than alien totalitarian rule. Unfortunately, however, this is not the choice that life offers to us. What individual states and alliances must decide is whether it is worth running a small risk of nuclear destruction to circumvent a more substantial risk, sooner or later, of a hostile nuclear threat leading to subjugation.

We shall consider these political issues later. All I am stressing here is that the owl fully acknowledges the complications. For example, it does not follow from the clear irrationality of nuclear war (as I see it) that the possession of nuclear weapons has not helped to deter major war between the superpower alliances. They could have done so. The issue hinges not on whether nuclear weapons are 'usable' but whether superpower leaders have *thought* they might actually be used and have altered their conduct in consequence. Even so, the key questions for the owl are not general ones about whether nuclear arms can deter but, for example, how far they can do so without increasing the chances of nuclear war.

As I have said, the owl believes, however reluctantly, that

nuclear weapons will now be perennially re-inventable and great powers will always be gravely tempted to redevelop them in times of crisis, if only as a precaution. On this analysis, nuclear weaponry will always be waiting in the wings, however far we cut it back. Few if any nuclear powers are therefore likely to take 'abolition' seriously, however vividly their public rhetoric calls for it. Their real interest will be in arms reduction and arms control, quite another approach.

The owl would never, however, suggest that nuclear arms would be of any real use in combat. He sees their only rational purpose as deterring their use by anyone else. It is theoretically possible to use a few nuclear weapons at sea without disastrous human or environmental consequences but the breach of the critical psychological barrier makes even this *caveat* almost futile. The owl, therefore, wants to move towards a situation in which at most they provide an ultimate counter-threat to any threat of nuclear blackmail and therefore to the policy of what we shall be calling Minimum Defensive Deterrence or MDD.

The Moral Crunch

I promised earlier to return to the moral tangle. Doves will rightly insist I do so since I have found myself driven to accept that the retention of nuclear weapons to deter their use by others can, if rarely, be justified. This they will find profoundly unacceptable. But before they cast me into outer darkness, let me utter a few words of defence.

First, I am thinking of the situation of say, the United States *vis-à-vis* the Soviet Union. As I understand it, not even CND demands that Washington should unilaterally dispense with all its nuclear weapons before Moscow has done so.

Secondly, my key criterion has to be the avoidance of nuclear war rather than the intrinsic evil of the weapons — which is a complex proposition, easier to feel than to argue. And the avoidance of war is a practical, empirical matter, not a 'purely' moral one (if indeed there is such a thing).

Thirdly, I see the Superpowers' understandable retention of at least some nuclear weapons as no valid excuse for other powers, say Britain or France, to keep or acquire them. This discrimination will sound unjust to smaller powers; I seek only to be practical in the situation as it now is.

Fourthly, agreement to the Superpowers' retaining some nuclear weapons means no automatic assent to their current nuclear policies. As I shall suggest, these should be radically changed.

Fifthly, I persist in a violent revulsion against the very idea of a nuclear threat. A friend, the author Patrick Rivers, says I am nevertheless recommending MNI — Minimum Necessary Immorality. He is right. He thinks this is outrageous. I fear that anything else is impractical or worse.

Sixthly, I hope the policy of minimal dependence on nuclear threat can be a passing stage on the road to a world order that could wholly dispense with it. (Although that would presumably depend on ultimate sanctions even more powerful than those which the nuclear miscreant could himself apply.)

I confess to grave doubt as to whether my position (or the Vatican's or much of the Church of England's) could confidently be called Christian. It is certainly a long march away from the Sermon on the Mount. But I do hope it cannot be written off as an obviously immoral response to the nuclear world as we find it.

A Residual Role

What is the eventual objective of the owl's policy? It is gradually to ease nuclear weapons into a purely residual role, to ease them into the incidental margins of future history. We must learn to see them not just as obscene but as basically irrelevant to practical defence arrangements rather than, as now, their ostensible core. Nuclear weapons cannot be magicked away but, as Stan Windass[5] has interestingly suggested, they might eventually be ritualised like a Lord Chancellor's mace that *could* kill but is used only as a symbol of authority. On this view, nuclear warheads would become an ultimate and all but unusable deterrent capacity in a world that had grown beyond its nuclear adolescence. This situation, however, is a virtually impossible achievement whilst most Western leaders — and many elsewhere — are convinced that the Soviet Union still represents a potential threat. To this subject we now turn.

8

Two Troubled Giants

America wants peace; the Soviet Union wants the world.
Former President Richard Nixon[1], 1988

Long before Mikhail Gorbachev became a household name, many distinguished people were calling the Soviet threat grossly exaggerated. Yet until recently at least, the Pentagon[2] has still been saying it sees no reason to conclude that the talk about 'reasonable sufficiency' from Moscow 'represents a renunciation or even an alteration of the inherently offensive Soviet military strategy.' Some other Western governments — not all — privately take a similarly jaundiced view. Indeed, Sir Geoffrey Howe on Panorama overtly greeted Gorbachev's April 1989 visit to Britain with accusations that he was 'seeking to beguile public opinion' with one proposal after another while the reality remained that of 'this huge bear' still looming over Europe.

Capabilities and Intentions

However broadly we redefine security, a major test of policy has to remain the military capabilities and likely intentions or long-term ambitions of the potential adversary. Strong capability without hostile intent is not worrying; nor is a hostility allied to a poor capability. Western Europe does not see the huge military strength of the United States as a threat, or not a direct one.

Both capabilities and intentions are hard to judge, especially in a closed society. Although reconnaissance satellites can read number plates, they cannot assess the condition of the tank, the training, discipline and morale of its crew, nor, on which side a Polish crew would fight. Estimates are also often highly subjective.

There are few effective checks on official exaggerations; witness the history of scare stories about an alleged East – West bomber-gap, a missile-gap and other Soviet 'windows of opportunity'.

Assessing 'intentions' is still more problematic. We have a profound tendency not only to seek an enemy figure but then to caricature him; we project upon him not only our darkest fears but some of our own worst features. The enemy's ruthlessness at once justifies and increases our own. *His* hostility is unforgiveable: *ours* is defensive. To the satisfactions of humbug, we add the pleasures of self-righteousness. Moreover we see the enemy not just as absolutely wicked but as icily efficient, not only unscrupulous but devilishly well-organised.

Soviet history is certainly stained with much horror and blood, not all of it in the Stalin era. Nevertheless, the muddle, mess and torpor that any of us may witness for ourselves in the Soviet Union alone casts doubt on the diabolic view. An increasingly bankrupt ideology and a frail national unity built largely on fear and frankly authoritarian management scarcely makes the strongest basis for adventurism. Any master plan for world revolution locked in the Politburo's bottom drawer could only be a comic document of vain rhetorical ambition woven around political irrelevancy. Such kits cannot work, whether aimed at revolution or reaction. There are far too many unknowns. The Soviet Union is certainly ruthless and militarily powerful, however inefficient, and has long been hostile to the capitalist system. But none of this amounts to a master plan, any more than does the existence of opposite hankerings amongst some post-war American administrations. (When does an aim of making the world safe against Communism become an imperial quest? If we sometimes have a problem of interpreting our potential enemy, so does Moscow.)

Extreme hawks claim that the Soviet Union is too profoundly perfidious for any agreement with it to be dependable; that it must not be lived alongside but beaten. By contrast, many doves have always seen the Russians as misunderstood and embattled former allies with bitter memories of successive Western onslaughts and interventions and mortal fears of encirclement and attack. In their view, the Soviet Union is too weak or too peace-loving for the West to have need of strong defences or, presumably, any defence system at all. These opposite extremes seem to me almost equally facile and misleading.

Personal Impressions

My first childhood idea of the Russians was as the wicked comic book foes losing against the valiant Finns, all in white on skis. Later, however, they became our heroic allies, led by the courageous Stalin who liberated half Europe from Nazism. Then came the Cold War, the shocks of the Berlin air lift, Hungary 1956, Cuba 1962, Prague 1968 and so on. While never becoming a Cold War warrior, I came to see the Soviet Union as at once powerful, unsqueamish and, if basically defensive in outlook, fully prepared to attack if necessary and certainly to avoid any defeat.

Our first visit to the Soviet Union, a few years ago, was a revelation of complexity compounded by ambiguity. My wife and I flew into Moscow one October night in the Andropov era and the huge clinical airport, bare but for a few political slogans, was indeed an Orwellian caricature. So were the dark, wet, empty streets on the way to the gargantuan ghetto of a hotel, barred, it seemed, to all Russians apart from security people, spivs and call-girls.

We at once tested those stories about being followed everywhere by taking the Metro, rumbling between palatial stations, to emerge on to the wet moonlit cobblestones of an empty Red Square. It was silent save for the *clunk*, *clunk*, of a few goose-stepping guards outside the main Kremlin gate and the mumbled singing of a few drunken students somewhere behind St. Basil's amazing onion-domed cathedral. We were quite alone. (No one followed us then or later, in a dozen cities.) We stood transfixed by being so suddenly at the heart of what people have variously seen as Mother Russia, the fount of revolutionary hope, the 'evil empire' or the potential epicentre of the most awful war in history.

Here certainly was the nerve-centre of a prodigious state power. Beyond those high walls, straight through that arch with its few smart sentries and traffic lights, were the controllers and commanders of the whole system: the Armed Services, the Government and Party apparatus, the economy, the public services, the Press, the KGB, the Gulag, the whole panoply of near-imperial power stretching from the Baltic to Vladivostok. Across Red Square flapped some banners with revolutionary slogans torn by the wind; over by the GUM department store, someone giggled in the shadows.

During our ensuing tour, a thousand warring impressions were added: the friendly questions ('American'?); the meat queues and the often marvellous concerts: the brutal architecture and the grandiloquent monuments; the neat shepherded primary school children at a Lenin shrine and the old women birch-brushing the streets. Then, in Central Asia, there was the jolly curiosity of the round-faced Khazaks at a wedding outside Alma-Ata, the site later of a race riot; the stiff Victorian values preached to us at a cultural centre; the Uzbek stonemasons' dedication in repairing the mosque-museums at Samarkand and the drab apology for a Moslem seminary at Tashkent. Here indeed was a modern city where the Asian poor stalled their house-cows off narrow streets only a hundred yards from the high-rise, 'European' shopping centre. We had forgotten that the Soviet Union is also a Third World country.

Reassuring the Dissidents

How can we make sense of such mixed impressions? We must first reassure the Russian dissenters that we recognise that Soviet society has long been one of quite fearful oppression and that, despite many recent improvements, Soviet authoritarianism remains evident in the Party's almost total control of the media, its denial of the rights of organised political opposition, its abuse of due legal process and its cruel arbitrariness.

To register such abuses is not to deny that there are some partly mitigating historic causes or that some régimes identified with the West, like South Korea, Chile or Turkey, have features in the same league of infamy. But we must think clearly; the Soviet system remains substantially oppressive and stupid, if also one now bravely attempting reform. It sprang from nobly eglitarian ideals but also out of a cruelly feudal, secretly-policed society and it adopted a profoundly dogmatic and materialistic philosophy. Despite some real insights, Marxism-Leninism does permit the use of individuals in their millions as incidental means to huge ends instead of their being free to work out their own small destinies. A revolutionary society became a profoundly conservative one in which the power and privileges of the ruling élites mocked the high motives of the founders. The members of the so-called *nomenklatura* were often cynical 'radish Communists', red on the outside but white within: people who learned young that promotion, good money and foreign travel were hard to get without a Party card. Not surprisingly, the grand design was largely forgotten.

Greed, injustice, stupidity, humbug and different sorts of oppression stain every society but here they are by-products of totalitarian controls which are especially horrifying to Westerners because they provide virtually no safe or effective means of protest. The recent improvements are, as yet, more symbols of aspiration than achievements of dependable substance. Most elections are still essentially a farce, the printed word is closely watched, the law does not yet rule, organised opposition is still dangerous. As we heard for ourselves, any dissent may be regarded as anti-Soviet activity and suspicious contacts are promptly reported by Party narks. Stepping out of line invites sanctions which are beyond effective appeal. No doubt the economics teacher in Tbilisi still fears demotion for expressing his heterodox views: Moslem Khazaks probably still cannot buy the Koran and people met in the park at Sochi will still get into trouble if they come for a drink in your hotel. Much of the paraphenalia of domestic Soviet tyranny is trivial and grotesquely paranoid. People are not beaten up in the streets. Instead you see a drab (if often cheerful) citizenry to whom politics in our sense is still largely denied.

Such judgements sound harsh, even dangerous, to those who ache above all for peace between the blocs. Yet stable international arrangements cannot and should not depend on people glossing over harsh truths, let alone refusing to see them. Sensible relationships do not depend on approval of each other's political systems. Our task is to manage our antagonisms and differences, not to pretend they do not exist. Few any longer doubt that the Soviet Union is now embarked on a radical programme of economic and even political reform. *Perestroika* (restructuring) is essential and therefore *glasnost* (openness) is virtually inescapable. But will a stronger Soviet Union be safer to live with? Should the West still regard the Soviet Union as fundamentally expansionist? Or is it, basically, a deeply troubled empire now intent on halting its slide into Third World status and securing its own survival?

Soviet Imperialism?

No nation is intrinsically imperialistic and it is especially ironic when the British, French, Germans or Belgians utter this charge against the Russians, having themselves blithely carved up Africa as recently as 1884. Expansionism is born of circumstances, ambitions and opportunity, not of some intrinsic national or racial evil. The post-war extension of Soviet power across Europe was primarily to establish a defensive glacis to prevent any future war being fought on Russian soil (with the loss of another 20 million people), but it would surely be naive to imagine that Moscow would scruple further to extend its sway in Europe or elsewhere if it were safe or possible to do so. Few great powers in history have ever shown such restraint. But *safe* is the word. Moscow has generally been extremely careful to avoid action likely to risk a major war; Cuba in 1962 was a dramatic exception.

Any Soviet bid to seize part of Western Europe would create even larger dangers. Anyway, why inherit a war-torn landscape filled with once rich and still stroppy Western democrats who would prove even more difficult to dragoon than the East Europeans? In fact, the only country where Soviet forces themselves have crossed the post-war East–West divide is Afghanistan and even that proved too much for them.

Essentially, the Soviet Union is now far too weak to risk foreign adventures, let alone conquests. Indeed in power terms it is now clearly in retreat. Nor will this situation change in the forseeable future. There is no economic depth to the superficial military strength. It is way behind several of the Western (and Asian) powers in electronics, computer science, robotics, lasers and so on. This gap is still widening. In terms of production and of income *per capita*, the Soviet Union has been a very poor performer. Its total gross national product (even including the East Europeans') is far behind Western Europe's and is remaining almost static. Seventy years after the Revolution, Russia is still humiliatingly dependent on Western supplies of wheat, let alone technology.

Mikhail Gorbachev has to perform a second Russian revolution if this moribund society is to get moving or even stay intact, for he also has to meet the frustrations of the Armenians, Khazaks, the Baltic peoples and the Ukrainians. Meanwhile the Central Asian nationalities are far out-breeding the Russians and nearly half the Soviet Army is expected to be Moslem by origin (with Russian as second language at best) within the next decade or two — a fact of some interest to Islamic fundamentalists.

The Soviet Record Overseas

Another great constraint on any remaining Soviet ambition is its tenuous hold over Eastern Europe, a volatile mixture of very different societies — witness the tension between Hungary and Romania — in a pressurised container. In Europe, the Soviet Union has, therefore, become a *status quo* power, more concerned to retain its fragile general hegemony (while trying to spread *glasnost*) than to extend it. Meanwhile, as I have seen for myself, the differences between, say, Czechoslovakia and Poland, now, astonishingly, with a Solidarity-led government, are probably greater than those between any two Western European countries.

The Soviet Union's performance in the Third World has been no more impressive. Soviet 'anti-colonialism' already looked fraudulent before Afghanistan and, to African and Asian ears, Marxist ideology affords little understanding of nationalism, tradition and tribal identity and none of religion; it appears not only abstract, dogmatic and grossly materialistic but incapable of delivering the good things of life.

Soviet ventures in the Third World have been expensive and not notably successful: witness the prodigious wasted investment in Nasser's Egypt and, later, in Somalia. In Angola and Ethiopia it has been frustrated. Cuba and Nicaragua offer some (very costly) encouragement but its Indo-Chinese policies have long contributed to the tensions with Peking.

Despite a recent easing of relations, the looming presence of a potentially hostile China must especially worry Soviet policy-makers. They contemplate well over a billion energetic Chinese swiftly multiplying their economic strength over the coming decades, with the increasingly active help, no doubt, of Japan. Eventually, Moscow might be confronted, horror of horrors, by a Sino-American alliance.

Some say that an economically wretched and internally unstable Soviet régime could prove more, not less, dangerous: they see the dying giant lashing out across the European Central Front in a final act of desperation. But if Soviet strength and Soviet weakness are held to be equally threatening, what coherence could Western policy ever have?

The Gorbachev Factor

President Gorbachev is no born-again liberal but he is intelligent, sophisticated, persuasive and courageous. He is going not only for economic reform but for the reduction of privilege, censorship and the abuse of human rights. He seems more politician than technocrat.

His concerns are in the widest sense moral. He explicitly diagnoses his country's sickness in terms of apathy, alienation, deformation and stagnation. He calls for a more open society, denounces rigid and over-centralised rule and speaks of a 'spiritual crisis' with a brutal self-criticism unequalled in any Western society.

Some hawks dismiss all this as little more than propaganda, while some doves have gone overboard the other way, seeing Gorbachev as a wonder-working convert to human rights, mother-hood, apple pie and perpetual peace. Nevertheless, a man who has impressed Margaret Thatcher and Jean Kirkpatrick as well as somewhat softer natures is a very considerable figure.

Moreover, his actions have so far gone along with his words. They have included a long nuclear test moratorium that met no response, some extraordinarily disproportionate concessions to secure the INF Treaty and striking flexibility over some of the START issues, on compulsory on-site inspection and other vital technical matters. There was also powerful corroboration for his new policy of 'defensive sufficiency' in his remarkable speech to the United Nations in December 1988 in which he specified major unilateral reductions and withdrawals of men, arms and offensive equipment to be achieved by 1991, including about half the Soviet tanks in Eastern Europe. (Surveillance will soon establish whether these moves materialise.) In May 1989, after the NATO Summit, the Warsaw Pact offered to slash by about half its troops and conventional arms stationed in Central Europe and Gorbachev promised a further cut in Soviet defence expenditure of 14 per cent over the next two years and more cuts beyond that.

Excitement . . . and Caution

What is now happening in Soviet policy-making and in the Soviet Union itself is certainly exciting. Friends just back talk of staggering changes in the atmosphere; the Soviet press carries denunciations of KGB corruption; the first real elections have started in factories; and there have been distinct relaxations in relation to political prisoners, religious worship and even public protest. The new Congress of People's Deputies, inaugurated in fifteen days of passionate controversy and no little democracy in mid-1989, was witnessed by 90 million on television. When a party is clearly divided, it is equally clearly no longer infallible. One has to wonder if there has been a sort of moral change: Soviet diplomats attending our *Dunamis* open forum in London are talking with an unprecedented openness and modesty, in public as well as private. They no longer pretend to have all the answers, or virtues. Nor, remarkably, do they nag about Western crimes and failures, however real.

Despite all this, the excessive optimism of some doves can only put hawks on their guard (and peace campaigners to sleep) and impede constructive change. The Russians are not ten feet tall but nor, the hawks insist, are they four feet tall. They are neither the old devils nor the new saints. They remain powerful and their behaviour will considerably depend on Western firmness.

The owl does not need to trust the goodwill of the Kremlin or believe that Stalin's latest heir has had a 'change of heart'. He banks on something much more dependable, the Soviet Union's objective need for radical economic reform and hence the progressive reduction of international tensions and military expenditures. This, together with full verification in the field, could provide the basis for remarkable progress.

This said, however, the obstacles are as impressive as the opportunities. The survival of President Gorbachev's leadership may not be essential to a continuing cautious Soviet foreign policy but probably he alone could enable the USSR and it allies to succeed and settle down within the Western-dominated world economic system rather than vainly persist in hoping to destroy it. His energy and vision are probably even more critical if we are to create a saner and safer global order. In this wider and longer term perspective, his loss or replacement would almost certainly be a tragedy. Rarely has so much, for so many, depended on one man.

President Gorbachev's survival against the forces hostile to his reforms is, however, far from assured. He has to produce results, not least more sausage in the shops. He needs luck, and not too many Armenian earthquakes, ethnic disturbances and other disasters.

A Divided Western Response

Will the West help or hinder the Soviet leader's complex and hazardous venture? Most West Europeans and their governments — even Britain, a relative laggard — have been very positive. Too many Americans, however, are still accusing him of pretending weakness and warmth to mislead and divide the West, while making the Soviet Union stronger for the next round of the struggle with world capitalism. This is sheer fantasy but at the time of writing (June 1989), it is too early to see whether President Bush's new administration can be persuaded not only to co-operate energetically in radically reducing the military confrontation between the blocs but in positively assisting the new Soviet economic reforms.

Such co-operation should not be too much to ask but many doubts remain. Not least in West European eyes, the US has been becoming little less problematic than the Soviet Union. After a very slow start, President Bush's first major NATO initiative of May 1989, discussed later, was rather impressive. Nevertheless, there has been growing European anxiety in recent years about the nature of many American policies and an even deeper ambivalence towards American society and power in general.

Reappraising Our American Ally

With Mikhail Gorbachev's first arms control proposals in 1987, a majority of Britons were already seeing the United States as 'a greater threat to world peace than the Soviet Union' and a majority of West Germans wanted Bonn to co-operate equally with the United States and the Soviet Union. Such views are often denounced as Left-wing anti-Americanism or wimpish neutralism but this misinterprets the hope that Gorbachev has brought and the doubts that many West Europeans have often concealed. Many distinguished Americans themselves agree that Washington has often pursued bad, hypocritical, illegal and sometimes dangerous policies. The critics may love much about America; they love freedom and are not 'anti-American'; I am one of them.

Revisiting America recently, I was struck again by its immense contradictions. In parts of Florida, let alone Chicago and New York, the contrast between private affluence and public squalor is larger than ever. Alongside the classic grandeur of the capital itself, there are still the sleazy black and Chicano slums that first shocked me 30 years ago. My paediatrician wife was amazed to discover that this rich country ranks as low as 19th for infant mortality. It is as if Uncle Sam cannot resist making it easy to caricature capitalist society: the spendthrift opulence, complacent suburbs and Bible-belt humbug alongside poverty, racism, crime and the neglect of welfare. It is a society that trumpets its economic successes and ignores profound inequality; proclaims opportunity and presides over deep injustice; despises its poor and has little regard for the loser. Americans are passionately devoted to individual rights and staggeringly neglectful of their collective responsibilities. They can celebrate an American dream in *Dallas* and live a nightmare on the New York subway. They have political rights galore yet half the electorate do not vote. Americans are deeply involved all over the world but know little about it. They are profoundly greedy of its limited resources and unconscious of that greed. They are still guzzling gas at low prices and are still prepared to 'nuke' anyone who gets in the way of 'their' supplies from the Gulf. National self-indulgence is justified as a strategic necessity.

Many Europeans, however, too easily forget some of America's startling virtues. Compared to Britain, let alone Communist countries, its openness is amazing. Go to Washington (including Congress and the Administration) if you want information about British defence. Wherever you go, you rediscover the vibrant energy of America, the disarming candour and optimism, the personal warmth and generosity, the sheer zest and amplitude of it all. Much of American life is ugly, greedy, violent, myopic and sick. No less of it is intelligent, sophisticated, caring, daring and open to change.

Moral Equivalence?

Many Europeans, especially doves, argue that American economic injustices should weigh as heavily with us as Soviet political injustices, that democracy can have many meanings and that, one way and another, US equals SU. I understand the argument but reject it. The US is broadly a good form of society with immense faults. The SU is a bad form of society with only limited virtues.

Yet this whole debate is surely rather futile. Both Superpowers have their dark shadow side and neither has the right wholly to condemn the other. In any case, no degree of evil on either side, 'equal' or not, could possibly justify obliterative warfare. And the more evil an 'evil empire', the less justified could be the slaughter of its subject millions. People too often speak as if 'the good guys' are entitled to do what they like to 'the bad guys'. It is a most peculiar argument. In any case the world has been growing ever more doubtful whether it wants to be 'saved' by either the Ugly American or the God That Failed.

Will 'Containment' Continue?

The critical question is whether the United States will persist in its basic post-war policy of containment as it is usually presented, as the reasonable resistance of further Soviet gains, or as one of aggressive pressure and 'rolling back'. A classical official statement of 1950, document NSC-68[3], is still relevant and explains much. It explicitly saw the Soviet Union as imbued with 'an aggressive expansionist drive', stating:

> ... the policy of containment is one that seeks by all means of war to (1) block further expansion of Soviet power, (2) expose the falsities of Soviet pretensions, (3) induce a retraction of the Kremlin's control and influence, and (4) in general, so foster the seeds of destruction within the Soviet system that the Kremlin is brought at least to the point of modifying its behaviour to generally-accepted international standards ... Without superior aggregate military strength, in being and readily mobilisable, a policy of 'containment' — which is in effect a policy of calculated and gradual coercion — is no more than a policy of bluff.

This tough version of the policy is still essentially supported nearly 40 years later by wide tranches of Washington opinion. A euphemism like 'induce a retraction' means 'force a retreat'. 'Fostering the seeds of destruction' is plain enough, as is 'calculated and gradual coercion'. 'Superior military strength' on top of this virtually amounts to what I have called Imperial Crusade.

As the simplest exercise in therapeutic role-reversal, we should re-read the NSC-68 extract with 'United States' and 'Washington' substituted for 'Soviet' and 'Kremlin'. Would it not seem to confirm the most drastic accusations of Russian ambition and perfidy? Moreover the frequent United States military interventions in the Third World have not only often been wrong in motive, clumsy in execution and bitterly cruel in impact (like the blanket bombardments of Vietnam and the secret bombing of Cambodia) but frankly illegal, as in Grenada, Libya and Nicaragua, and hence contrary to the 'accepted international standards' of which the policy itself speaks!

On top of all this, America's European allies have often despaired about its clumsy incompetence (especially obvious in the Iran-Contra affair) and failures of even elementary consultation (as over SDI and Reagan's extraordinary offers at the Reykjavik Summit).

New Limits to American Power?

Irrespective of Western Europe's ambivalence towards American policies, however, it has to be noted that a formidable set of economic difficulties is gradually constraining the United States' power to pursue them. It is now common ground that America has been spending and borrowing too much and saving and investing far too little. From being the world's greatest creditor nation, it has become its greatest debtor. Its budget and current account deficits are foreign-funded, its once world-lead in technology has been eroded. The domestic American infrastructure needs rebuilding. The primary and secondary education system is widely seen as a disgrace, a bar to economic progress and a recipe for crime and urban disorder. Furthermore, American dependence on foreign oil imports has again risen to about 50 per cent, making it, and perhaps world peace, hostage again to Middle Eastern instabilities. Meanwhile, Japan's immense economic and technological power is growing, the European Community gears up for its 1992 market integration and China and much else of Asia is lurching forward at unexpected speed.

It seems clear that the Great Republic should not and cannot continue to try to lord it over an increasingly multipolar world and that when the rival Superpower is in an even worse state and talking a new defensive language it should actively collaborate in constructing a new order. Unfortunately, no great power easily relinquishes the popular pre-nuclear illusion that a nation cannot be too strong, especially where the 'Vietnam syndrome' still prompts many Americans to 'stand tall'.

As the distinguished American historian Barbara Tuchman[4] once put it, the Americans are not warlike, but they *are* violent. 'We have been anti-militarist in thought and sentiment while remarkably combative in character and practice.' A belligerence which is at once impulsive, impatient, optimistic and self-righteous does not make for confidence amongst either antagonists or allies. The United States could indeed become a positively dangerous ally again, not least if President Bush's keenness to earn a second term induced him to play up to a notably conservative, isolated and over-patriotic electorate.

As against all this, there is a much more enlightened and cautious segment of American opinion, Republican as well as Democrat, that is alive to the limits of force and sceptical about saving impulses. The new economic and budgetary constraints and the influence of America's friends and allies will mostly favour more realistic and conciliatory policies.

Putting the American equation together with the Soviet one, there seems to be a reasonable chance of more constructive policies. The process will, of course, need to be gradual and not interrupted by shocks, like another Afghanistan or Nicaragua. It will hinge on positive confidence-building — a matter of style and rhetoric as well as actions. (Words are also actions.) Many in both super-power administrations will need convincing that present policies are far less safe than they look. This is our next subject — the last bit of excavation of the old thought structures before we assemble some new ones.

9

NATO's Current Policies: Pseudo-strength, Genuine Confusion

It is the business of military strategists to prepare for eventualities and it is the fatal error of such strategists to create eventualities for which they must prepare.
Reinhold Niebuhr, theologian, 1892-1971

The basic NATO orthodoxy is still that the Soviet Union is by its nature aggressive in disposition, expansionist in its ultimate intent and capable of posing a mortal threat to the Western societies. NATO's fundamental aim, therefore, is seen as that of deterring any form of Soviet aggression against its members and, if deterrence fails, to use any means necessary to preserve the integrity and restore the security of its nations.

The Soviet bloc is also seen as having so marked a superiority in conventional forces in the European theatre that NATO has to threaten to use nuclear weapons against any substantial aggression whether nuclear or conventional. This policy of Flexible Response was first devised to avoid the perils of all-or-nothing massive retaliation involved in the trip-wire philosophy of the Dulles era—effectively blowing up the house to stop the thief. Under Flexible Response, the United States and NATO are said to be able to choose between a variety of military options depending on the circumstances of any aggression such as its weight, persistence and degree of first success. These options of conventional, tactical nuclear, theatre nuclear and, ultimately, strategic nuclear weapons are meant to allow a 'graduated response' to any escalation in the

Soviet attack rather than compel NATO at once to make what is called a General Nuclear Response (GNR) and hence open a general unlimited war.

This strategy has been offered in softer and harder forms but, generally speaking, the West has seen it as wholly compatible with negotiating arms control and disarmament agreements, the reduction of political tensions and the improvement of economic and cultural relations. This twin-track approach is seen as firmly based on nuclear deterrence but entirely open to the building of confidence, dialogue and détente.

Many of us have come to think NATO's policy deeply flawed but millions of Westerners and most Western governments (of most political colours) find it basically reasonable and essentially defensive. They say it only really envisages the selective use of nuclear arms to demonstrate the political will to escalate if aggression were persisted in. NATO would never fire the first shot but, once fired upon, must be free to respond as it sees fit — including the option of firing the first nuclear shot, probably itself a 'demonstration' in a thinly-populated area.

Doves, of course, reject this policy root and branch. They denounce any dependency on nuclear threats and many of them reject any military alliance, and NATO as such, not just its policies. Nevertheless, the only chance of affecting the hawks' judgements — and they are the people in the driving seat — is not to deny their premises but to ask, as does the owl, how far NATO's policies are really coherent and whether they achieve their object safely.

NATO Rhetoric versus Reality

Like many others, I have come to the conclusion that NATO's present policies are neither coherent nor safe. Nor, until recent changes at least, have I thought Soviet ones any better. But our concern is with the policies formulated in our, Western, name which can endanger us as much as the Russians. Moreover, our main hope of affecting Soviet policy is clearly through amending our own.

Any genuinely self-critical NATO supporter would, first, admit that 'deterrence' has been used to justify every sort of Western doctrine and armament, whether defensive, retaliatory or potentially aggressive. The doctrines have included Balanced Collective Forces, Massive Retaliation, Mutual Assured Destruction, Counterforce, Escalation Dominance and the Seamless Web. What started as down-to-earth defensive rhetoric has obscured huge differences over theory and practice between the NATO allies, within their governments and amongst their peoples. 'Deterrence' has become a catch-phrase with which to justify—or condemn— almost anything.

Many subscribers to this vague doctrine in its nuclear form think it sufficient to point to the alleged fact that nuclear weapons have preserved the peace of Europe and prevented world war for four decades. Yet, if so, they have reduced a small chance of a European war at the cost of virtually guaranteeing cataclysm if it did still occur. Moreover, the man who leaps from the 50th floor may well shout out as he falls past the fifth that he is OK so far.

It is more than possible, in fact, that, since 1945, the Soviet Union has never thought the attempted conquest (and ruination) of Western Europe worth even the conventional damage to itself. Possession of a retaliatory nuclear capability could indeed help to deter a nuclear attack (members of CND have admitted as much) but it does not follow that, without one, there would have been a Soviet attack. Nor would it follow that it is right to retain and plan to use nuclear weapons in the ways that NATO does or that the United States and the United Kingdom do (which are not entirely the same thing). Only the simple-minded think they must accept NATO as it is or have no NATO at all.

NATO has no single agreed rationale either for the use of nuclear weapons or for the way in which the West should generally relate to the Soviet world. The rationalisations of different generals and ministers are as various as the personalities themselves and as the audiences to which they are selectively addressed. A former weapons designer tells me that he automatically distinguishes NATO 'policy' from NATO 'actions' since they are not only divorced but each possesses its own momentum. Two critical cases of confused doctrine will illustrate the position, Flexible Response and SDI, or 'Star Wars', which, though not formally anyone's definite policy, has still not been rejected by any NATO member.

Case One: Flexible Response

The first question is whether a limited nuclear war, conducted in 'flexible' stages, is as workable in practice as it sounds in theory. Many high commanders just don't believe in it. There also seems to be something of a gulf between the (mostly sincere) rhetoric of Western governments and the realities confronting practitioners such as the military target planners. Desmond Ball[1] has shown that those in Omaha, for example, have their own ethos and objectives and that the complications and limitations of their work are rarely understood by their ostensible masters in Washington. Many of the factors arising amidst the typical 'fog' of actual war would, he says, be unprecedented and unpredictable. No pre-planning could take adequate account of the behaviour of enemies and allies, the early damage done or the consequent availability of particular forces for particular tasks. On top of all this, there is the huge but partly unpredictable impact of electro-magnetic pulse (EMP) — a sharp and extremely powerful surge of energy that is an atmospheric by-product of nuclear explosions — on military communications, radar and other electronic systems which are integral to all modern C_3I functions. Ball concluded from these and other factors that the idea of fighting a limited, highly controlled, nuclear war was a chimera, as was any notion of maintaining a step-by step control as nuclear war gradually escalated. Most military commanders would probably agree with this. A former Permanent Under-Secretary of the British Ministry of Defence, Sir Frank Cooper[2], has said that the idea of controlled escalation was 'always nonsense'.

Another highly-rated authority, Paul Bracken[3], goes further by doubting whether the United States could even control a nuclear alert: the kind of command and control system this would require has never been built, because it is not known how to do it. As things are, he concludes, limited nuclear attacks on the Soviet Union would initiate 'an uncontrollable cascading sequence of actions and reactions'.

Despite such fundamental handicaps, Flexible Response virtually assumes that a nuclear war could be limited and controllable. It depends, after all, on the Russians crying 'halt' when the escalation becomes too painful. But since the Soviets achieved strategic parity, it has been doubtful how far they would find Western nuclear threats credible.

Flexible Response also tacitly assumes that the prime danger of war arises from simple intentions rather than from inadvertence or miscalculation in a festering crisis in, say, the Middle East. Nor is Central Europe itself at all safe. The Russians take the Inner German Border to run down the middle of the Elbe, while the West says the two banks are the borders and the river is an international waterway. What if a West German survey boat (or gunboat) asserts the Western view by sailing along the Eastern bank? On the Eastern view, its penetration of their half of the river is an act of invasion and Russian armour and artillery are brought up in strength. Western forces then do likewise. Conflagration could be close.

This is not fantasy: such a crisis occurred in 1966 and the local Western commander, a British Brigadier, was given discretion to open fire — 'in self-defence'. Had he done so and been overcome by superior force, NATO strategy was (and is) to fight conventionally, mostly with armoured coverial troops initially, and then with major combat forces, until (we are told) the superior Soviet tank armies are close to a breakthrough. At this point, granted political authorisation, the West might well fire a 'demonstration' shot and then a few short-range battlefield nuclear weapons. It might then fire more. The next stage — quite possibly Day 2 or 3 — would be to use air- or sea-launched intermediate-range weapons (of which NATO still has plenty) against targets in Eastern Europe. The last stage would be the 'release' of long-range missiles, including the United States land-based strategic armoury, to strike first military and then general ('countervalue') targets deep in the Soviet Union itself.

Defenders of present policy say that the nuclear threat should be enough to deter any serious attack but there is no doubt whatsoever that the forces of both sides are ready to 'release' at very short notice at any one of these levels, or all of them.

'Then we will blow up the world'

Some years ago a United States Deputy Assistant Secretary of Defence, Morton Halperin, said: 'The NATO doctrine is that we fight with conventional forces until we are losing, then we will fight with tactical nuclear weapons until we are losing, and then we will blow up the world.' This may sound a crude over-simplification but it is a masterly encapsulation of some amazing facts. The doctrine of Flexible Response is held to justify the threat and the use of every conceivable type of nuclear weapon — missiles, shells, mines, bombs — in one of the world's most crowded regions. This could hardly be thought a rational war, leave aside a just one. If deterrence failed, the doctrine could lead to the virtual extinction of both East and West Germany and their neighbours. The

European 'theatre', as it is called by American strategists from their distant seats, would be disembowelled.

The doctrine also assumes that the Russians can remain prodigiously self-controlled and rational under apparently remorseless escalation. The doctrine is superficially logical but in practice suicidal and, therefore, stupid. It is also not especially credible to Moscow: 'Behave, or I'll kill you . . . and myself!'

Flexible Response would have been more genuinely flexible if NATO had abided by the original proposals of December 1967 which would have provided sufficient Western conventional forces and ammunition to resist a Soviet assault for four weeks, rather than the few days which they might now have, before resorting to demonstration shots and all that would probably happen thereafter. The Americans were always (very sensibly) keener than the Europeans on the longer conventional phase but the Europeans have tended to want a tighter linkage with American nuclear power — a 'seamless web'. NATO has, therefore, persistently failed to have adequate conventional forces and stocks and has planned in general for early nuclear use. This said, many believe (Morton Halperin[4] for example) that NATO members have agreed nothing definite beyond using a demonstration shot to indicate that the war is getting out of hand.

Soviet 'Offensive Defence'

In Soviet eyes, all this is rather menacing and, *if* there is going to be a new war in Europe, the Soviet Armed Forces must of course win it. This means that Soviet forces would have every reason to hasten to destroy the major NATO threats from land, air and sea before they can be deployed. 'flexibly' or otherwise. So far as was possible the destruction would be by conventional means, but, once Western nuclear weapons were used, mayhem would be almost inevitable. Moreover, the sooner NATO is thought likely to use them in a crisis, the more swiftly will the Soviet Union seek to pre-empt them. Soviet targets for blanket treatment would be NATO nuclear forces and air fields, its communication apparatus and its lines of supply, including ports and marshalling yards and, perforce, many cities. In fact, the Soviet Union could readily take out all Western Europe's most critical military and industrial targets in a single massive nuclear onslaught. (And, of course, *vice versa*.)

Washington would then be forced to decide between opening a mutually suicidal inter-continental nuclear exchange with the Soviet Union or to abandon Western Europe. Europe (and American troops there) would be past fighting for and, unless the President thought a suicidal retribution was somehow obligatory, cold reason could well dictate a cessation of hostilities. By that stage, however, strategic nuclear exchanges between the Superpowers might have been triggered already by the blinding anger unleashed on both sides by the first atomisation of European soil. If so, of course, Flexible Response would have failed even more conspicuously.

Some hawks say Moscow's refusal to play the escalation game is only its 'declaratory' position and that, in practice, it would respond only tactically to NATO's first tactical use. (Only a few little Hiroshimas along the Rhine!) I would not like to place bets on this. Nor should NATO. The Warsaw Pact, like NATO, is equipped and trained to go nuclear from the start, if considered necessary. If there were to be another war in Europe, the Russians would naturally try to win it beneath the nuclear threshold — without incinerating Europe. Nevertheless, their determination to minimise damage to the Soviet homeland cannot be exaggerated. Their strategy would, (at least until recently) be one of offensive defence, just as NATO's policy at least began as one of defensive deterrence.

The Inflexibility of Flexible Response: A Simmering Scandal

In this light, NATO's obvious preparedness for the prompt use of nuclear weapons is the more dangerous because so much of its tactical nuclear armoury has to be held far forward, on the surface and 'at the ready', in positions which could tempt Soviet forces to attack or even seize it first.

NATO's readiness for early use is the result not only of avoidable conventional weaknesses but of traditional West German insistence on 'forward defence'. This makes Flexible Response even less flexible. General John R. Galvin, current NATO Supreme Commander, was frank in addressing the Senate Armed Services Committee in 1988:

> Instead [of traditional defence in depth] our strategy relies on the threat to escalate the conflict by employing nuclear [sic] weapons to increase the costs of

aggression beyond any level the attackers would be willing to pay. Forward defence contributes to this strategy of deterrence because the Soviets recognise that any aggression will be met immediately by NATO defending every inch of Western soil, and they realise that they will be unable to attack NATO without running grave risks of nuclear retaliation.

This reference to the early use of nuclear weapons is not mere talk. Since NATO only has about one week's reserves of ammunition, petrol bowsers and so on, such a stage could be reached very swiftly. (Technical officers in the British Army on the Rhine have told me frankly of their frustrations and fury over this.) For far too long, the public has failed to see that this situation is simply outrageous. The West's problem on the Central Front has centred less round a fearful Soviet conventional strength than an avoidable Western conventional weakness. The West has been prepared to use cheap nuclear explosives as a substitute for adequate anti-tank capabilities, ammunition stocks and so on and as its main instrument of both deterrence and defence. Nor do all the the West's plans look 'defensive' from Moscow.

'Aggressive' Doctrines in NATO

The West's reputation for essential defensiveness, let alone intellectual coherence, took a knock in 1982 when the United States Army, not NATO as such, adopted worldwide the so-called Airland Battle doctrine. This seeks not only to destroy the attacker with all available ('integrated') forces but with deep strikes on the second and third echelons of the enemy's reinforcements and supplies coming up from the rear. In Europe this would mean launching massive attacks, some probably nuclear, on massed formations and transport 'choke-points' deep inside (in other contexts 'heroic') Poland and even the Western parts of the Soviet Union.

This United States Army doctrine has worried many in NATO on several counts. Militarily, it involves diverting (anyway inadequate) conventional forces from defending territory against the Soviet's powerful Operational Manoeuvre Groups. Politically it is, and looks, more aggressive since the same sorts of attacks would be involved in a NATO *blitzkrieg* on the East. Strategically, it also invites military pre-emption if war seems to be becoming probable.

NATO has not accepted Airland Battle but nor has the United States Army dropped it: more confusion. Apologists claim that the strategy could not be employed in the absence of NATO members' agreement — but can any of us imagine Washington in crisis awaiting agreement from Copenhagen or Athens? Meanwhile, since 1984, NATO has adopted a related strategy called Follow-on Forces Attack (FOFΛ). This doctrine also involves the interdiction of reinforcements but not, it is claimed, the deep penetration of Warsaw Treaty territory, the launching of pre-emptive attacks or the use of 'integrated' nuclear, conventional and chemical forces. (It depends on proven technologies like remotely-deliverable mines and the JP 233 airfield runway cratering munitions.) FOFA, it is claimed, is not meant to win the war but to 'win the defence'. But the capability itself is as ambidextrous as is the Russians' for their own 'offensive defence'. In fact, there is a reciprocally reinforcing mirror image between the alliances: each sees itself as essentially defensive and sees the other's capabilities as potentially aggressive. And in terms of capability *both* are quite right. There are built-in nonsenses on both sides.

Guilty Secrets

Flexible Response is a conspicuous example of the mess into which defence policy can get into through an addiction to traditional military 'strength' compounded by political compromise and electoral calculation. Politicians have few, mostly primitive, ideas about strategy which they largely leave to their military experts — who naturally like to please their bosses and also have their own inter-service axes to grind. Nor do they always show especial insight. Flag Officer Submarines, recently told *The Independent*[5] that British submarines will patrol anywhere their Soviet counterparts go, including close to Russian territorial waters. He is reported as saying: 'I do not like no-go areas. If there's a place where the enemy is likely to go and I cannot go, it worries me,' What would the Admiral's reaction be to Soviet submarines hovering close off Plymouth Sound?

The same peculiar double standards are evident in the extraordinary way in which most major Western arms purchases have been decided. In the British case, former ministers have told me that Labour's decision to modernise Polaris with Chevaline was taken in secret by only a handful of them, and that the Conservative Cabinet's decision to adopt Trident was taken in about 20 minutes. It is deeply perturbing that large and expensive acts of (unilateral) rearmament should be carried out with so little public, Parliamentary or even Cabinet discussion.

Case Two: The Astonishing Saga of SDI

Confusion has been almost laughably evident in the case of the Strategic Defence Initiative (SDI), a saga that is not yet finished since President Bush will probably continue with much of the content even if the 'package' is downgraded.

In starting the SDI ball rolling in March 1983, President Reagan aimed for no less than a revolution in Western security policy — the rendering of nuclear weapons 'impotent and obsolete'. He wanted to replace deterrence with defence but he had a hidden agenda of maximising America's technological advantages in all kinds of weaponry and meanwhile spiking the guns of the growing American 'Freeze' movement by presenting himself as a great peacemaker. Richard Perle, one of Weinberger's deputies, certainly thought this way. It is also quite possible that, in his simple-minded way, Reagan genuinely believed American science could actually deliver a marvellous choice: a secure peace or American victory.

Defensive Stability and SDI

In its first pure form, SDI sought security via defence rather than retaliation. It would, hence, finally expel humanity's nightmare of only a single miscalculation bringing fiery ruin to all. The concept flatly contradicted the assured mutual vulnerability that underlay most previous strategic policy. Only with the second version, SDI-II, which was limited to the 'point defence' of American military targets, would the idea of security through deterrence be reinstated. In that version, nuclear weapons in general are not made obsolete; they are merely made safer from each other.

Most scientific observers are anyway extremely dubious as to whether the system could work at all, let alone perfectly. The required computer power for automatic instantaneous battle management amidst the prodigiously complex 'architecture' of the system would be staggering. And how could its comprehensiveness be tested, except in combat? Only a few strategic missiles need to get through to cause chaos. Moreover, the enemy could create complicating counter-measures like decoys and jamming or merely saturate the defences with extra waves of (relatively cheaper) missiles. Furthermore the orbiting satellite system would be highly vulnerable to interceptor-type anti-satellites, orbiting space-mines and ground-based lasers. Only a small hole would need to be punched through the shield to make a way for the main attacking missiles.

At best SDI would be profoundly destabilising: an antagonist possessed of sword and shield is far more dangerous than one with a sword alone for he can attack in relative safety. Although President Reagan did at first offer an SDI shield to the Soviet Union, the offer was less than convincing since he was even refusing to sell them personal computers! In effect, the reciprocal vulnerability of mutually assured destruction would be ended by SDI, and Washington could do more or less what it liked. The Kremlin might then decide it had no alternative but to strike first. Even were the SDI 'umbrella' leaky, the Russians would have reason to fear it. Although useless against a downpour of Soviet missiles, it would be invaluable against the much thinner drizzle of missiles that had survived a deliberate American first strike. Moscow, therefore, sees an allegedly defensive system as potentially quite the opposite — and Moscow is right.

SDI caused consternation throughout NATO, whose members had not been consulted, and also in China. Might not the United States be tempted to retire to its continental fortress, leaving Western Europe horribly vulnerable? Would not an arms length stale-mate between the two Superpowers give Moscow a free hand in Europe? Moreover, President Reagan was now denouncing the West Europeans' precious deterrence as 'a Mexican standoff' in which each antagonist had a pistol pointed at the other's head! The essence of NATO's (and British, French and Chinese) policy was undermined in a few theatrical phrases. The irony was that, morally, the President was basically correct about this: the only small trouble was that his particular remedy was likely to make the condition worse.

Learning from SDI

In its first form, SDI was a Utopian dream of world peace without threats of nuclear retaliation. By definition, however, in creating the means for defending the United States it would create means for attacking the Soviet Union safely. Moreover, the space-based defences necessary for destroying incoming Soviet missiles would also be able to mount a pre-emptive attack on Soviet anti-satellite defences and hence on all the eyes and ears of Soviet defence. These capabilities increase the tension in any 'war may be coming' crisis and foster 'precautionary' moves which further heighten reciprocal fears. Each side might then be making very quick decisions about whether to strike first for fear of the other doing so.

The nightmare has been vividly summarised by Thomas Schelling[6]:

> A modest temptation on each side to sneak in a first blow . . . might become compounded through a process of interacting expectations, with additional motive for attack being produced by successive cycles of 'He thinks we think . . . he'll attack; so he thinks we shall; so he will; so we must'.

At the time of writing (November 1989), SDI is an expensive research project with decreasing Congressional support and a highly uncertain future. On the hustings President Bush said he would continue to pursue the programme but financial exigencies may well enforce a slow-down. SDI probably remains at best what James Schlesinger called 'a collection of technical experiments and distant hopes'. That is what it must remain. One critical lesson of SDI is that reassurance between the Superpowers (and Allies) is essential to stability. Another is that the 'junior partners' in NATO must never again go supinely along with daft ideas as they did in this case, whether or not they can get a very few commercial contracts out of it.

Other Concerns about Western Policy

Apart from the confusions and dangers already outlined there are many other reasons for re-examining Western policies.

> ▷ The underlying incoherence of Western strategy as evidenced at the 1987 Reykjavik Summit, when the whole foundation was undermined without warning or consultation in only two days.
> ▷ Some continuing ambiguity as to whether the United States most wants deep cuts of strategic weaponry or to preserve SDI and thereby weaken the SALT II (Strategic Arms Limitation) agreement.
> ▷ The increasing integration of nuclear with conventional forces, not least in Western Europe, and the development

of war-fighting deployments and doctrines in which nuclear weapons are no longer the 'ultimate deterrents' of politicians but the early resort of colonels.

▷ The adoption of launch-under-attack doctrines and hardware and the enlargement of the pre-delegated authority of local commanders of nuclear forces.

▷ The continued presence of large United States naval forces in the Arctic and Barents Sea in close and threatening positions to the Soviet Union by way of 'offensive sea control'.

▷ Frequent provocative naval manoeuvres in or close to Soviet territorial waters (as in the Black Sea in February 1988) as part of a policy that, in the not over-subtle words of Admiral Carlisle Trost, United States Chief of Naval Operations, 'can signal menace to any potential troublemaker'.

▷ The forward deployment of large integrated nuclear and conventional forces, including United States Marine forces on the Aleutians, all the way round the Pacific Rim and the Soviet land-mass and the consequent danger of a nuclear war spreading from, for instance, a conflict in the Korean peninsular.

▷ Plans to 'modernise' short- and medium-range nuclear forces in Europe to fill gaps allegedly left by the INF Treaty, rather than go full tilt for nuclear as well as conventional arms reductions in Europe.

▷ An interventionist American spirit combined with fierce rhetoric and the maintenance of United States Rapid Deployment Forces for long-range power projection, for example against Libya.

▷ Western reluctance, on various highly questionable grounds, to pursue a Comprehensive Test Ban Treaty (CTBT).

▷ Western failure to increase the effectiveness of the Non-Proliferation Treaty (NPT) and of complementary International Atomic Energy Agency (IAEA) safeguards.

▷ An underlying ambivalence, in the United States especially, as to whether to sustain a strongly confrontative posture towards Soviet Communism or to assist President Gorbachev's efforts for domestic reform and external defensiveness (while also vigorously testing his sincerity).

▷ The increasing military irrelevance of a stiffly deterrent NATO posture to a period in which the Iron Curtain is visibly corroding, the barriers falling and democratic movements are gradually and non-violently seizing power within the old citadels of Communist oppression.

▷ The political inflexibility of NATO's posture, bleak and visionless, when the shape and future of all the major Western and Eastern institutions including the European Community and both military alliances need to be radically reassessed along with the role of US forces (and of nuclear forces) in Europe.

The Fundamental Lesson: Re-appraisal

NATO seems still ensnared by the idea of preparing for war in the honest belief that this is the way to avoid it. Yet not only is nuclear war the worst of all possible outcomes but many of our 'deterrent' preparations are destabilising and probably, in the long run, unsustainable. We have, in fact, constantly taken defence-related decisions incrementally and 'instinctively' with no clear grasp of our overall goals. Robert McNamara, has recently said of his own unrivalled experience of nuclear policy making[7],

> Each of the decisions, taken by itself, appeared rational and inescapable. But the fact is that they were made without any reference to any overall masterplan or long-term objective. They have led to nuclear arsenals and war plans that few of the participants . . . would, in retrospect, wish to support.

The failure to re-examine the fundamentals of policy may reflect less of an obsession with 'nuclearism' than a genuine fear of the uncertainty that letting go of Nurse Terror might entail. Arguably and ironically, President Reagan was one of the few statesmen who have so far challenged the accepted nuclear wisdom. At all events, a combination of essentially unusable pseudo-strength and genuine confusion about aims will not diminish the dangers as miniaturisation, lasers, particle beams and other new technologies produce new spirals in the arms race. Continued proliferation, the splitting open of the old agenda, the arrival of Gorbachev and the growing sense of flux makes this a good, nay vital, time for basic re-appraisal.

PART III

From Competitive to Co-operative Security

10

The Philosophy of the Owl: Co-operative Security

> The dogmas of the quiet past are inadequate to the stormy present. The occasion is piled high with difficulty, and we must rise with the occasion. As our case is new, so we must think anew and act anew. We must disenthrall ourselves.
>
> Abraham Lincoln's message to Congress'
> 1 December 1862.

Such has been the power of pre-nuclear military logic that we were already about three decades into the nuclear era before former insiders began publicly to question NATO as well as Warsaw Pact policies. Among the American critics were Robert McNamara, to whom I have often referred, McGeorge Bundy, a former US National Security Adviser, Jerome B. Wiesner and Herbert Scoville, both former United States Presidential Scientific Advisers, United States Admirals Noel Gayler, Eugene Carroll and Robert Laroche and former American Ambassadors like George Kennan and Thomas Watson (both to the Soviet Union), Gerard Smith and Jonathan Dean.

In Britain, the respectable dissenters have included the late Lord Mountbatten, Field Marshal Lord Carver — both former Chiefs of the Defence Staff, Lord Zuckerman, former Chief Scientific Adviser, General Sir Hugh Beach, former Deputy Commander in Chief, United Kingdom Land Forces, as well as many other former — and serving — air, sea and land commanders. All have seriously questioned various aspects of NATO (and British) policy without being 'unilateralists' or subscribers to any other pre-packaged bundle of opinions.

117

All these people are former practitioners whom no one could accuse of political naivety or military ignorance. All would still wish NATO to have appropriately strong defences and none of them would, I think, reject the idea of the West retaining an ultimate and credible nuclear threat, certainly as long as the Soviet Union did so. Nevertheless, all would regard NATO's (and the Soviet Union's) present dependency on nuclear weapons as excessive and unnecessarily perilous and any nuclear use by anyone as a disaster. Their emphasis would not be on 'military balance', let alone 'superiority', but on military dispositions that give best hope of curtailing crises and avoiding nuclear use. People of this stature do not all think the same but Bundy, Kennan, McNamara and Smith[1] wrote together one of the most celebrated critiques in which they came out for a policy of No First Use, quite contrary to NATO orthodoxy.

In parallel with this train of thought, many strategists and international theorists have been arguing, as we have seen, that détente is more important than disarmament as such. The latter can become yet another area for competition and conflict; positive political moves towards confidence-building are needed even more. Meanwhile, thinking about Third World poverty and environmental degradation has been providing a new global perspective.

Co-operative Security

Emerging from all this, the broad outline of a new wisdom is gradually becoming discernible. As I see it, the hawk has basically emphasised deterrence and the dove has emphasised disarmament. The owl, in contrast to both, goes for co-operative security. In essence the new wisdom says of East – West relations that the hawkish principles of Containment, Comprehensive Deterrence and maximum strength must be replaced — but *not* by the dovish principles of Appeasement, Unilateralism and deliberate weakness. Instead, it says, we should develop the owlish principles of Minimum Defensive Deterrence, Maximum Mutual Reassurance and far-sighted Global Reform.

Taken together, these three owlish principles amount to a policy of co-operative rather than competitive security: an appropriately three-track response to humanity's triple crisis — East – West, North – South and Man–Nature. It is a policy which envisages not only East and West but North and South co-operating to minimise the danger of large-scale instability, let alone war, and hence enabling humanity to concentrate on its most serious long-term challenges. In this sense it could be seen as a new Grand Strategy, an overall design that must eventually supplant NATO's much narrower Comprehensive Concept of 1989.

Co-operative Security requires us to aim for what United States Admiral Noel Gayler has called a 'general nuclear settlement' but this will take many years, perhaps decades, to achieve. Nor will it ever be complete. Even if nuclear abolition suddenly happened overnight, maintaining the ban during periods of crisis could be even more difficult than sustaining stability at low agreed weapon levels. During the crisis, the incentive for one or other antagonist to produce a potentially decisive single nuclear weapon would clearly be tremendous.

Why Abolition is not Feasible

This, of course, means we cannot accept President Gorbachev's proposal for the *total* elimination of nuclear weapons by the year 2000 as being at all realistic. One may wonder if he really believes in it himself. Quite apart from such a transformation being politically inconceivable within so short a period, both sides would be bound to secrete some nuclear warheads in case the other was doing so. Elimination would only be honoured in the breach. It may indeed be safer for both Superpowers to know that the other has some nuclear capability than for either of them to hazard an unreliable guess that the other does not and be tempted to take advantage of it. 'He may be re-making so we must re-make' would probably be more destabilising in a crisis than the reciprocally known possession of a few nuclear weapons. For the Superpowers, therefore, 'some nukes' could be safer than 'no nukes'. In any case, any existing nuclear power could almost certainly re-make some nuclear weapons within a few weeks, even starting from scratch, so 'abolition' would, at best, be 'delay'. Moreover neither Superpower would conceivably denude itself of nuclear arms while there is any serious fear, sooner or later, of a nuclear challenge from any other power, say China, let alone a 'terrorist state'.

It follows, therefore, that we must think not in terms of a once-and-for-all solution but of a gradually extending set of processes and agreements, working from a conviction that, as the late Olof Palme[2] put it, 'international security must rest on a commitment to joint survival rather than on a threat of mutual destruction'.

This also happens to be the original spirit of the United Nations Charter, a sadly neglected document, whereby collective security assured through the Security Council would provide the context of confidence necessary to arms control and disarmament. Moreover, war prevention, including peace-making and peace-keeping, is usually and directly more fruitful than disarmament. In a period when the counting of military hardware has become ludicrously obsessive, we have neglected the other side of the coin. As Hugh Hanning[3] has rightly said, the joint Superpower view of disarmament expressed by John McCloy and Valerian Zorin way back in 1961 needs re-amplification now. It should, they said, be 'accompanied by the establishment of reliable procedures for the settlement of disputes and effective arrangements for the maintenance of peace'.

What we have often had instead is a mainly American reluctance, partly for domestic political reasons, to recognise that useful agreements with the Soviet Union are actually possible. At one time, Ronald Reagan called SDI a choice between Soviet promises and American technology — a simply ridiculous dualism. What we need are no-one's promises but verifiable agreements rooted in a clear appreciation of mutual interests — survival, for a start. This is what Mikhail Gorbachev seems to be going for; the problem now is not convincing the West to be nice but to be sensibly self-interested.

The common interests of the two Superpowers are far more extensive than Cold War rhetoric ever allows. Both sides are, at root, agreed on the critical need to avoid major war, let alone nuclear war. They both agree on the need to reduce the damage if they should fail and to reduce Third World and other instabilities that could further spread dependency on nuclear weapons or actually precipitate war. On longer term calculations they also have shared interests in the relief of Third World deprivations and in a more dependable international economic order, including common access to vital resources. They are also both interested in expanding their bilateral trade and other exchanges as well as in developing the rapidly-growing body of multilateral international agreements on air and sea transport, communications, environmental threats, epidemic diseases and so on. Not least, they both have an urgent interest in reducing their immense defence budgets, to reduce their national debts and meet social needs and consumer appetites.

The West has, however, often acknowledged these common interests grudgingly rather than welcomed and boldly built upon them. It has emphasised its suspicions of the East and the need for military strength and the utmost caution. Almost perforce, therefore, it finds itself preparing for war in the course of 'deterring' it, rather than building the kind of peace that would make nuclear arms all but unnecessary. Nor have the East's often crude rhetoric and actions much improved matters. Both are partly to blame but both have good reasons for building a new regime of co-operative security.

No Military Use

A new policy for the West, as also for the East, could start from a single proposition — that nuclear weapons have at best only one use, that of deterring their use by anyone else. As Robert McNamara[4] has put it, 'nuclear weapons are not weapons — they have no military use whatsoever, except to deter one's opponent from their use'. This is not just a moral proposition but a practical one. It is not just wicked, it is irrational to wield weapons that destroy more than they can save, immolate friend with foe and the innocent masses along with the guilty few. And it is surely daft to initiate what would almost certainly become an unlimited and hence virtually suicidal nuclear war.

It seems likewise daft to say we might justify the selective use of small nuclear weapons at sea. The casuist can always weasel his way across dividing lines: he or she will say that some nuclear weapons are smaller than some conventional ones, that civilians would not suffer and that there would be little environmental damage. No casuist, however, can bridge the critical psychological gulf that lies between use and non-use. Any soul of any sentience, let alone any political observer of any perception, would gasp at the breach of what Robert McNamara[5] and his co-authors call 'the one clearly definable firebreak against the worldwide disaster of a general nuclear war . . . the one that stands between all other kinds of conflict and any use whatsoever of nuclear weapons'.

If the only purpose of nuclear weapons that seems at all rational is to maintain a kind of minimal existential deterrence, a second proposition follows naturally: West and East must learn to live-

and-let-live. Whether we call this co-existence or détente, or by a new term with different reverberations from either, may matter less than that its basic intentions are understood and pursued. As Donald Brennan[6], a professional military expert, used rather shockingly to say 'we should prefer live Americans to dead Russians, whenever a choice between the two presents itself'. And rightly assuming the reverse preference in the Russians, he asserted a common interest in live Americans *and* live Russians.

Many Western apologists would claim we have live-and-let-live now. As we have seen, however, the West remains deeply ambivalent about it because it means working primarily for stability and only residually for relative advantage. Détente means active co-operation within a conflict that is acknowledged to be unresolvable rather than maintaining pressure with the aim of 'prevailing'. It means an end to adversarial arms control negotiations and souped-up propaganda battles about human rights. It involves very deliberate efforts to create safer international structures — a somewhat pedestrian and not always popular cause. It means losing your enemy and all that that can involve including a bloated sense of national or ideological virtue, a hate figure around which unity can be forged (in both senses) and an economic dynamic much coveted by some (not all) of the ruling groups.

Co-operative Security plainly cannot depend on minimum deterrence alone. The careful management of suspicion is not sufficient for the building of long-term security. That needs not only positive efforts to create reassurance on both sides but the larger agenda of Global Reform to give added point, profit and warmth to the enterprise. Let us briefly examine these other two requirements, vital to the owl, before returning to what hawks and doves alike will still regard as the bottom line — the nuclear issue.

The First Principle: Mutual Reassurance

As Professor Sir Michael Howard has often stressed, security inevitably involves reassurance. Domestic public opinion has to be reassured that its interests and values are being safeguarded and at a reasonable cost in treasure and lives — and, one might add, civil liberties. Allies need to be reassured that they will be fully considered and consulted and will not be left in the lurch. Most of all, and perhaps surprisingly, each of the would-be foes needs to reassure the other, as far as is possible, about its intentions and capabilities so that escalation of suspicion does not lead to war by inadvertence.

Each adversary needs to be reassured that their own military or political moves will not be dangerously misinterpreted, for instance that their precautions against attack will not be misread as preparations for attack. For safety's sake, both sides have to understand broadly what the other is up to. Both will be seeking advantages, both will sometimes pull a fast one, but neither will want to risk war. Both recognise that there is quite often smoke without fire and sometimes fire without smoke. Both need to know which is which.

This means a most difficult balance has to be sustained. Just as too threatening a deterrence can lead to instability through provocation, so also can too much reassurance through complacency. The would-be aggressor must not be led to believe the victim will not react; he can hardly be told just what outrages he can get away with. There can be too much 'transparency' as well as too little.

A degree of uncertainty is therefore necessary to deterrence and hence to stability. On the other hand, too much uncertainty can also be fatal to stability. Both sides need to recognise by what ground rules they are playing. When each wishes to deter the other from doing certain things it is as well if they both know roughly what these are.

Yet this is to put the business of mutual reassurance in far too chilling a way. As more powerful and ingenious measures of verification are put in place, the old suspicions of surprise attack can subside and attention turn to positive measures to avoid, reduce or manage the conflicts that are bound to arise. As communication and understanding improve, an atmosphere can jointly be created where regional conflicts can be mitigated and even resolved — Afghanistan, Namibia and Angola are recent examples. Meanwhile, new subjects for active co-operation can be explored — the Middle East, for instance, or South Africa — and both the diplomatic and the public atmosphere will be greatly improved.

Mutual reassurance should not, however, be left to bureaucrats and politicians alone. The role of private and organised people-to-people exchanges (in the media as well as in the flesh) can be highly potent because they operate at the level of feeling as well as calculation. The 'enemy figures' are increasingly humanised and sheer curiosity (and mutual advantage) can counteract the caricaturing of the propagandists.

The Second Principle: Global Reform

Of the three owlish principles that of Global Reform is plainly the most positive and far-sighted. As we shall see later, its pressing agendas of the relief of Third World poverty, the healing of North–South divisions and the combating of environmental degradation could provide the crucial avenue for East and West to escape their mutual obsession. Mutual Reassurance is also aimed at that objective but it naturally focuses on the disease: the patients also need a positive reason for living.

Global Reform should not be interpreted as a mere token or charitable gesture towards Third World poverty. What is at issue is not just the generosity of the rich, West and East, but the common survival of all, the poor and the prosperous alike.

On any number of fronts, from the economic to the political, social and environmental, the collaboration of East and West, and of both with other major blocs and nations, is rapidly becoming essential to a sustainable way of life on this planet. Such collaboration may require not only the fullest use and adaptation of existing inter-governmental institutions but the creation of new ones.

The Third Principle: Minimum Defensive Deterrence

Doves will denounce any dependence whatsoever on even the remotest nuclear threat. I have shown why some nuclear weapons (or their potential) will continue in existence and why therefore our species' best hopes seem to lie in radically diminishing their role — rather than going for the chimera of total abolition. In short, Minimum Defensive Deterrence is almost certainly the very best that anyone, of West or East, and including the doves, can expect in the next few decades and our joint efforts would be far better aimed at this than at a Utopian goal. (The British Bomb as such we examine later.)

If this is so, the main task of dove and owl alike is somehow to satisfy the moderate hawks that their prime security needs can be met despite drastic cuts in nuclear armoury. Convincing them will not be easy. Many hawks will be frankly scornful of Minimum Defensive Deterrence. Even moderate ones would insist on a fully Comprehensive Nuclear Deterrence on the lines currently employed by both NATO and the Warsaw Treaty powers. A useful first step would be to persuade both extremes that deterrence and détente can be mutually helpful. An alliance strong enough to deter aggression can be confident enough to make concessions, do deals and build up co-operation. Equally, constructive confidence-building can enlarge the common interest in peace and reduce some of the dangers that cold deterrence alone could bring. As one strategist and commentator, Christoph Bertram, has put it 'Deterrence reassures détente; détente reassures deterrence'. This is not far from the 'twin track' commonplaces of traditional post-war rhetoric: Mrs Thatcher often speaks this way. But the test is much less the principle than the way it is implemented. Here, people can be worlds apart.

The Aims of Minimum Defensive Deterrence

Minimum Defensive Deterrence (MDD) is a strategy for 'real defence' (like 'real ale'); one within which conventional arms increasingly resume the roles that nuclear weaponry has usurped since 1945 (while of course being themselves cut to such minimum levels as the various processes of agreed reduction, verifications and confidence-building allow). Whether this process would be swift or slow would depend primarily on how the rival alliances responded.

The aims of MDD are, first, to avoid nuclear war or major conventional war; secondly, to satisfy the traditional requirements of national defence and the international order — the preservation of independence, freedom and so on; and thirdly, to increase general stability by slowing the arms race, reducing potential provocation and allowing more effective crisis management. All these are essential to providing conditions for co-operation rather than continuing to stare down endless decades of nuclear peril.

The policy involves both superpowers retaining a minimum of nuclear forces for the essential purpose of dissuading the adversary from actively threatening or using their own nuclear weapons. The policy is defensive in that, so far as possible, both sides abandon what might be construed as offensive military strategies and capabilities. It is a policy of deterrence in that it acknowledges unashamedly that it would meet serious aggression with terrible, if conventional, punishment — and, only if finally pushed to it, with nuclear use.

This is the owl's great parting of the ways with both hawks and doves. Hawks do not hesitate to depend on nuclear arms to deter conventional attack. Owls refuse point-blank to do this — or to prepare to do it. The option of first use of nuclear weapons is considered by hawks both proper and sensible and NATO's nuclear dependency has been fundamental. Owls utterly reject this. They will not develop or deploy nuclear weapons for battlefield use, regarding them as worse than useless for the purpose.

Equally, however, the owl's policy of MDD also represents a decisive break with the doves. It takes defence needs seriously, it is unembarrassed by acquiring relevant military strength, it permits the superpowers to retain some nuclear weapons and ultimately, if in a very far extremity, it takes the risk that they might be used. This owl cannot dodge that implication.

I should, however, say that I cannot think of any plausible circumstances in which I could personally justify pressing the button. Even surrender would be less wicked, and insane. Nevertheless, I am prepared to accept that the least worst defence arrangements we can contrive could involve some ultimate risk of using the minimum nuclear deterrent. But this still puts my position far nearer the dove's than that of, say, Richard Harries, Bishop of Oxford[7], (who is himself no outright hawk) who declares, that 'in view of Soviet non-nuclear strength, it is right that for the time being NATO keeps open the early use of nuclear weapons as a possibility'.

I reject that view which, however qualified, amounts to willingness to justify nuclear war-fighting. My own position does not. It is not 'war-fighting' in any real sense to maintain an ultimate nuclear threat (and only that) and in some extreme circumstances be effectively forced to apply it.

Yet in no sense is MDD a weak or wimpish policy. The main burden of deterrence and defence falls on the conventional forces — themselves increasingly horrendous, as NATO is always saying — because they can be effective without being obliterative or suicidal. These forces should be fully able and ready to inflict unacceptable losses on an aggressor. The minimum nuclear force is only intended to deter nuclear threat or use, even though the fact of possession would by itself inevitably help dissuade any attack. (State A may decide never to use nuclear weapons against a non-nuclear attack but State B can never be entirely sure of this.) I stress again, however, that this inescapable element of existential nuclear deterrence is no excuse whatsoever for NATO (or anyone else) failing to organise a sufficiency of conventional defences.

Both the aims and the general 'dual track' philosophy of this approach would be acceptable to most NATO apologists; the gulf most clearly yawns, when one comes to the level and kind of arms being held and for what purposes. MDD would certainly require a series of profound changes since, for a start, nuclear weapons would no longer be available for anti-tank roles. It would also clearly separate nuclear and conventional forces and disassemble all currently 'integrated' forces. In practice, NATO would have to adopt a policy of No First Use (to be discussed later) and freeze some current weapon developments. Some of these moves would be made in their own right ('unilaterally' if you will), if only because they anyway suit NATO's own interests, but many would depend on the Soviet response.

In the process, deep cuts could be made in the nuclear armouries of both sides. Eventually such measures could probably lead to reductions in the numbers of nuclear warheads in American and Soviet hands from about 20,000 each to something like 500 each. That is the figure at least that Robert McNamara[8] now advocates. These would, of course, remain devastating armouries each equivalent in megatonnage to about 30,000 Hiroshimas with thousands of Chernobyls thrown in.

These proposals will disconcert many moderate NATO supporters. They will point to the danger of becoming vulnerable to a single disarming blow, to the especially sensitive problems of comparability at low levels of weaponry and to the risk of MDD 'making the world safe for conventional war'. Meanwhile outright hawks will say that the policy allows the Kremlin to persist in its various oppressions and fatally depends on trusting it. On this, I must stress at once that, adequate or not, MDD is not dependent on anyone's change of heart. It builds neither on the dove's fragile foundation of sentiment nor on the hawk's perilous foundation of absolute fear but on a hard-headed recalculation of mutual interests supported by rigorous verification.

Designing a Minimum Nuclear Deterrent

A minimum nuclear deterrent, a key feature of Minimum Defensive Deterrence when applied in the East–West context, is the smallest nuclear force capable of deterring an aggressor from using nuclear weapons or threatening their use. It is not necessary for such a force to be large enough to threaten the total destruction of the aggressor's society but only credibly to threaten more loss than gain, such as the destruction of a few substantial cities. Doves will be rightly horrified at this but at present whole nations, not just cities, are at risk. Meanwhile, hawks who doubt whether a few cities would be sufficient hostage, should ask for what gain would the United States risk the annihilation of more than New York, Atlanta and Los Angeles or the Soviet Union of more than Leningrad, Kiev and Tashkent?

If minimum nuclear deterrence is to work, each side's nuclear force must plainly not be so small or vulnerable to tempt the aggressor into launching a pre-emptive first strike to destroy it. Too few, as well as too many, nuclear weapons can be destabilising: either extreme can make people trigger-happy. A minimum force must, therefore, have enough warheads to suffer the loss of some through accident or incompetence and sufficiently mobile or deeply buried in rock or sea to be effectively invulnerable to enemy attack. Most advocates have favoured submarine-launched ballistic missiles (SLBMs) but want some other missile types too.

The most dependable formula would probably have the minimum number of single nuclear warheads scattered on the maximum number of platforms. Multi-headed missiles would mean too few platforms and too many problems over verification. A typical design, like that now proposed by the (American) Council for a Livable World[9], would be up to 1,000 single warheads on each side. These would be more-or-less evenly divided between small submarines, with, say, Trident I missiles; widely dispersed bombers with air-launched cruise missiles; and land-based (say Minuteman) missiles.

For mutual reassurance, the weapons and delivery systems should also so far as possible permit ready satellite or other verification of numbers and deployment (if only as to where they are *not* located). This means agreeing to exclude visually ambiguous dual-purpose weapons. Much current nuclear armament would be unsuitable. The American Trident D5 missiles (also being acquired by Britain) would be too sophisticated in that they will be threateningly accurate in a first-strike role and long enough in range (7,400 km) to hit Soviet missile silos anywhere in the Soviet Union.

The targeting plan for a minimum force is critical. By definition the force would not be numerous or accurate enough to destroy the opponent's nuclear force because that would make both sides constantly nervous. The minimum force must therefore be aimed at soft targets like population centres, industrial areas or oil-fields. Even 20–30 warheads could do immense damage to these. McGeorge Bundy[10] has written of the enormous gulf between the thinking of political leaders and that of the think-tank analysts setting levels of 'acceptable' damage well up in the tens of millions of lives. As he rightly says:

> They are in an unreal world. In the real world . . . a decision that would bring one hydrogen bomb on one city of one's own country would be recognised in advance as a catastrophic blunder.

Threatening even a few cities with immolation looks like a reversion to the hideous old doctrine of Mutual Assured Destruction (MAD): human beings by the million would be the ultimate hostages to good order. There is, however, a vast difference between the two doctrines. Under MAD, the threat of a huge nuclear assault was meant to be the prime basis of Western security: an all-or-nothing response to any sort of serious aggression. MDD retains some nuclear weapons in order to keep them out of the military equation. MAD said we needed nuclear weapons, and in great quantity, to deter aggression. MDD says no one needs them except to neutralise the opponent's nuclear weapons.

We should also note that, in any case, no other nuclear strategy whether Countervalue, Counterforce or whatever, would enable the urban millions to be saved once war broke out. There are said to be 80 'military targets' in Moscow alone: how do you 'take out' a few of them without incinerating the whole area? The Pentagon's regularly updated Single Integrated Operational Plan (SIOP) is said to contain literally tens of thousands of alleged military targets: that is what comes of having too many missiles (on both sides) for which to find a use. President Carter's version known as SIOP-5D contained 40,000 Soviet targets! It was said not to include cities 'as such' but it could not avoid including barracks, supply depots, ports, marshalling yards, vital road junctions, communication facilities, industrial plants and military and political headquarters and hence, in practice, every major centre of population. Some of us may not see a huge moral difference between being killed as a hostage or as incidental 'collateral damage'.

How Minimum is Minimum?

Some would say a true minimum nuclear delivery force would be too minimal to be safe because in any crisis it would enforce an all-or-nothing choice as to nuclear response. MDD does not, as they say, 'degrade gracefully' by allowing half-measures like a warning explosion or a carefully limited counter-attack. The 'minimum plus' that I have described would allow the former if not the latter. The limited nuclear attack is undesirable since it takes one back into a nightmare cycle of 'what ifs?' that brings instability and, in the end, madness: a type of analysis that misses out all the factors we have emphasised — the political context, our capacities for verification and confidence-building and the astounding fact that only one modern nuclear warhead could do quite unprecedented damage. The sceptic essentially claims that MDD deprives us of limited or escalatory nuclear war. It does. But few really believe there could be such a war anyway. Moreover, it would almost certainly be less disastrous to lose a small nuclear war than to 'win' a large one!

Another standard objection is that, almost by definition, a minimum nuclear force cannot be used to defend against a conventional attack but, as I have said, that should anyway be met by conventional means. No encouragement should be offered to ideas of defence by incineration. Moreover, the right context in which to judge MDD is not the blatantly unreal one in which it is translated straight into today's Europe of huge confrontative armies but circumstances in which, perhaps over a few years, both sides have agreed, with verification, to deploy and plan on a much more defensive basis. We explore this critical aspect of the puzzle in the European context later.

I have agreed that the 'minimum' should be plainly sufficient, since a very small system would be too vulnerable to enemy first strike or a technological leap in the accuracy, mobility or hardening of the other side's missiles. The force also has to be numerous enough to be largely exempt from cheating, and sufficiently 'strong' to reassure a conservative electorate.

Is MDD Even a Starter?

Despite being denounced by extreme hawks as perilously wimpish and by extreme doves as intrinsically wicked, minimum *nuclear* deterrence as part of a broader policy of minimum *defensive* deterrence has advantages to a surprisingly wide variety of interests.

Many doves would see it as a giant stride in the right direction. Many hawks would see it as a less-nuclear but still robust defence which upholds NATO and rejects doctrinaire unilateralism. Both would approve its abandonment of a confrontative military structure and what should be the reduced risks of war by miscalculation.

The policy also offers the military the means of recovering proportionality and hence its claims to rationality and honour from the present toils of indiscriminate destruction. It also allows the military to retain force levels that are smaller but still genuinely 'second-to-none' and to recover an intelligent flexibility in conventional defence ('real defence') planning that the nuclear obsession has made almost impossible. In general it also offers greater stability — a relatively stark situation with simpler command and control problems and no 'use-them-or-lose-them' dilemmas.

Might the policy be negotiable with the Soviet Union? The chances are not at all bad if President Gorbachev stands by his new strategic thinking and positive attitudes to verification. (He claims to want total abolition.) Moreover the old guard (on both sides) would be reassured by retaining what would still be capacities for immense nuclear destruction within a policy that would be at once cheaper and less inflammatory than the current one.

Nevertheless, the policy described presents very real difficulties, not least for the multi-membered West, and no sensible owl would expect to resolve them all at once. It will not allow nuclear defences against mass tank attack (but that should not be necessary anyway); it allows only some indirect nuclear 'deterrence' of conventional attack (at most at the level of French 'pre-strategic' nuclear signalling) and, to much of the public (especially the American), it may look too fragile. MDD does, however, have the powerful advantages I have spelled out and is far less riddled with inconsistencies and paradox than the present NATO orthodoxy. Nor is the policy in any way vague. Even a decision in principle to adopt it would lead to early changes in planning, force deployments and weapon requirements.

It is also an approach that has attracted support from highly experienced men like Robert McNamara and Field Marshal Lord Carver. The latter[11] told a UN symposium at Florence in 1987; 'It would be much cheaper and less dangerous to abandon the search for nuclear superiority, abolish all counterforce systems and reduce nuclear arsenals to much smaller numbers, designed solely for retaliation'. I entirely agree.

11

Co-operative Security in Practice

If we will disbelieve everything, because we cannot certainly know all things, we shall do ... as wisely as he who would not use his legs, but sit still and perish because he had no wings to fly.

John Locke, *Essay Concerning Human Understanding*, 1690

Co-operative Security can be exciting because it promises greater security with less nuclear risk, less expense and much more scope for wider co-operation. Yet it can also be very boring, not only in lacking the big brave slogans of full frontal confrontation, or high-minded renunciation, but in its evident dependency on piecemeal options. It offers no simple striking formulae but the hard graft of the gradual process that was for many years my own life in diplomacy.

An East–West antagonism that has grown in stages must also be unmade in stages. About the precise content and timing of these stages we are bound to be uncertain and need to be flexible. Priorities will shift as circumstances change and opportunities serve but we should rehearse the main components. These will already be familiar to some, but I trust they will take on a new significance when the underlying motive is no longer that of mutual fear at a lower level of arms but of mutual stability at a higher level of confidence.

For East and West to agree to renounce nuclear war-fighting and counterforce strategies and adopt safer sorts of armaments, deployments and plans would represent a triumph of diplomacy even if the remaining deterrent forces far exceeded the desirable

132

minimum. The key obstacles are less the size of the arsenals than the mutual suspicions they symptomatise.

Détente before Disarmament

The problems are political before they are military. This is why many strategists and politicians are now being gradually persuaded that, if anything, détente comes before disarmament and could in time change the East–West relationship in some of the fundamental ways that the Sino-Western relationship has been changed — or had anyway before June 1989. After exploring some of these, we will come to the acid test of Europe.

The necessary agreements and measures now needed between East and West can be treated in four broad categories — direct superpower relations; regional conflicts; arms control and disarmament; and human rights. Of these, the first and second are of overwhelming importance. The third category, arms control and disarmament, usually put first, is where improved confidence is reflected rather than created. And, as I shall (rather bravely) argue, human rights must come last.

We shall take these categories in turn but let me first stress that if most of their content seems to reflect the old preoccupations with East–West conflict and weaponries rather than the new global agenda of Third World poverty and environmental degradation, there is a good reason for it. In essence, the old hawk will not be persuaded of the new messages from the young doves unless the hawk's grim anxieties are dealt with in roughly his own terms. The reader will recall that the owl sees honest and valid concerns from *both* sides of the traditional debate. Provided that point is grasped much of the technical detail in this chapter may, gentle reader, be skimmed or even skipped.

I. Direct Superpower Relations

High-level Meetings

As I well remember, professional diplomats are highly cautious about letting their leaders loose on each other. Few of them are house-trained, as they put it. Nevertheless the value of personal contact at the top levels, and the energising impact it can have, often makes the risks worth running. The dangers of public expectations running too high would be reduced if summit meetings were more frequent, regular and informal, and hence less dramatic: the Malta summit of November 1989 made a good start. Much would be learned through travel in the opposing bloc. As it is, the higher the decision-taker, the less likely is he to know the country and people he is negotiating with.

Risk Reduction

There will always be sudden crises of confidence so we need to eleborate risk reduction and confidence-building measures (CBMs) to reduce the chances and the consequences of miscalculation.

The existing Hot-Line arrangements have been improved but still are very inadequate. Moscow and Washington need proper Risk Reduction Centres with permanent joint staffs (not just temporarily designated Embassy officers) to develop procedures and negotiate an agreed Crisis Consultation Period before military deployments and alerts intensify the tensions. (Such consultation is already provided for following dangerous incidents at sea and unidentifiable nuclear explosions.) There should eventually be an International Monitoring Mediation Service, ideally under United Nations auspices, as a supplementary safeguard (and important face-saving device). Such a service, based perhaps in Sweden, would sustain real-time surveillance of the opposing strategic missile fields and other nuclear forces through satellites, radar and other means. It would also provide another building block towards an effective UN military agency.

Review of Alert Systems

Both Superpowers must have survivable capacities of command, control, communications and intelligence (C_3I), otherwise they could swiftly be blinded and any hope of effective crisis management or indeed of preventing, limiting or stopping a war would have gone. The 'hardening' of communication channels would reduce the dangers of ill-judged or panicky initiatives being taken by, for example, missile submarine commanders who have been given pre-delegated (if circumscribed) authority to fire.

All existing warning and alert procedures need radical review. Over the past two decades they have been increasingly integrated with the nuclear weapon firing systems until now there is a global system of sensors, radars and satellites that can almost instantly flood information to the central command system. This tight coupling is demanded by the unprecedented speed and destructiveness of a single nuclear attack: one Soviet submarine could wipe out Washington and most of the American bomber force in a few minutes. And *vice versa*. The system must therefore treat each 'small' threat as capable of producing a massive convulsion. This in turn means that false alarms, misread signals or computer failures can have prodigiously multiplied effects. New tactics of launch-on-warning, rather than launch-under-attack, are deeply worrying. Moreover safeguards tend to be relaxed (for swiftness of response) at precisely the times of tension when they are most needed.

In effect the United States and Soviet alert systems are now being tightly coupled to each other. A Soviet military movement, whether real or apparent, provokes an American precaution which in turn precipitates a Soviet reaction. This mutually reinforcing action-reaction process may become a jockeying for tactical position between two sides each determined to fire their own missiles first if (as they think) there is anyway to be a war. Paul Bracken[1], a well respected and unhysterical commentator, has said:

> In certain respects, American and Soviet strategic forces have combined into a single gigantic nuclear system. What cements the coupling is the warning and intelligence systems of each side. If the situation were not potentially so grave, we could discuss this as science fiction!

Restraint of Intelligence Operations

All this reinforces the need for restraint on aggressively intrusive intelligence-gathering operations which deliberately provoke the 'enemy' to expose his capabilities. For example, the United States Navy's 'Holystone' mission, exposed in 1975, sent specially-fitted attack submarines into Soviet territorial waters to monitor Soviet SLBM tests and even plug into the military communication cables strewn across the ocean floor. Equivalent Soviet penetration of American waters would have caused outrage: it caused a fair bit in neutral Sweden's waters. Where 'transparency' is especially desirable, the Superpowers should organise it either by mutual agreement or unaggressively.

Confidence-Building Measures (CBMs)

As we have seen, mutual reassurance, especially against surprise attack, is a key to security. Confidence-building measures of various sorts in the European context have been the subject of talks ever since the agreement on prior notification of troop manoeuvres in the 1975 Helsinki Final Act. Since then the exchange of information, military observers and intrusive inspections has been further developed. (The underlying principle was dramatised when the INF Treaty provided for Soviet observers to go to Greenham Common and Molesworth amongst other Allied bases to verify its provisions, and, of course, American observers *vice versa*.)

In January 1989 the 35 signatories of the Helsinki Accord finally agreed that there should be Conventional Forces Europe (CFE) talks to pursue conventional arms reductions 'from the Atlantic to the Urals' as a successor to the ineffectual Mutual and Balanced Force Reduction (MBFR) negotiations, as well as talks with a wider membership aimed at a follow-on Conference on Confidence- and Security-Building Measures and Disarmament in Europe (CDE). Both need yet more energy put behind them.

Enthusiasm for CBMs can of course never be total. If handled badly or used cynically for propaganda or allowed to degenerate into mechanistic invigilation they may actually delay better understanding. Nevertheless reciprocal inspection, including challenge inspections at short notice, are highly relevant to the verification of agreements on air, sea and land manoeuvres and exercises, of force levels in sensitive areas or in general and to nuclear test and missile firings. In some of these respects progress has been made, in others as yet not. The Soviet Union used to resist 'intrusive' on-site inspections as a 'spies charter' but President Gorbachev's relaxations are now inducing some Western leaders to mutter about commercial secrecy! The West cannot have it both ways. CBM's are relevant wherever in the world the potential alternative is a vicious circle of warning, precaution, counter-measure and so on down to hell.

Exchanges on Strategic Philosophy

Many, including Henry Kissinger, have urged these exchanges as enabling each side to understand what the other considers its vital interests. It is therefore refreshing to see a Soviet Chief of Staff touring American military bases (and the Pentagon) and a United States Secretary of Defence paying a return visit to Soviet facilities. Such engagements may reveal new areas for useful negotiation but are anyway symbolically powerful expressions of the idea of co-operative security.

Threat Reduction Agreements

The curtailment of Soviet nuclear missile submarine (SSBN) operations near the American coast (which allow the United States bomber bases only five as opposed to 25 minutes warning time of missile attack) might be traded against all or part of the similar but larger American submarine dispositions in Soviet waters. Agreement not to make threats against each other's capital and national command centres would do even more to curtail unsettling anxieties about possible 'decapitation' and reduce the itchiness of fingers during crises. (There is evidence that many Soviet naval forces are now being withdrawn unilaterally to home waters.)

The chances of nuclear war would be substantially reduced by agreeing terms for reversing the forward deployment of NATO fleets under its Maritime Strategy. These fleets are highly threatening in that they are capable on their own of taking out most of the USSR's strategic missile capability as well as its largely home-based fleet.

Non-interference with Sensors

It would be sensible to ban interference with warning and assessment sensors including observation satellites. Attempting to blind one's opponent (even just by smashing his spectacles) can be more harmful and provocative than a blow to the body. President Gorbachev, amongst others, has suggested a special global verification system for peaceful work in space.

High Speed Arms Control

Post-nuclear military logic also demands attention to possible ways of terminating both conflict and war itself by measures of 'high speed arms control' such as short-notice restrictions on aircraft movements and the sequential surfacing of missile-carrying submarines to demonstrate their positions. Each side has a tremendous interest in the technical efficiency and discipline of the other because forces that cannot be reliably controlled cannot be reliably deterred. It has, therefore, been suggested that each side should quietly tell the other when its forces, however accidentally, act differently than their — mostly overheard — signals have ordered! (The Pentagon may well follow Soviet military signals and forces more closely than does the Kremlin itself, and *vice versa*.) All such arrangements contribute to what Paul Bracken[2] has called nuclear 'rules of the road' and hence broader political understanding.

Economic, Technical and Cultural Co-operation

In the longer run, understanding will depend more on mutual profit than reciprocal precaution and many are very willing to do business. In addition to the familiar ones in the grain trade, barter dealing, technological transfer and commercial loans, many opportunities could arise from the new Soviet willingness to participate in world economic arrangements like the GATT and the IMF. The main obstacles and inhibitions may now be Western. Nevertheless, sheer appetite, public and private, will no doubt prevail. Greed has its uses. Fears of the Russians thereby becoming rich enough to outface the West in world markets are absurd. On this score both East and West should rather watch the Pacific Rim!

Superpower co-operation could plainly be greatly reinforced in traditional areas like transport and communications, where it must mostly be multilateral, and in new headline subjects like environmental protection, international terrorism, drugs and AIDs. In their quiet way however three other dimensions may be as significant as any: the cultural, the televisual and the personal. A Leonard Bernstein or a Yevtuschenko can do as much to weaken military obsessions as any number of hard-nosed trade deals. And so, if more gradually, can the thousands of reciprocal individual and group contacts made by tourists and technicians, students and conference delegates. Through technology and cheap travel, much of diplomacy is being quite usefully privatised!

II. Regional Conflicts

It is widely agreed that a Third World War is more likely to be sparked off in the Third World than in Central Europe and this emphasises the need for regular superpower exchanges on all the troubled regions such as Central Asia (including Afghanistan),

South-East Asia, Central America (including Nicaragua), Southern Africa (including South Africa) and the Middle East (including the Gulf and the Palestinian – Israeli conflict). Some governments would understandably see this as Superpower 'interference' and even as a threat of global Superpower 'dyarchy' but such suspicions will subside if the Superpowers demonstrate that their aim is not competitive intervention but precisely its avoidance. Their handling of their relations with China, especially after the recent repression, will need particular sensitivity if new fears and instabilities are not to be generated.

The Superpowers must perform a balancing act — realistically recognising the power they are bound to wield, while neither oppressing the local states, nor allowing their own inevitable rivalry to become destabilising. Local initiatives, regional bodies and the United Nations, with active help, should be left, where possible, to make the running. The Superpowers will be wise to avoid playing either regional bosses or joint policemen. Ideally they will both recognise that reconstruction at home depends on contraction abroad. American temptations to wield the big stick, as over Libya, should be resisted: its own long-term interests would be far better served by helping to fund United Nations peace-making and peace-keeping machineries and encouraging the development of purely regional arrangements or organisations — a subject too huge to dilate on here.

III. Arms Control and Disarmament

Stabilising Redeployments

Some of the American forward deployments of integrated nuclear and conventional forces right round the Pacific Rim (from the Aleutians, down to the Indian Ocean and the shores of Africa) are highly questionable when serving a strategy of 'offensive defense' that has doubled forward deployed US firepower since 1980. A former US Navy adviser has called the result 'a pathological instability'. This extravagant and futile strategy — carefully delineated in a book by Peter Hayes[3] and others — reflects the brash philosophy declared by the then Navy Secretary John Lehman in 1981: 'Nothing below clear superiority will suffice'. Reductions and redeployments will plainly encourage equivalent Soviet moves: if not, they can readily be reversed.

Nuclear-Free Zones

The nuclear-free zones of local councils may be little more than propaganda gestures but agreements like the 1967 Treaty of Tlatelolco prohibiting nuclear weapons in Latin America and the 1985 Treaty of Rarotonga in the South Pacific are path-breaking, if still incomplete, precedents for similar arrangements for other areas including Africa and the Indian Ocean.

Introducing such zones in, say, the Balkans where East and West meet, would be much more difficult but not, in principle, impossible. Obviously no such arrangement can secure any area's immunity from nuclear weapons (none of us can be immune) but it can inhibit their introduction into it.

Deep Cuts

Oddly enough, deep cuts in strategic missiles, as hoped for in the Strategic Arms Reduction Talks (START) negotiations, may be no more stabilising in themselves than some of the less dramatic possibilities summarised so far. Sharp, 'small' weapons held close up against the enemy's side are more likely to provoke war than many more large ones held in the rear. The strategic arsenals could be cut by four-fifths and still end the human story. Nevertheless, deep cuts would do much to hasten wider progress and the proposed cutting of the Superpowers' long-range nuclear weapons by nearly 50 per cent would be a marvellous beginning, provided it did not induce complacency.

Most useful of all would be the elimination of war-fighting weapons. The arsenals would already be halved by scrapping the 10,000 short- and medium-range nuclear weapons on each side. It is simply crazy that every United States (and presumably Soviet) artillery unit and all but its smallest surface ships should be capable of nuclear fire. The remaining 10,000 or so nuclear weapons on each side could be cut to about 3,500 by eliminating multiple-warheaded missiles and reducing to five the maximum number of nuclear weapons carried by each bomber. Further reductions of warheads would hinge on reducing the number of launchers. We should remember, however, that a remaining, say, 2,000 warheads of 100-kiloton yield would be equivalent to well over 10,000 Hiroshimas.

Especially in Europe, to which we come later, deep reductions in conventional forces are also necessary.

Reductions in Destabilising Arms

As Dr. Paul Rogers[4] has pointed out, even a START agreement involving deep cuts could simply dismantle obsolete systems and encourage the shift towards offensively-oriented counterforce systems.

Missile systems capable of first-strike or pre-emptive use, like the highly accurate American MX and Trident II and any successors to the Soviet SS-18 or SS-24 missiles, are particularly destabilising. So are weapons that are themselves highly vulnerable and also, therefore, incline the enemy to strike first. A third category is comprised of the dangerously ambiguous dual-capable (nuclear and conventional) systems which are so intractable for verification purposes. One especially complex example is the sea-launched cruise missile (SLCM) which would best be flatly banned within the START negotiations. Effective verification on these weapons, however, requires some form of on-board inspection which Washington has so far adamantly refused. Another example in the START context is the ICBM in a mobile mode such as the Soviet SS-24 rail-mobile and SS-25 road-mobile systems and the various mobility options for the American MX and Midgetman missiles. If verification provisions cannot be agreed, a straight ban would again be needed.

Freeze

Many weapon systems are suitable for an agreed freeze when no more radical restraint proves possible. A freeze could also be applied to the production, testing and deployment of particular kinds of nuclear-capable artillery, the production of fissionable material and the development and deployment of equipment for 'Star Wars' programmes on either side.

Freezing an existing imbalance of arms can however make an otherwise transient instability permanent. (In 1982 a freeze would have stopped Pershing II and Cruise but not the Soviet SS20.) Where possible therefore, deep cuts (or verified abolition) are greatly preferable.

Comprehensive Test Ban Treaty (CTBT)

A ban on all nuclear weapons testing would do as much as anything to inhibit the development of new weapon systems. The tragic failure of the early 1960s negotiations was largely due to a Soviet refusal to accept more than three annual on-site inspections and an American insistence on eight. We now know that three would have sufficed. Decades later, the West is still using dubious 'technical' objections to delay and even refuse, agreement. Seismologists, East and West, say modern equipment could detect banned test bomb explosions of less than one kiloton. The Foreign Office denies this but, with that practised British humbug I once deployed myself, pretends it wants to overcome the difficulties. Recent United States administrations absurdly claimed that a Comprehensive Test Ban Treaty (CTBT) would magnify the Soviet threat. The truth is that both the United States and Britain want to test their new warheads. Former weapon designers say the other Western excuse — that testing is essential to maintaining the reliability of nuclear stockpiles — is bogus. No such test was made up to 1980: stockpile inspection is enough.

It was sad and bad that the long voluntary Soviet moratorium on nuclear testing which ended in February 1986 was not reciprocated. President Gorbachev has called a CTBT 'the simplest, most explicit and effective step' towards stopping the arms race and says the Soviet Union is now ready to accept both internal monitoring stations and on-site inspection. If this is bluff — and I do not believe that it is — the bluff should be called. Already, in May 1986, non-governmental American scientists were allowed to establish a seismic station at Semipalatinsk. An earth scientist tells me 70 automatic tamper-proof seismic stations could be installed in the Soviet Union for the price of one nuclear test. If necessary it might be done by a group of Third World countries, or even by private enterprise!

The road to a CTBT could be paved by an agreement for declining annual test quotas or phased reductions in the permitted yield. Such a process is reversible but it would offer hope. The prize is immense. We should all go for it: nothing else would so effectively curb the arms race and it is impeccably respectable for those who mind about such things: very much Harold Macmillan's baby from the start.

Extending the Nuclear Non-Proliferation Treaty

A CTBT, together with reductions in superpower nuclear armouries, would do much to sustain the Non-Proliferation Treaty

(NPT) which could otherwise be at risk of virtual dissolution at its 1995 review conference through the nuclear 'have nots' losing faith in the goodwill of the nuclear 'haves'. Nuclear proliferation is plainly a major long-term threat to global stability.

Urgent, too, is the amplification and strict enforcement of International Atomic Energy Authority (IAEA) safeguards, not least on the United Kingdom and West Germany. Only then could effective pressure be brought on non-signatories tempted to go for nuclear capability.

Britain has failed to conform to the full nuclear inspection provisions of the Euratom Treaty while urging others to do so. It has also persisted in the illegal civilian and military co-processing of plutonium, expanded its plutonium production well beyond civil needs and had to admit 'confusion' and 'lack of consistency' in its nuclear materials accountancy. On official figures, about two tons of civil plutonium have been put to some other use or are missing. That is enough for 400 nuclear bombs.

Until there is a clear, strong, international policy the present disorderly and squalid malaise of greed, evasion, incompetence and smooth lying will continue in Britain as elsewhere. There is an implicit pessimism as well as cynicism in the policies of many 'street-wise' governments that make big money out of Japanese nuclear waste while cocking a snook at their own solemnly-sworn obligations. Once again the root lies in a live-for-the-day hedonism that pays no respect to the prospects for succeeding generations.

Curbing the Conventional Arms Trade

The rival alliances' competitive arming of Third World powers is in no-one's eventual interest but, equally, the legitimate self-defence interests of small nations must be respected, an obligation which doves too easily forget. Recipient as well as supplier states need a voice in creating fair and sensible guidelines. Reporting of all military expenditures and arms transactions to the UN would help, but is not very likely. The monies involved are fabulous. The Western powers alone are fiercely competitive for juicy contracts from such countries as Iraq and Iran, or, indeed wherever a market exists. Their great cry is that if 'we' don't get the contract the French or Germans or Italians or whoever, will. Meanwhile the 'military-industrial complex', against which President Eisenhower warned in the 1950s, is as strong as ever and as relevant to export sales as to Alliance arms procurement. The 'revolving door' links between defence contractors and defence officials is as ill-disciplined in the United Kingdom as the 'Rent-a-General' system in the United States. Meanwhile the British Government proudly claims to have become the world's third biggest arms exporter.

Banning Chemical and Biological Weapons

Of the chemical weapons, the incapacitating nerve gases are so devilish that front-line troops of both alliances now have to be equipped with cumbersome protective clothing. The production of binary warheads, in which the active nerve gas is generated *en route* to the target, is meanwhile making chemical weaponry much easier to create, handle, transport and deploy. Chemical weapons are now talked of as a sort of Third World nuclear-substitute (favoured by some Arabs as a counter to Israel's bomb).

The need for much more far-reaching and rigorous controls than those in the 1925 Geneva Protocol was dramatised by Iraq's terrible actions against the Iranians and its own Kurds and by Libya's alleged preparations. Some notably constructive British initiatives in favour of a comprehensive ban offer some hope of success and American obstruction seems to be lessening. New efforts to make progress are under way following the Paris conference in January 1989 and the Soviet declaration that the destruction of its stocks would proceed shortly.

Biological weapons threaten the spread of some of the foulest diseases and a Convention in 1975 prohibited their development, production or possession. Both Superpowers, however, conduct 'defensive research' and it may not be possible by technical means to verify that no one is going beyond that. Nevertheless the agreement symbolises and strengthens the profound horror humankind has always felt about war by toxin and bacteria and this in itself is not a negligible sanction. A similar agreement may soon, incidentally, be needed on weaponry based on molecular biology.

Safeguarding the ABM Treaty

In the 1972 Anti-Ballistic Missile (ABM) Treaty the Superpowers agreed, in effect, that efforts to create an efficient anti-ballistic missile system would at best cause a new arms race and at worst give one or other side a dangerous war-fighting ascendancy. This was a prime reason for West European misgivings over SDI. The ABM Treaty should in fact be strengthened. First, any alleged violations should be dealt with as the treaty prescribes and by on-site inspection if necessary. Secondly, SDI research should not be pursued even where it only threatens the Treaty. Nor are deep cuts in Soviet strategic weaponry to be expected if SDI is pursued. Thirdly, the Treaty needs beefing up to forbid the testing or deployment of anti-satellite (ASAT) weaponry which could blind the opponent and hence precipitate war. Such a ban was proposed by President Carter in 1977 but the talks were abandoned after the Russian invasion of Afghanistan. Why depriving the world of an agreement not to militarise space was thought especially to help the Afghans or punish the East was never clear.

As the late Olof Palme's Commission[5] rightly reported in 1982:

> Negotiations for the limitation and reduction of arms ... are not gifts to an adversary or rewards for his good behaviour, but rather a means of pursuing common security and profiting from shared interests.

IV Human Rights

There seems to be a parallel confusion in Western minds about the highly sensitive issue of human rights. NATO leaders force the item high on almost all East – West agendas and are predictably counter-attacked over their own domestic injustices. No nation likes being put in the dock and Moscow is infuriated when the West shows double standards and humbug over torture or the equivalent in so called Free World nations like Turkey, Chile, Indonesia and, in their time, Spain and Greece. (And indeed the United Kingdom, in Northern Ireland). As a NATO member, Turkey's performance is horrendous, now arguably worse than the Soviet Union's, yet we just let it pass.

Soviet conditions are plainly improving but if they deteriorate again we must ask whether there can be any serious competition between progress on human rights and on human survival where these two conflict. Nor, in a tense atmosphere, are they likely to be improved anyway. Is a beleagured state likely to become more liberal? The usual Western argument that reliable deals cannot be struck with violators of human rights is palpably false. International deals — as with Turkey's membership of NATO — hinge on common interests and dependable verification, not on angelic characters on either side. Refusal to make deals with nasty people is simply childish. With nice ones you scarcely need them.

I hope I shall not be misunderstood. Human rights, broadly interpreted and universally applied, are fundamental. The Helsinki Accords of 1975 rightly established them as one of the main general conditions of peace in Europe and gave signatories the legal right to investigate. Western persistence in the slow tortuous Helsinki process has achieved much and is perfectly legitimate so long as we remain impartial and non-propagandist and do not act to the detriment of stability. To cut off one's nose to spite someone else's face has never been wise.

Conclusion

In few if any of the areas we have explored is total verification and, therefore, total confidence possible. Yet our present condition is also one of risk. Moreover it is the total structure of co-operative security that needs to be examined. A or B may be able to cheat here or there but the benefit of a single infraction is most unlikely to be decisive, whereas the consequences of discovery are likely to be severe. Within the right overall context, therefore, self-interest is likely to dictate what natural virtue will not. All this said, the creation of co-operative security between the Superpowers will critically depend on sustaining security where they most critically confront each other, in Western Europe, to which we now turn.

12

The Security of Western Europe

> Viewed dispassionately, the huge East–West military con-
> frontation in Europe seems to have passed its high point,
> politically if not militarily, and to be in decline.
> Former United States Ambassador Jonathan Dean[1].

In Brussels in October 1979, Henry Kissinger[2] excited a controversy that has still not been resolved and is now very likely to
revive. Essentially he said that once the Soviet Union acquired the
power of direct nuclear retaliation, the American pledge to launch
a nuclear war on behalf of Western Europe was,

> bound increasingly to lose its credibility and public acceptance, if not its
> sense — and so would the Alliance's defence strategy. For the strategy now rested
> on the threat to initiate mutual suicide.

Kissinger[3] was roundly criticised for undermining NATO strategy but he remained wholly unabashed:

> For more than two decades, the West has hid its head in the sand and ignored
> the inevitable . . . The legacy we are left with is a precarious combination of a
> NATO reliance on nuclear defence, trends towards nuclear stalemate, growing
> nuclear pacifism, and continued deficiencies in conventional forces.

Even hawks, therefore, have long had doubts about a key element
of NATO's philosophy.

Dependence, Abandonment and Entrapment

An old maxim had it that NATO's main aims were to keep the Russians out, the Germans down and the Americans in. In its earliest days there were two threats — the old one of a resurgent Germany and the new one of Soviet expansionism aided by domestic Communism, as in France and Italy. American help to Western Europe was swift and substantial but there has always been a basic geo-strategic asymmetry: the United States is 3,000 miles away while its European allies are face-to-face with Soviet might. The Warsaw Pact has short, internal, cross-land lines of communication. NATO has to depend substantially on long, external supply routes with all the expense, delay and hazard of air and sea passage.

This asymmetry has also meant Western Europe playing host to large, resident American forces and therefore, almost inevitably, being seen from Moscow as providing a forward base from which the United States can threaten the Soviet bloc. From Washington, the Alliance is seen as absorbing the German problem and preserving overall stability along 'freedom's front-line' in an essentially defensive manner. (The Soviet Union can equally legitimately see these deployments as part of an American 'crowding' that stretches from the Canadian and Norwegian North through Turkey and Pakistan to Korea and the Aleutian Islands.)

Western Europe's dependency on American strength is inevitably accompanied by resentment and tensions. The Europeans get increased military protection and reduced military costs but less freedom of action. They also have fears of abandonment at one extreme and entrapment at the other, of either being deserted or of being sucked into a war of American rather than European choosing.

The United States naturally has the opposite fear. One of the oldest questions in NATO strategy is whether Washington would risk Chicago to save Hamburg. Some Western loyalists, like Kissinger, have doubted it. So did the authors of the 1988 Pentagon-sponsored report, *Discriminate Deterrence*[4], who said that in defending their allies and their interests abroad, the Americans 'cannot rely on threats expected to provoke our own annihilation if carried out'.

In one sense the Americans cannot win. Any moves to reduce European fears of abandonment, like installing Cruise and Pershing 2, incidentally increases European fear, and not only in the peace movements. Any American relaxation of its guard, as in negotiating these systems away, arouses fresh fears of abandonment, especially in the Germans and the British.

Nor, in American eyes, can the Europeans win. The United States looks at the Soviet Union eastwards as well as westwards and it is not entirely clear to many in California and the mid-West why a prosperous and sometimes fiercely competitive Western Europe, comprising more people than either the United States or the Soviet Union, should need many divisions of expensive American troops as well as massive American nuclear forces. From their perspective, the distant and culturally-conceited Europeans are mean about their own defence, shameless in their demands on the New World, unreliable about providing military or even political support to the United States 'out of area', and condescendingly critical of much American policy. Why cannot the West Europeans, they ask, defend themselves? It is not a wholly unreasonable question.

A Real Turning Point for NATO

Many West Europeans have drawn the same conclusion form their concern about Flexible Response — a strategy meant to bind transatlantic security interests together but also liable to incinerate Central Europe. And, even in the eyes of its supporters, each of the three legs on which Flexible Response has ostensibly stood has now been severely weakened. First, NATO's conventional strength has not been significantly enhanced, despite the appeals of the last Supreme Allied Commander (SACEUR) General Rogers, amongst others. Secondly, the land-based INF weaponry is being removed and the early use of battlefield nuclear weaponry has come to look suicidal, especially to the West Germans. Thirdly, the credibility of the ultimate sanction, United States strategic missiles, has been eroded by Kissinger's question, reinforced by the rhetoric surrounding SDI and the Reykjavik Summit.

The essential choice now facing the NATO governments — though some of them are still to see it — is whether to try to rebuild Flexible Response, plus a fully credible United States extended nuclear deterrence over Western Europe, or to go for Co-operative Security. Let us first glance at what the former, hawkish, alternative would involve.

All three legs of the triad would demand attention. Conventional forces would need much strengthening and hi-tech modernising (unless there had been very big Soviet cuts meanwhile). The escalatory steps then represented by battlefield and intermediate nuclear weaponries would also need not only 'updating' but increased accuracy and destructiveness. Finally the credibility of the United States strategic bottom line would need to be regained through marked changes in American rhetoric and practice in relation to nuclear deterrence in general and to strategic initiatives like SDI and START in particular.

It is doubtful whether much of this can happen. What hawks try to dismiss as the Gorbachev 'charm offensive' has profoundly affected West European — and much American — opinion. Bellicosity and even up-tight defensiveness are looking dated and there is neither the public will nor the public purse, especially in the United States, to undertake new expenditure. Budgetary squeezes may well lead to further American troop reductions in Europe and certainly renewed pressure for more European burden-sharing. There may be some modernisation of battlefield and air- and sea-launched intermediate nuclear forces but, pushed too far, this will antagonise West German and other opinion and undermine the general NATO consensus. And whatever Washington did about the strategic leg of the triad, the awkward question of whether Hamburg is worth Chicago would still remain. Meanwhile, NATO's apparent reluctance to respond positively to the Soviet President's offers would slow down his reforms, possibly prejudice his survival and certainly appear unstatesmanlike to the wider world.

The resuscitation of Flexible Response therefore seems very unlikely — even if the theory endures as a cover story for a sorry reality of a virtual all-or-nothing trip-wire. Yet that provides the worst of all worlds — apparently 'strong' defence at high expense with a built-in propensity, as immoral as it is self-destructive, for first and early nuclear use. We must, I think, seek defensive arrangements in Europe that are far less dependent both on nuclear arms and on transatlantic linkage.

Soviet Conventional Superiority?

Any big change of NATO policy must plainly start from assessing the real operational significance of the disparity between the conventional strengths of each side. In strict numerical terms the Warsaw Pact itself now admits its forces are larger in some — though not all — respects. But what does this amount to? The argument can be endless but some of the typical errors and distortions are easily sketched. NATO estimates include Polish and Czechoslovak divisions of dubious loyalty and Soviet units needed for internal security duties. They meanwhile exclude their own Spanish forces and fail to mention that Western divisions are usually much larger (as well as much more effective) than those of the Warsaw Pact. In actual serving manpower the two alliances are fairly equal. The Warsaw Pact admits to twice the number of tanks but very many of these are old and ill-maintained and far more vulnerable to anti-tank systems than NATO's battle tanks. Nor does the West count 5,000 American battle tanks held in European stores. The observant will notice that, since the Soviet Union has promised unilateral cuts in its tank forces, Western pundits are beginning to claim that these will make the Soviet army sleeker and hence *stronger*! (Western propaganda is no less shameless than Eastern but it also assumes innocent idiocy in its target audience.)

NATO assessments especially neglect Western technical superiority in weapons like the M1 tank, the Bradley fighting vehicle, the Apache attack helicopter and the F-15 and F-16 fighters. They also underplay the notable technical, air-fighting and bomb delivery capabilities of the NATO air forces. NATO air defences are expected to destroy 4−5 enemy aircraft for every NATO aircraft lost in combat. NATO navies also have a considerable superiority in numbers of aircraft carriers (US-11 − USSR-0), in other major surface combatants and amphibious warfare ships, and indeed in world-wide aggregate tonnage. (The West's insistence on the exclusion of naval forces from the current Vienna talks is grossly unrealistic since NATO's naval superiority could itself be a major factor in a European 'land' war. Yet NATO at first tried to exclude the air forces as well — for 'objective' technical reasons.)

A key question is whether Warsaw Treaty tank forces are sufficient to head a successful *blitzkrieg* attack on the Central Front like Hitler's in 1940 — the gut fear of many Westerners. If attempted by the Soviet bloc's standing forces, before mobilisation, it looks as if about 57 divisions would be up against only 28 in NATO Europe. The NATO divisions, however, are larger, better equipped and more competent so the overall ratio of strength is probably no more than 4:3 in the bloc's favour (even prior to the Gorbachev cuts). Yet, even with the advantages of surprise, any attacker would traditionally want 3:1 superiority to have a good chance of success on alien and hostile terrain. It is also generally agreed that a Soviet attack *after* the mobilisation of both sides would be even more hazardous.

Broadly these are the conclusions of most independent studies. For example the IISS Military Balance[5] of 1987 said 'the conventional overall balance is still such as to make general military aggression a highly risky undertaking for either side'. *The Economist*[6] concluded a major study of Western capabilities in similar vein. My clear impression from numerous conversations with people professionally engaged, including some at NATO headquarters, is that this judgement is reasonable.

The two sides are not all that far from a broad parity of quantity plus quality and this is not really surprising: as a British Atlantic Committee study group[7] has rightly pointed out, NATO spends considerably more on defence than the Warsaw Treaty countries. The latter are said to spend 15–17 per cent of their GNP on defence but as their GNP is far smaller than the West's, this is grossly misleading. Both sides cheat, fiddle and define weapon and manpower categories to suit themselves; and NATO is smarter at all these things.

NATO does have some real disadvantages: serious linguistic complications, a disgracefully wide variety of weapon and communication systems and, with 16 members, great trouble in reaching a common view of anything. On the other hand, Soviet troops are mostly poorly educated, often weak in the Russian language and lacking the characteristic flexibility, commitment and high morale of Westerners defending their liberties. Pehaps I lay more stress on those factors than other people: I do not apologise.

Quite apart from the risks of military defeat or stalemate on the Central Front, the Kremlin would also have to prepare to meet substantial American attacks from the East and Chinese attacks along their long common frontier. Soviet–Chinese relations are currently improving but if there were a Superpower war — the last thing China wants — Beijing would certainly not want the Soviet Union to win it. All this leaves aside the dreadful possibility for Moscow of revolt in some of the Warsaw Pact armies and of major civil disturbances and sabotage in Eastern Europe, even perhaps in some of the Soviet provinces. Moscow would also, of course, expect immense conventional damage to the Soviet homeland even if no nuclear weapon were fired.

Why Does NATO Exaggerate?

If there is now virtually no chance of a deliberate Soviet assault on Western Europe, why do senior NATO politicians persist in speaking fearfully of the Warsaw Pact's 'overwhelming' conventional superiority? I think the reason lies more in political needs than military realities. Western leaders especially fear that the democracies might lower their guard. This regular NATO cliché has something to it — the public has a natural hatred for war and waste but also a lazy unwillingness to think issues through.

But West European governments also have a special interest in actually maintaining NATO's conventional inferiority. Without it, they would find it hard to justify their demands for a large American conventional and nuclear presence in Europe and hence the critical triggers of the United States strategic nuclear forces. It is no wonder that there was much annoyance when, in December 1987, a Western European Union parliamentary committee[8] criticised the inconsistency and credibility of NATO statistics, pointing out that the Soviet Union had only 1,400 modern T-80 tanks in service compared with the West's 4,800 modern M1s. But the key point is that NATO's main problem is not the conventional (or nuclear) strength of the Soviet Union but, as it sees it, the frailty of the trans-Atlantic link. To this we shall have to return.

Causes for Concern

Although most NATO generals (and defence ministers) would agree that a deliberate Soviet assault on Western Europe was most unlikely in the forseeable future — and that the needs of *perestroika*, and the recent quiet revolutions in Eastern Europe, reinforce this judgement — they would classically insist that Soviet intentions could change if NATO's will or capabilities were greatly weakened. Moreover, even with a genuinely strong NATO there are circumstances in which war could arise whatever the intentions of either side. Nor can NATO generals wholly discount the idea of a wild sally arising from a power struggle in the Kremlin or a left hook being thrown to seize Hamburg as a bargaining counter to stop, for example, another

American attempt to overthrow Castro. President Gorbachev, they might opine, seems a sensible fellow and ministers may approve of him but we cannot instantly rebuild neglected defences the day after he has been slotted into the Lenin Tomb. Nor can we be unprepared for the conflict that neither he nor we wanted. It is by being properly prepared that we, the military, can best help to avoid such a situation ever arising.

Doves naturally find such talk pessimistic, depressing and shocking. It is certainly simplistic, because ill-judged 'deterrents' can themselves precipitate conflict, but there is still a core of common sense in it. Doves cannot consistently argue that the dangers of unintended or miscalculated war are substantial and then insist we drop our guard because the new Russian intentions are benign. Furthermore generals are rightly paid to prepare for the worst, not the best, and could plausibly point out that, although the Kremlin is now talking about a 'non-offensive' military doctrine, Soviet Army plans and deployment have yet significantly to change. Ever since 1945, Soviet staffs have believed that, however it may start, the next European war would be won (and Russia defended) by a high-speed Soviet tank assault. In the 1970s, indeed, Marshal Nikolai Ogarkov developed the idea of acting so fast as to deprive NATO of time even to debate the use of nuclear weapons.

The new Soviet Defence Minister, General Dmitri Yazov, endorses the new defensive thinking and is said to have personally conducted the 'Autumn '88' exercises in the Ukraine on that basis. Nevertheless NATO Supreme Commander, General John Galvin, like others, is almost bound to remain sceptical until there are very substantial changes on the ground. A reasonably independent report[9] at the end of 1988 said Soviet forces in Europe 'not only exceed the reasonable needs of defence . . . but are . . . configured and deployed in a fashion which favours high-speed, short-warning, offensive or counter-offensive operations'.

Following President Gorbachev's United Nations speech of December 1988 and later pronouncements, this may well change. Meanwhile the Cold War is thawing and the Iron Curtain is fast dissolving. Look, for example, at the remarkable pace of political change in Hungary, East Germany and Poland. Western leaders must therefore be prepared to move fast and creatively to meet what may soon prove to be radically changed conditions. If, meanwhile, they must to a degree play safe on the military side, the sensible response is not to mock their fears but to suggest better ways of meeting them.

Reassessing NATO's Conventional Defences

Western Europe needs to retain defences adequate to repulse any major Soviet attack, however started, and hence to avoid feeling politically overawed by Soviet power — a condition that would itself be highly unstable. Yet we have seen how NATO's existing defensive plans are, as Robert McNamara[10] puts it, 'far more likely to destroy Europe than to defend it'. Moreover, as he says, 'whatever deterrent remains in NATO's nuclear strategy is eroding rapidly'. The practical problem is therefore two-fold. The first is how to organise far better conventional defences for Western Europe, which is dealt with in the rest of this chapter. The second problem, dealt with in the next chapter, is how to reduce NATO's high dependency on nuclear weapons.

Most military authorities would agree that whilst NATO's forces do not need to 'balance' or match specific Soviet capabilities, they must be strong enough to throw the gravest doubts on the prospects for any plausible attack. The prime military tasks would be to counter the initial Warsaw Pact assault, to achieve air mastery over the battlefields, to interdict the Pact's follow-up formations and to disrupt its regional command and control systems while safeguarding NATO's own. Providing these tasks, especially 'interdiction', are not perverted into (or interpreted as) aggression by other means, none of these aims — on either side — is incompatible with an essentially defensive posture.

Some capacity for counter-attack is essential to defence, otherwise the antagonist could add all his own defensive forces to his attack. He could also mass those forces in safety behind his own lines and, once he had unleashed his offensive, largely monopolise both initiative and surprise. But a necessary capacity for local, tactical counter-attack is not the same as a strategic capacity for massive counter-offensive (or offensive) deep into enemy territory. The difference may be one of degree but it is crucial.

Means of Defence

In addition to the counter-attack on the enemy's forces ('counter-force') and threatening a general counter-offensive (classic 'deterrence'), there are two other basic means of defence. One is to obstruct the enemy force by means of obstacles and fortifications. The other is, so far as possible, to avoid presenting the enemy with lucrative targets for heavy weapons — *ie* to disperse, to melt into the forest while attacking the enemy along the flanks, in the dark and so on.

NATO's defences have primarily been based on the first two of these four means, 'counterforce' and 'deterrence'. To achieve more effective territorial defence and better chances of avoiding nuclear war, many strategic specialists since the 1970s have laid increasing emphasis on the other two means — obstruction and removal — within a wide variety of non-offensive or non-provocative defence plans.

Non-offensive Defence Plans

The variety of plans offered by such specialists as Horst Afheldt, Lutz Unterseher, Norbet Hannig, Major General Jochen Loser, Albrecht von Muller and Andrzej Karkoszka have been well summarised in the *Bulletin of the Atomic Scientists*.[11] Some of the plans would change overall strategy, others would revamp tactical operations; some call for unilateral moves, others would depend on bilateral agreements; some call for reductions, others do not. Some place all the weight on static defence, others share it with mobile defence, using tanks. All, however, seek to create forces that can provide a reliable defensive system without provoking Soviet fears of attack or risking war by miscalculation. One highly readable formulation is that by the British author Stan Windass[12] who employs the acronym FORT standing for Firepower and Forward Defence; Obstacles; Rear Area Defence; and Transparency.

These are rather technical military issues but, as they are taken seriously by many retired and serving NATO officers, let me sketch a few of them.

Defence in Depth

NATO's present conventional defences are as brittle as an egg: hard on the outside but soft within. Too many German politicians have insisted on not sacrificing an inch. A realistic defence would resist any massed attack all the way, fighting on its own chosen terrain rather than necessarily on the border. Maximum use would be made of headquarters and support troops all of whom, including the women, should be trained in small arms. Territorials and locally-recruited militia units (on Swiss or Yugoslav lines) would be expanded and upgraded and, like reservists, be highly trained in the optimum fighting techniques for their own local environment whether marshlands, forests, mountains or, as often as not, town and city streets. West Germany has two million men in its General Reserve: with an effort there could be seven million men (and women) in Central Europe alone, with specific duties to defend the transport and communication systems as well as port facilities, storage depots and other critical rear installations which are otherwise too vulnerable to Soviet *Spetsnatz* agents, paratroops or, indeed, direct attack.

As things are now, NATO's shortage of pre-prepared barriers and impediments means in turn that covering forces need more warning time and could be caught by Soviet artillery or aircraft before they could move. Moreover, NATO's ammunition stocks and transport systems are excessively concentrated and not sufficiently inter-operable. Dependence on early reinforcements from the United States is also high. It takes two weeks to air-lift an infantry division across the Atlantic and longer for a mechanised division; a C-5 air transport takes one tank at a time and a division needs about 250.

Instead, then, of having to resort quickly to battlefield nuclear weapons, it is suggested that the (largely theoretical) Soviet *blitzkrieg* would be met by a 'thicket' defence in which deliberately-placed ditches, canals, embankments, tree plantings, and other anti-tank obstacles and minefields are added to existing natural features to help slow and divide the attack, and to divert enemy forces towards calculated concentrations of fire. These would be provided by anti-tank aircraft and helicopters and, on the flanks, from a static 'web' of light infantry commandos with deadly anti-tank weaponry, mines and mine-throwers. These forces would be complemented by a well-practised artillery network and mobile armoured formations, 'spiders' which would not be so large as to present easy targets (or offensive threats).

This is not to propose a new Maginot Line buried in concrete (although that was by-passed, rather than overcome). It exploits in depth what Clausewitz long ago noted, that defence is intrinsically 'the stronger form of war'. The attacker is by definition on alien, unfamiliar territory, at increasing distance from his sources of supply and, while the defender is concealed and among friends, the attacker is highly visible and thoroughly hated. (Both Vietnam and Afghanistan stand in fearsome witness to this.)

In addition to military measures, the civilian populations of democratic societies should be capable of effective non-violent defence or 'social resistance' through strikes, sabotage and non-co-operation in occupied areas. The likelihood of such action could alone have some dissuasive effect on a would-be aggressor. (Some doves would depend wholly on such a strategy; I can see it only as a useful supplement.)

Emerging Technology (ET) and the Automated Battlefield

The attacker may have the initial advantage of surprise but every day thereafter his vulnerability increases. Moreover, the 'transparency' of the battlefield is now greatly amplified by day and by night through satellite surveillance, fibre-optics, infra-red imaging and image intensifiers.

The computer chip and other technologies are rapidly creating a substantially automated battlefield, as Frank Barnaby[13] has called it, in which enemy forces can be located, tracked and targeted almost instantaneously through the use of data-links, computerised evaluation and automated fire control. Micro-electronics have produced the remotely piloted vehicles and drones used by the Israelis in the Lebanon, the air-launched TV-guided Maverick homing missile that was battle-tested in Vietnam, the British Army's highly sensitive ground sensors on the Irish border, and the deadly Exocets that sank the £100 million HMS *Sheffield* in the Falklands war. Nuclear weapons aside, a Third World War would be as different from the Second as that was from the First.

There have been startling advances in 'conventional' explosive power, guidance systems and warhead design. A single salvo of 12 rockets from one version of the multiple-launch rocket system (MLRS) will explode 10,000 grenades over an area equivalent to six football fields. The 'fire-and-forget' anti-tank missiles, from land, air or sea, will seek out their target on their own and these autonomous missiles could soon be up against robot-driven vehicles with their own 'smart' weapons, whether wire or laser-guided, heat-seeking, radar-homing or electro-optical.

Conventional combat is rapidly becoming more technical, more capital-intensive, longer in range and ever more deadly — especially for any advancing or otherwise visible force. Emerging Technology (ET) is shifting it into a cruel competition of so-called survivability where stealth and mobility are vital and open *blitzkrieg* can spell suicide. Where only the hidden survive, the attacker is doomed. The cost and military trade-offs can be huge: the M-1 tank is over 170 times the cost of the TOW-2 missiles used in my 'Hellarm' exercise; the F-15 aircraft is 600 times the cost of the Stinger missiles; the Aegis cruiser is 2,000 times the cost of the anti-ship missiles that could instantly sink it.

ET does, of course, have problems: technical, practical, operational, bureaucratic and financial. It is not an infallible hi-tech fix. Human factors remain critical: service morale and organisation, strategy and tactics, imagination and courage. There is also still a need for basic competence, as dramatised by the United States Navy's Aegis cruiser shooting down of the Iranian airliner in 1988 (such competence demands constant, intensive and often live training, despite the inconvenience and occasional danger to the public. Without training, however unpopular, the huge effort and cost of replacing nuclear arms with conventional ones would be effectively wasted and necessary minimum defences undermined).

Conventional Arms Reductions and Zones of Disengagement

Some of these emerging technologies could encourage an emphasis on defensiveness on both sides even if only pursued unilaterally, but far greater benefits all round could come from negotiating verifiable force reductions and zones of disengagement. The old Mutual and Balanced Force Reduction (MBFR) talks in Vienna produced no agreement in 14 years and became a propaganda sideshow. President Gorbachev proved to be prepared to break the log jam, partly by unilateral withdrawals, partly by asymmetric cuts. The substantial unilateral cuts he announced in his United Nations speech in December 1988 included not only an overall reduction of half a million servicemen, much artillery and many aircraft but the withdrawal and disbandment of six tank divisions from East Germany, Czechoslovakia and Hungary together with many assault units.

New East–West negotiations on conventional arms opened in Vienna in March 1989 with the Russians seeming to make all the running with assorted new offers while internal NATO divisions intensified. A bold bid to regain some Western initiative was somewhat unexpectedly provided by President Bush at the May 1989 NATO Summit when he challenged Moscow to reach an agreement on conventional forces within a year. As part of a masterly policy package to defuse NATO's crisis over the 'modernisation' of short-range nuclear weaponry, he distracted attention by proposing the negotiation of a 20 per cent cut in United States troops in Europe and that combat aircraft and helicopters should after all be included in the Vienna talks. Mr Bush also called for full implementation by 1992 or 1993 of an agreement including a reduction in the numbers of tanks on each side to 20,000.

The Soviet Union itself proposes not only parity in tanks, armoured personnel carriers and artillery pieces but in tactical aircraft, helicopters and anti-tank weapons and in troops as such. At some stage it is also likely to propose, say, a 75 kilometre demilitarised zone on both sides of the Inner German Border.

In the Conventional Armed Forces in Europe (CFE) talks that are now under way, NATO should further test President Gorbachev's shift towards defensive sufficiency. It should be bidding for big cuts on both sides not, as at present, for levels of arms that mean very small reductions in its own forces. Moreover, if for example the quality of the best Soviet battle tanks, like the T-80, still induces some Allied fear of a massed surprise attack, NATO should propose a mutual total ban on heavy mobile weapons like tanks, big artillery and bridging equipment from a strip, say, 50 kilometres (31 miles) wide on each side of the border.

A former Deputy Commander in Chief, United Kingdom Land Forces, General Sir Hugh Beach, has said it would increase confidence if the zones were 150 kilometres deep. Professor Dieter Senghers[14] amongst others has suggested that such zones of disengagement could also exclude attack helicopters and (a subject of the next chapter) battlefield nuclear weapons. There could also be limits on the numbers of fighting troops and on ammunition stockpiles. Inspection could be by officers of the opposing alliance or by neutrals.

These zones would not be wholly 'demilitarised'. The border areas are militarily far too vulnerable and politically far too sensitive for that. Partial disengagement would, however, ensure that neither strip contained forces capable of launching a heavy surprise attack. Sir Leon Brittan[15], a former Conservative Cabinet Minister, is amongst those who have called for a tank-free Central Europe, a concept also commended by Zbigniew Brzezinski. Nor would such zones be incompatible with the other ideas discussed, including the elaboration of physical barriers and fortifications within the zone, the stationing of mobile tank forces behind them and overall force reductions.

The stabilising effect of the zoning would be further enhanced by the kinds of confidence-building measure sketched in the last chapter and likely to be further developed within the talks that are continuing the Helsinki process. If the present momentum is sustained in these and in the Conventional Force Europe (CFE) talks, the agreed measures could include overall limits on the numbers of specified weapon types from the Atlantic to the Urals, with sublimits for the Central European states or for 'ready', non-national and other units. NATO is already making proposals of this kind at the CFE negotiations but it is crucial that it eventually also pays attention to other relevant arms, including aircraft, helicopters and naval forces — and to their quality as well as their quantity.

A Preliminary Conclusion

Even the best of the various proposals I have sketched are likely to face significant problems of cost, complexity, seeming inflexibility and political resistance. It is an immense and technical subject. Nor will it be easy to re-fashion, re-train and re-deploy Western (and Eastern) defensive forces. The owl will not be dogmatic and recognises that radical change will be a matter of years, not months. There is no single clear-cut saving formula, no resounding clarion call. The clear message is that there is no clear solution. Yet all the ideas we have discussed are essentially and verifiably defensive and therefore do represent a dramatic change from the present eyeballing confrontation. And since Flexible Response is becoming increasingly perilous and incredible, we simply must now move decisively in this other direction. Critical questions remain, however, as to how Western Europe can reduce its present high dependency on nuclear arms, even against conventional attack.

13

Reducing Nuclear Dependency: An Audacious Response to President Gorbachev

> So far as redressing any conventional imbalance goes, reliance on the early use of nuclear weapons is simply no answer.
>
> Field Marshal Lord Carver[1]

NATO's muffled and divided response to President Gorbachev's remarkable energy and boldness is in danger of making the West appear so inflexibly obsessed with old problems as to neglect new opportunities; or, as one United States Congressman said, like a bunch of accountants faced with a man of vision. This has been bad for the public consensus on which NATO's prospects must depend. But most of all, wider global interests and morality itself—the only final justification for any alliance—demands that the West keeps moving constructively.

Three Major Proposals

This does not mean the West need go overboard for the new ideas but three early and major shifts of NATO nuclear policy commend themselves. None of them are irreversible if President Gorbachev should prove less co-operative in practice than he so far sounds in theory, although I believe all three make sense in their own right. Together with bold movement towards conventional force reductions and newly-defensive deployments, they would go a long way

162

to stabilising Central Europe and weaning both sides from their addiction to irrational weapon systems. All three proposals will be counted perilous heresy by the hawks and mere cosmetic compromise by some doves. As usual, owls will have to fight on both flanks.

The First Proposal: Agreements About Nuclear First Use

I have argued that the West's willingness to use nuclear weapons against a non-nuclear attack is unnecessary, inflexible and potentially suicidal. It may be some deterrent but it is not defence. Flexible Response does not, as some of its believers claim, provide some merely 'theoretical' nuclear options: it involves NATO having nuclear artillery, missiles and mines at the ready in perilously 'integrated', well-trained nuclear-plus-conventional military units. The nuclear warheads are not even generally stored in hardened sites, precisely because they are to be used first.

NATO speaks of a graduated and selective nuclear response with weapons used[2] with 'discrimination and precision' and 'in a deliberate politically-controlled way'. These are nice moderate words — yet only a fraction of NATO's arsenal of battlefield nuclear weapons would cause a million or more casualties: Russian, East German, West German, Dutch, British and so on. The distinctions made are quite spurious in real battlefield terms. As the British Atlantic Committee[3], including a distinguished group of senior ex-officers, long ago said: 'The concept of controlled, step-by-step, escalation is impractical nonsense in an unpredictable and largely uncontrollable and chaotic situation.' The firing of nuclear weapons would also precipitate a mighty Soviet reprisal. The essence of Soviet doctrine seems clear: no limited wars. Start using nukes, they say, and we shall throw the lot at you. Many of our own field commanders would probably react in the same way unless under very tight control. As long ago as 1959, George Kennan called First Use 'a fateful and pernicious principle' and our weaning away from it the key to any coherent strategy. This remains true.

It used to be assumed that NATO would hold back nuclear use until facing conventional defeat but NATO nuclear planners[4] are now speaking openly of 'demonstration shots'. General Bernard Rogers[5], the previous SACEUR, also admitted this shift to even earlier nuclear use.

What can be done to reduce this menace? The Soviet Union made a declaration of No First Use in July 1982 at the United Nations and asked for a Western response, for which it still waits. Sceptics have always protested that mere declarations are of virtually no value. They are right: in a crisis mere promises would cut no ice. But that oversimplifies the problem and the possibilities. What we need are not declarations vainly aimed at constraining the use of nuclear weapons in time of war but measures and agreements carefully designed to constrain their deployment in time of peace. We need not a *declaration* but a *policy* of No First Use. This policy would require drastic changes in strategy and force structure. Military commanders would have to provide fully effective, and long overdue, conventional defences against any non-nuclear attack. They would also have to be instructed not to use their battlefield nuclear weapons unless opposing forces went nuclear first. The Central Front would then become far more crisis-resistant.

Interestingly enough, the effectiveness of a new NATO policy of No First Use may not depend on trusting the Soviet Union's equivalent declaration (or policy), or *vice versa*. What is essential is for the military on both sides to have to take their own political superiors seriously by making their own nuclear forces genuinely less accessible, less vulnerable and less provocative. Distrust between the opposing powers will of course remain but both sides should feel safer. Moreover, many of the consequent redeployments, training measures and staff doctrines would be verifiable and therefore susceptible to formal agreements.

As for the famous four, Bundy, Kennan, McNamara and Smith,[6] said in their seminal *Foreign Affairs* article in 1982, a policy of No First Use would not only help the West's relations with the Soviet Union but reduce the pressures on both sides for new nuclear forces and 'bring new hope to everyone in every country whose life is shadowed by the hideous possibility of a third great twentieth century conflict in Europe — conventional or nuclear'.

This said, nothing except actual verified nuclear abolition — probably itself a pipe dream — could wholly guarantee either side against nuclear first use. It may therefore be best to start with a set of East – West agreements providing for No Early First Use. This would be close to what General Bernard Rogers seemed to mean in saying he would like to reach a situation in which he could 'almost guarantee' No First Use. We are very far from that at present.

The Second Proposal: Purging Europe
of Battlefield Nuclear Weapons

Whatever happens about No First Use, the West must stop depending on battlefield nuclear weapons as a substitute for conventional anti-tank munitions. In a crisis these smallest and shortest-range nuclear weapons would be quite the most dangerous of all: the first to be deployed, the first over which junior officers got discretion to fire and the most likely to be thought 'proportionate' to a local emergency.

Most of the battlefield weapons, primarily artillery and short-range missiles like Lance (70 miles), are necessarily deployed in West Germany and it is there or next door they would go off, slaughtering soldiers and civilians, friend and foe, in dizzying numbers. Even conservative West Germans are now at best ambivalent towards them. As one Christian Democrat spokesman saw it, 'the shorter the range, the deader the Germans'. German farmers have long resisted the burial of atomic demolition munitions on their land. Nuclear anti-aircraft missiles, now withdrawn, were also recognised as especially daft, not least since aircraft now have to fly very low to avoid radar detection. Thousands of obsolescent nuclear artillery shells have been (unilaterally) withdrawn by NATO and public opposition stopped the physical introduction of neutron (enhanced radiation) shells, although large stocks of them are held at the ready in the United States. The theory for the use of battlefield nuclear weapons sound superficially rational: imagination plus simple realism quite destroys the case for them.

Despite all the military and political complications, NATO still has over 2,400 battlefield nuclear weapons in Europe (and nearly as many other nuclear weapons). On present plans the first serious trouble would lead to the nuclear shells for NATO's self-propelled artillery being rushed out from a hundred front-line storage depots to the highly mobile vehicles of national armies spread out from the icy wastes of Norway to the remote valleys of Turkey. Once any heavy fighting began, any serious hope of firm political control over nuclear use would evaporate. And what tasks could they actually serve? Experienced American commanders like General Maxwell Taylor and Admiral Noel Gayler have said they were unable to devise plans for using them.

This amounts to saying that battlefield nuclear weapons are militarily useless — too destructive for the battlefield and too small for ultimate deterrence. Nevertheless, for political reasons their reduction would be fiercely resisted and would have to be done in very careful stages. Much Western opinion has been persuaded that they are somehow defending 'our boys'. What we should probably first work for is a number of unilateral cuts on both sides, followed by a superpower agreement on the disengagement of the remainder, including the old 70-mile-range Lance missiles, from specified frontier — an accord that would certainly first require substantial 'asymmetrical' reductions of Soviet armour.

The USSR had already promised some early reductions of its SCUD and other short-range missiles when, in May 1989, Mr Gorbachev promised unilaterally to withdraw 500 short-range missile warheads from Europe. NATO may well follow with big cuts in her own arsenal in 1989 to follow earlier ones — for which NATO deserves credit. Even so, while the USSR seems prepared to negotiate the total elimination of at least land-based nuclear missiles from Europe, some NATO governments want to update about half of its tactical nuclear weapons — missiles, bombs and shells — of which only 10 per cent could still burn Europe to a frazzle, and, in a crisis, at virtually no notice.

Moreover some of the new designs and deployments being considered could produce other complications. The new nuclear artillery shells, though fewer in number, will be more versatile and will no longer require the prior dispatch of a 'spotting round' which enabled the gun itself to be spotted. This means that the new equipment will be much more threatening. Furthermore, the new mobile American mission teams, with their kits of nuclear warheads, will now be able instantly to take over, for example, the 80 Dutch 203 mm (8 inch) guns and so make them nuclear capable without any serious chance of Soviet verification. Similarly, all the big NATO artillery, spread right round the Alliance, could become potentially nuclear, and hence far more suspect to the Warsaw pact, even though the actual number of nuclear shells is cut. Such clever arrangements need the closest watching: the public — and the protestors — too easily assume that fewer warheads necessarily mean greater safety.

A somewhat equivalent difficulty attends current NATO ideas for basing extra Dual-Capable Aircraft (DCA) in the United States but regularly exercising them from European bases. This would amount to an unverifiable and 'deniable' reinforcement that would fall outside any would-be agreement on European aircraft force-levels. The Soviet Union also has objectionable dual-purpose short-range weapon systems, including the Frog-7/SS-21 and the SS-1c/SCUD B, but it has agreed in principle to a 'third zero' or 'triple zero' arrangement that would remove all these short-range nuclear systems from the European theatre on the same lines as the INF Treaty bans the intermediate-range missiles. That is what we ourselves should be going for. For a start, the Soviet Union would be removing far more land-based nuclear missiles that the West.

The third zero seems a long way off however and a half-way stage will probably be needed. One possibility would be the one recommended by the distinguished Palme Commission[7], namely a 150 kilometre zone free of nuclear (and chemical) weapons on either side of the Inner-German Border. Sir Leon Brittan[8] has since called for a tank-free Central Europe in exchange for NATO foregoing its land-based battlefield nuclear weapons. Perhaps other senior Conservative figures will follow before long.

Ultimately, some truths are simple and the humorist got it right when he said NATO had created a new nuclear grenade with only one problem: its crater was wider than anyone could throw it. In more sober military terms, a roughly equivalent nuclear exchange would destroy more of the highly concentrated Western forces and populations than the Eastern. As Lord Carver[9] has said, the notice that the West could redress an unfavourable conventional military situation by resorting to the use of nuclear weapons is nonsense. 'You would only add a nuclear defeat to the prospect of a conventional one.'

The Third Proposal: Deferring Modernisation

Although the INF Treaty of 1987 provides for the destruction of the land-based missile systems of between 500 and 5,500 km range, it — like the measures discussed above — leaves untouched the considerable air- and sea-based nuclear missiles of equivalent range that can also hit most of Eastern Europe and some Soviet territory. These include the missiles on the American Poseidon submarines committed to SACEUR, many other sea-launched missiles and those carried by the United States F-16 and RAF Tornado aircraft stationed in Britain and the continent.

Though legally consistent with the INF Treaty, such 'modernisations' would substantially reduce its point and seem a desperately negative and unintelligent response to Soviet initiatives. At present there is a somewhat imprecise NATO agreement in principle to modernise but the policy has so deeply worried West German, Belgian and other opinion as to prove the most divisive issue to hit NATO since Cruise and Pershing. Some of the weapons in question are genuinely old and, if retained, minor technical modernisations are virtually inescapable but many have said large scale modernisation would at least be postponed until we see whether the Soviet leader means what he says.

The British, especially, believe early modernisation to be essential and have refused to contemplate negotiations with Moscow towards a 'third zero'. In some of the toughest Summit negotiations NATO has ever seen, the West Germans and their many NATO sympathisers achieved something of what they sought in May 1989. It was agreed in principle, and against strenuous British opposition, to negotiate over short range nuclear forces (SNF). This negotiation however was to begin only after the agreements eventually reached at the Vienna CFE negotiations on conventional arms were being implemented and, even then, would only be for a 'partial' reduction in SNF.

It can be seen therefore that, although there are rival interpretations, this NATO agreement does seem to rule out a 'third zero' and also to allow the funding and quiet development of the modernisations to proceed unchecked. It may therefore later be seen as only a cosmetic operation to protect the West German Christian Democrats against electoral discontent while the military processes continue largely undisturbed.

One of the worrying twists in this context is the threatened use of NATO's conventionally-armed M-270 multiple-launch-rocket-system (MLRS) as the launcher for a Lance nuclear replacement as well. Tentative plans call for the design of a nuclear missile of 450 km range (just short of the INF lower limit) which would take account of West German concerns about very short-range systems and also be suitable for the nuclear interdiction of Soviet reinforcements under the United States Army's (controversial) Airland Battle doctrine. The Soviet Union's difficulties would be multiplied by not knowing which of the 1,000 or so M-270 launchers had nuclear, as opposed to conventional, warheads. But the more critical point is that any arms control efforts to limit or ban land-based nuclear missiles tied to the MLRS would be very much more difficult to negotiate and verify than if they were fired from their own dedicated nuclear launchers. The latter could be scrapped in an INF type agreement reducing essential conventional capabilities. Once the two systems are tied together, a third zero might be indefinitely postponed.

These are complex technical subjects but plainly ones of immense significance for Central European stability. It would be genuinely tragic, indeed scandalous, if decisions on weapon designs taken now should result in NATO being virtually unable to agree to a third zero, no matter how co-operative the Soviet Union proved to be. There is evidence[10] that this is the way some officials are already thinking.

The subject of modernisation raises, in acute form, the inadequacy of public and parliamentary knowledge and supervision of defence questions, not least in Britain. In a timely survey of this issue, Oliver Ramsbotham[11] has shown how the defence community has monopolised the decision-making process and how its excessive secrecy has fed the idea that it is monolithic and sinister. This he calls 'an antibody produced by the defence community itself' which has spilled over into general hostility towards NATO as a whole.

A Weakening of NATO?

Many NATO leaders would regard any one of these three bold initiatives as imperilling not only NATO's defences against *blitzkrieg*, but European-based nuclear deterrence and hence Europes's coupling to the American nuclear umbrella.

As to the first fear, I will not repeat myself about suicide being a questionable form of defence. On the second, the European-based sea- and air-launched nuclear weapon systems available to SACEUR would be technically (and numerically) fully capable of extinguishing any of the Central European targets currently assigned to the land-based weaponries.

They would also be entirely adequate if, with Lord Carver and others, we believe that the only valid function of theatre (Europe-based) nuclear forces is to signal to Moscow that is could not use nuclear weapons in Europe with impunity. Indeed SACEUR's strike and bomber aircraft could then be converted to entirely conventional (and very useful) roles.

A Danger of Decoupling?

This is also part of the answer of the third fear, that of a decoupling from the American strategic umbrella, with Europe being left alone with the Soviet bear. If handled clumsily, American voters could indeed refuse to allow their soldier sons to be deprived of what they might see as their immediate nuclear protection, especially if they concluded that Europe was failing in general to show a robust spirit.

As against these fears, many leading analysts believe the West European preoccupation with decoupling is absurd, especially the concealed notion that Washington could or should be sucked into any new European war against its own self-preserving instincts. They believe, moreover, that American opinion will gradually be persuaded that nuclear firestorms are no protection for anyone and that an ultimate nuclear capacity could quite sufficiently deter Soviet nuclear threats or use. I agree. Eighty per cent of Americans do not even know that NATO is prepared to use nuclear weapons first. In the final analysis, NATO cannot possibly retain dangerous weapons and strategies just because American opinion might misinterpret a change.

Except in response to direct nuclear attack on his own country, it is in fact difficult to envisage any circumstances in which a President would press a button that would also inevitably bring catastrophe to his own country. If anything might make him do so, it would be the emotional and political pressure created by material threats to the American troops stationed in Europe for deterrent purposes. I, therefore, frankly favour their staying for some while yet. The United States contingent need not however be nearly as numerous as it is now (assuming Mr. Gorbachev's reductions actually happen). So long as even 100,000 American servicemen remained in Europe — less than a third of the present number — the Russians would scarcely risk endangering them. I am sure that American 'boys' are much more reliable instruments of transatlantic coupling than any number of Europe-based American warheads.

A Role for Historical Modesty

My conclusion is that, provided European pressures for my three proposals is gradual and not seen as 'anti-American' in motivation. Washington is unlikely to weaken its identification with NATO or deprive Western Europe of its strategic protection. American concern for Europe is, however, rooted not only in political sympathy but essentially in the self-interest of the Great Republic.

Although I have spoken of the key role of American troops, I do not mean to imply that the US would be sensible itself to threaten nuclear weapons to defend them against purely conventional attack: rather, NATO's conventional forces should be made sufficient. What provides the nearest to an ultimate safeguard alike for Western Europe and those American troops is that the Russians could never be sure how any military conflict involving the superpowers would end — even if each only had near-minimum nuclear forces. That modesty before the misty Bar of History is amply justified — on both sides.

Hopes for the Short Term

Despite President Gorbachev's long string of concessions and proposals, we have seen that NATO has plenty of scope to respond with its own radical agenda, one that would increase stability, reduce expenditures and encourage change in Eastern Europe as well as the Soviet Union. My proposals will make some feel nervous but so, much more, should the present state of affairs. And far more extreme proposals will otherwise challenge NATO's continuity including those recently made by Admiral Elmar Schmahling[12], a leading West German planner, for the direct dissolution of both alliances, something I certainly could not myself support. We should be conciliatory enough to help President Gorbachev but tough enough to test his flexibility and that of those around him. The alternative, after all, is to drag our feet over conventional reductions while pursuing nuclear 'modernisation' and thus give another boost to the arms race just when we have a perhaps brief chance to take advantage of the most far-sighted statesman of the century.

One can fairly add that most of Mikhail Gorbachev's ideas have a more Western than Eastern provenance. Ideas about co-operative security and defensive sufficiency have been explored in the West for many years and Russian strategists have explicitly credited Robert McNamara, for example, with teaching them about the special logic of the nuclear age. Now it is for Western leaders to learn from their own owls!

A Long Haul

We must, however, come back to earth. To remove the land-based nuclear arms, like the artillery and Lance, in Europe, let alone the air-launched systems, would alone count as a considerable political achievement. But, unless the START and similar overall negotiations make quite remarkable headway, it seems highly unlikely that the next decade will witness the departure from the Eastern Atlantic of the immense American naval nuclear capabilities, the British and French nuclear missile submarines or the American nuclear airbases in Britain. Nor in that case could we expect equivalent movement from Moscow which, unlike the United States, after all, is not 3,000 miles away and would be negotiating about its own geographical equivalent to Washington's Mexico, Caribbean and Central America. The eventual prizes for nuclear disengagement will be immense but it will be a long haul.

If all the radical steps rehearsed in this and the previous chapter were taken, the military arrangements would be far safer, but many questions about Europe's relations with both superpowers and its own general direction would remain.

14

Thinking Ahead: Europe's Choice of Future

> Therefore I say it is a narrow policy to suppose that this
> country or that is to be marked out as the eternal ally or the
> perpetual enemy of England. We have no eternal allies and
> we have no perpetual enemies. Our interests are eternal and
> perpetual and those interests it is our duty to follow.
>
> Lord Palmerston, March 1848

Each Superpower will plainly retain substantial nuclear forces at
least until the other one becomes willing, if ever, to disband its
nuclear forces. Right or wrong, this is a fact that the rest of the
world will have to live with. In the short term, say 5–10 years, I
have suggested that the best hopes for European, and all round,
security lie in East and West creating essentially non-provocative
conventional defence arrangements in Central Europe with a
greatly diminished reliance on nuclear weaponries. Provided both
powers are prepared to collaborate, this direction of policy need
not long remain controversial.

In the longer run, however, much greater and more divisive
questions arise and we must begin to address them. I believe the
next stage of the long European story must be written by the
Europeans themselves and without too much paralysing anxiety
about retaining (ostensibly) tight and formal American guaran-
tees. The transatlantic relationship may remain potentially crucial
and certainly needs to remain friendly, but Europe must take
much more responsibility for itself. For one thing, it may not have
much choice. Beneath their usually bland surface, Western European leaders increasingly fear that the days of the American
Empire are limited. The United States has become the world's

largest debtor and, under Reagan at least, was a badly governed, blundering giant. Moreover when the United States is not myopically parochial, it is increasingly turning its attention towards the Pacific, where Japan is seen as a partner no less consequential than Europe, and to the Gulf, Latin America and South Asia.

Meanwhile, amidst a severe balance of payments deficit, Americans have been witnessing serious European Community competition for world markets. Protectionism is inevitably gathering strength, 1992 is coming closer and Americans see no persisting reason why millions of rich Europeans should pay much less per head than Americans for the defence of Europe. About half the United States defence budget, some $150 billion, is still being spent on the defence of Europe compared with about $120 billion by its actual residents. This position is absurd.

At the same time, the rise of Mikhail Gorbachev, and what seems to be a collective Kremlin determination to modernise the Soviet Union's economy and society, has prompted a sea-change in European perceptions of the Russian bear. The bear himself now recognises he is not 10 feet tall. He is admitting faults, making big unilateral concessions and seems almost desperate for the technologies — and the breathing space — that détente and co-operation could bring. Europeans know he will never be a teddy bear: he is certainly someone with whom, as Mrs Thatcher said, one can do business.

The internal cohesion of the Warsaw Pact was weakening long before Gorbachev's arrival. In many respects Romania had already broken away and its conflicts with Hungary (and President Ceausescu's with Moscow) had become intense. Meanwhile, an increasingly pluralistic Hungary and Poland openly criticised persisting Czech oppression. East Germany long remained resistant to *glasnost* (and confiscated many Soviet journals) until the sudden, mind-blowing opening of the borders and the Berlin Wall dramatised the concealed ferment—and the irresistible demand for freedom—within a profoundly restless alliance.

Few Western leaders are likely to allow the new Soviet stance or East European confusion to be literally disarming. Mr Gorbachev may be calling for 'one common European home', but half his nation is in Asia and the rest is immured from Western Europe by Soviet walls and minefields, not Western ones. Nevertheless change is very much in the air and few really believe that Western

Europe's relationship with either of the Superpowers can long remain unchanged.

The main longer term options seem to be three.

▷ *A Modified NATO* with a far stronger West European voice and a policy of defensive deterrence with a gradually denuclearised Central Front but sea- and air-launched intermediate-range nuclear forces under SACEUR and a United States strategic nuclear umbrella.

▷ *A United Europe* based on a new European Security Community (ESC) which is de-coupled from the United States and dependent on its own conventional strength, backed by an Anglo-French nuclear force.

▷ *A Neutral Denuclearised Europe* in which both sides have become 'de-aligned' through an agreed dissolution of both hostile alliances and a Soviet (and American) military withdrawal to their own frontiers.

The first of these options is the least dramatic and perhaps the most likely for the next decade or two because, although some weakening of the Atlantic bond is almost inevitable and stronger West European co-ordination of policy-making, arms purchase and so on is long overdue, NATO as such remains popular.

Option II would enable Europeans to conduct their foreign and defence policy independently, not just before talking to Uncle Sam. One version sees a new Superpower, a Pan-European Third Force. This, however, would require Europe not only to develop comprehensive nuclear forces but a single central political and military command system — most unlikely to be achievable. A looser, conventionally powerful ESC could however gradually emerge from the present European Community framework, despite the problem of Irish neutrality.

A version of Option III, much favoured on the Left and by 'Greens', sees a loose association of newly non-aligned West European states and the present neutrals opening out to the East Europeans. Its 'members' could have different economic systems and foreign policies provided these did not conflict with military disengagement from the Superpowers.

A Curious Proposal

Most present West European leaders would far prefer Option I as the nearest to the *status quo* that they (somewhat naively) associate with past success and presumed present stability. The French are more open to European initiatives that dilute the American presence and Option II, the European Security Community, has distinct attractions for them.

The profound objectives that would be widely felt, rightly or wrongly, to Option III, a loose association of neutrals, have to do with the pride of ancient, once powerful, peoples but more with a sense that international politics forbids a vacuum and that sooner or later this new Europe would either be overthrown from without or disintegrate from within. Who, in truth, can know that another Hitler or Stalin will never turn up? Nevertheless many equally strongly object both to staying tied to Washington, as in Option I, or becoming dependent on a dubious Euro-bomb, as in Option II. These divisions of opinion could well become furious and unsettling.

Fortunately, however, it may be that, for the next decade or so, a temporary coalition can be formed between all the three factions. I say this because, curiously enough, the strengthening of the European pillar within NATO, as in Option I, would probably be a necessary stage in moving not only towards a reasonably self-sufficient European Security Community, (Option II) but also *towards* a denuclearised and non-aligned Europe (Option III).

Ironically enough, all routes go via NATO, 'Rightists' wanting a militarily self-sufficient ESC (or even a swashbuckling global Third Force) and 'Leftists' wanting a non-aligned, denuclearised Europe might both be persuaded to agree on three prior steps: first, the strengthening of the European voice in NATO; secondly, the removal of (mainly American and Soviet) tactical nuclear weapons from the Central Front: and thirdly, wider movement towards more general Superpower disengagement in Europe.

A neutral Option III Europe would only become possible after Superpower disengagement but this could well hinge on first creating an interim European security system, since an abrupt dissolution of the Atlantic partnership would not only infuriate the Americans but encourage the more ambitious Muscovites to sit still until Western Europe fell into its lap. In short, Europe needs American co-operation to help ease out the Russians — and, later in the same long process, the Americans could be eased out too.

Nor is this calculation cynical. It is not in the interests of the United States, economically or strategically, to remain intricately or expensively involved in the defence of Western Europe if — I say *if* — its freedom and security can be sustained by other means. Americans have rarely objected to 'burden-sharing'!

European Security and the Bomb

The first requirement of European security is not military, let alone nuclear. It is for Western Europe to become politically cohesive as well as economically strong, not least by renouncing its present petty nationalisms in both NATO and the European Community. Without this cohesion, Europe will remain fearful of the Soviet Union, even if all Soviet forces returned home, and also perhaps vulnerable to an eventual renaissance of a united Germany or the emergence of a dominating Franco-German alliance. Europe must also be strong if its immense global interests are to be pursued effectively. Neither United States nor Japanese policy-makers (or corporations) are conspicuously given to sentiment. Dove-like supporters of Option III would be naive to suggest that Europe could rise wholly above the growing global struggle for economic advantage and limited resources (even though its influence could still be highly constructive). Nor will European voters allow governments any choice in such matters.

Many supporters of Option III would agree that Europe should remain robustly strong in conventional arms: the critical question is how far it should depend on nuclear arms. We have noted that the United States strategic nuclear umbrella combines some danger with less than total dependability but, so long as NATO survives, that umbrella will remain in place. The question then arises as to whether a European nuclear deterrent of some kind is also needed within NATO or would be needed in a post-NATO Europe.

Both questions will be critical to Europe's future. Opponents of any European nuclear force say that the Russian bogey is overdone and that Moscow could not afford the domestic costs, the East European turmoil or the worldwide disgrace that would follow from any type of aggression, nor would it profit from the lands it had incinerated. Both extremes of this interminable argument seem to ignore irreducible facts. Just as hawks hankering for a European Superpower underestimate the obstacles to political and hence military union, so the eco-feminists seeking a nuclear-free and neutral Europe, fail to recognise that the French will keep their national nuclear armoury come hell or high water. Looking beyond NATO, therefore, neither a nuclear-armed European Superpower nor a completely de-nuclearised Western Europe are on the cards. What other options might there be?

Some have argued that a combination of the British and French nuclear forces (each comprising land-, air- and sea-launched weapons) would provide an adequate strategic deterrent for a post-NATO Europe. On the face of it, this would constitute Europe's own Minimum Nuclear Deterrent. It would however probably be too small and too vulnerable to fit the criteria I have described. Most of such a force would be easily pre-empted in a first strike, leaving only two or three missile-carrying submarines at sea. These could threaten to take out many major Soviet cities but could almost certainly be used only once and therefore only for retribution. That seems pointless (and therefore the more immoral). Furthermore the would-be aggressor could have considerable doubt as to whether the British or French would really employ their virtually minimum, once-and-for-all, nuclear force in defence of other Europeans, even West Germany. Neither France nor Britain has ever clearly promised to do so although the French have been getting closer to it. Nor, in such infernal matters, could any nation's word be wholly trusted anyway. Would Britain lay down Glasgow to save Hamburg? Would France lay down Lyons for Istanbul? Would either of them use up their last card except in 'last resort' defence of themselves? Can credible deterrence be built upon an incredible act?

The German Factor

The West German aspect of the debate is a further complication. The Soviet Union, always apprehensive about West German *revanchism*, would be frankly alarmed by Bonn's acquiring nuclear arms. Such a development would abruptly reverse processes of détente and any hope of Superpower disengagement from the European theatre. The French and British have sometimes privately justified their acquisition of nuclear forces by saying the Germans might otherwise be so tempted. In fact, however, no major party in Bonn would favour it: their thinking goes quite the other way. Most political groups, notably the SPD and the Greens, favour the maximum practicable denuclearisation in Central Europe provided it is not thereby made vulnerable to Soviet *blitzkrieg*. West German opinion tends to be schizophrenic. Ideally it wants movement towards the 'reunification' of the two Germanies but without sacrifice of its Western ties and American protection. It also wants the forward defence of every inch of its territory plus a virtually guaranteed United States nuclear response to any serious Soviet attack but without any nuclear damage to either Germany. An increasing majority within the German Armed Forces themselves apparently incline to this view. Attitudes towards American nuclear protection are ambiguous enough: an attempted Anglo-French replacement would seem even more hazardous.

An important connected question is whether the French, half in and half out of NATO, can somehow be brought back into NATO's command structure. They have provided the Rapid Action Force of troops ready for immediate combat on the Central Front and have said a French response to an attack on West Germany would be 'immediate and automatic'. Nevertheless, the full integration of French conventional forces within NATO would probably require 'Europeanisation' of the whole command structure and a distinct loosening of the American tie. Only then would French airfields and ports again become available to the combined defending forces.

Helmut Schmidt, the former West German Chancellor, has even proposed that NATO armies should be replaced by an enlarged Franco-German army under a French General and a French nuclear umbrella. This formula of an alliance-within-an-alliance would still allow substantial military contributions by the other NATO members (including the United States) but it would remove the American Supreme Commander and American nuclear weapons. Politically, however, this would cause an upheaval amongst American opinion and excite British and other fears of Franco-German hegemony. A more fruitful course is probably to pursue reintegration through practical measures like joint training and force-planning, joint discussion of strategy and the shared design, production and ordering of equipment.

'Pick and Mix': the Best Way Forward

In the medium term I have suggested that a reformed NATO is the best course, whatever long-term direction one favours. But what would that best be? Amidst the maze of hard facts, awesome possibilities and subjective speculations confronting us, my own inclination is for Western Europe gradually to work towards a non-nuclear European Security Community. First, then, it would aim so far as possible to dispense with its own nuclear weaponry, not out of high moral principle but pragmatically because a Soviet nuclear attack on Western Europe makes little more sense than a Western nuclear 'defence' of it. As to any remaining Soviet conventional threat, I have argued that a strictly conventional response can be fully adequate. Europe has the means to do it and no excuse for not doing it.

This long-term aim is not at all inconsistent with retaining the United States strategic nuclear umbrella within a reformed NATO for the immediately foreseeable future. A non-nuclear ESC would only make sense if the Soviet Union had clearly demonstrated its willingness largely to pull back from Eastern Europe (and the United States similarly from Western Europe) and if all concerned were agreeable to verifiably defensive arrangements on both sides of the old divide.

In summary, I prefer a formula which is not wholly Option I, II or III but has something of all three. We start with Option I, a reformed NATO, and slowly but deliberately move towards a European Security Community, Option II, except that, like Option III, this dispenses with its own nuclear arms. If someone says this is neither fish, flesh nor good red herring, I say political process is like that. Call it 'pick and mix' like the village sweetshop, if they must. Why not?

The Bottom line?

I must, however, confront one more weighty objection. Some hawks and some doves, if for opposite reasons, will insist on my exposing the nuclear 'bottom line' of these calculations. I would reply that even if the Atlantic Alliance had been wholly dissolved, which we must eventually expect and prepare for, American strategic nuclear forces would still constitute a considerable disincentive to any Soviet aggression in Europe.

Even if it had no more troops in Europe, Washington would still be seen by Moscow as concerned about the fate of the other Western capitalist democracies and, in particular, to stop the Soviet Union stealing their industrial muscle. The American deterrent threat would not necessarily need to be formal or overt to engender Russian hesitation. I believe this would apply even if the United States (and therefore the Soviet Union too) had got close to Minimal Defensive Deterrence. In essence, therefore I believe that eventually, perhaps within a decade or so, the residual Soviet threat after the Gorbachev era may only need to be balanced from Europe's point of view by its own conventional forces and by a residual American Extended Deterrent.

Such arrangements would be far from totally secure, but nor are today's. Moreover, the primary source of Europe's security is no longer military, let alone nuclear. The political flexibility and economic strengths of Europe (and the material needs of the Soviet Union) are for more germane: it is on these that new structures of mutually beneficial co-operation can be built. Why, to put it crudely, should anyone go to war when they can do much better out of stability, retrenchment and peace? It is not 'deterrence' that we depend upon so much as 'dissuasion' and that can in part be positive while being equally real. If the Russians are rational, they can add up benefits: if they are not, nuclear deterrence is the more profoundly unreliable.

The French and British National Deterrents

I have deliberately left the particular conundrums of the French and British nuclear deterrents to last because it is vital to deal with them in a much wider context than that of Britain's over-heated, confused and absurdly self-important public debate. Neither flag-waving hawks nor anxious doves will like that judgement but, just for a start, NATO's Flexible Response and its battlefield nuclear weapons are far more likely to precipitate war, yet are grotesquely neglected. My own conclusion is essentially the same as Lord Carver's[1] when he said:

> I do not believe that whether or not Britain keeps an independent nuclear force makes much difference to anybody else. If the French want to waste their money on these things, let them.

Such a conclusion is deeply shocking to many, not least in its robust earthiness. Until the respectable dissenters like Carver broke ranks, the British bomb had become a sort of litmus test for general political 'soundness' and I am often surprised by otherwise highly-questioning friends who just assume there can be no sensible case against it or assume that one must be a 'unilateralist' to oppose it. Some cool rigour will not come amiss on either side of an over-polarised debate.

What the French decide is up to them but, if they can indeed be expected to keep their *force de frappe* till hell freezes over, an interesting point arises. If such a force has any deterrent value against a Soviet attack, it must (if only for reasons of geography) help defend France's British neighbour too. In that case, Britain could just take the free ride that Italy, say, does now on the United States. Almost comically however, many Britons feel deep down that the French are the ultimate enemy and would thrill with patriotic horror at the idea. Indeed such people fear virtual French hegemony if Paris were to become the sole mistress of the Bomb in Western Europe. I think this argument is ludicrous but at once we see how murky are the depths that can be stirred.

As to the British Bomb, there is a crudely elemental justification that still sways a majority of my compatriots. This is that however evil these things are, if the Russians have them and we cannot finally depend on the Americans, then we must ourselves be able to tear an arm off the Bear. This argument is superficially quite plausible and about three-quarters of our MPs, bureaucrats and opinion-formers would go along with it. ('Very unpleasant of course but one must face facts.') That was my own view until I studied the subject.

For what are the 'facts'? If even the closest ally of the strongest Superpower needs its own absolute weaponry, which countries, worldwide, do not? Iran? Iraq? Argentina? South Africa? Libya? And if they do not, precisely why not? Would the impartial non-Briton be bound to agree? Such questions *must* be answered if the official British position, albeit one shared by every British government since the war, is to have any intellectual coherence or credibility. Nor does this argument depend on whether British relinquishment of nuclear weapons would actually dissuade anyone else. Either we are prepared to follow reason or our whole position is exposed as self-serving humbug. Reasons cannot be right for us but wrong for anyone else.

There are other profound embarrassments to which we fail to face up. Does not the standard 'last resort' argument imply a British readiness to initiate a nuclear war that its closest ally, the United States refuses to fight? If not, why have a 'last resort' capability? And since the Russians cannot tell one missile from another, could not the British Bomb precipitate an attack on its closest ally? And therefore a world war? Have not British motivations fundamentally been national pride and 'staying at the top table' (which we have not)? And should not the argument that London adds to NATO deterrence as a second (or third) centre of nuclear decision-taking, worry Washington no less than Moscow? The White House cannot assume British prime ministers will always be sane and safe. At Suez, the immensely experienced Anthony Eden was sick, irrational, impetuous and warlike. The late Leonard Beaton, the defence analyst, told me years ago that the Pentagon had confirmed to him that they maintained contingency targeting plans (amongst hundreds) to take out all nuclear weapons capabilities and command centres wherever they were, including Britain and France. The American military are serious people.

If a solo British 'release' really became imminent, both Superpowers would need and want — possibly by agreement — to take out our nuclear capacities without delay. Could Americans ever assault British bases? The British attacked and destroyed part of the French Navy in Oran and Mers el Kebir in July 1940. When you think about it, Britain's phasing out of its nuclear capabilities should be worth plaudits from Washington as well as concessions from Moscow!

One of the further arguments made for the British bomb is the general one about the unpredictability of international life: no one can know when it might be needed. Yet that too could justify a hundred nations going nuclear. Do we oppose proliferation or not? (Do as I say, not as I do?) Moreover, the alleged 'unpredictability' should make it easy to dream up many plausible scenarios for British 'release'. I have never heard one and Lord Carver, among others, thinks they do not exist. A serious British threat to the Soviet Union would be pre-empted; a one-off British attack as a retaliation would be suicidal and pointless. What then, one is asked, if Colonel Gaddafi had the bomb? This is now the question politicians get on the doorstep. It first of all assumes that both Superpowers were indifferent, that the world community was helpless and that we stood alone. All this is far-fetched. It is also far from today's realities. Britain has the bomb, Libya does not; nor do dozens of other countries which hanker for it. How do we keep it that way? Should not Britain be helping to lead bold moves towards a powerful non-proliferation régime rather than pleading a pathetically weak special case and adding hypocrisy to ineffectualness?

A Closet Unilateralist?

Plainly one does not need to be a 'unilateralist' or a knee-jerk 'anti-nuke', to conclude that it is militarily unnecessary, strategically destabilising and materially wasteful (and therefore also wrong) for Britain to have its own nuclear weapons. Nor is it at all contradictory to believe that the Superpowers are right to keep some of theirs, for the time being at least. Britain, after all, already has more nuclear 'protection' than almost anyone. And if, again I say if, nuclear weapons have helped 'keep the peace' in Europe, the American ones have done it. The British (and French) ones have been too few in comparison to matter.

As to 'unilateralism', if it is presented as a universal philosophy of making unconditional concessions in the hope of producing a change of heart, I have to reject it. Sometimes, of course, such unilateral moves do make sense: NATO has itself made several in its time. But, for the most part, 'something for nothing' is only right where it has a fair chance of producing something! As a philosophy, a combination of strategic multilateralism facilitated by tactical unilateralism has great advantages and is now widely supported, even in CND. One can however be against, even passionately against, the British bomb without being any kind of 'ist'.

The British Bomb and the American Bases

In keeping with my generally holistic approach of trying to see each issue in context, I do not myself see the British bomb as a suitable subject for dramatic gestures. I am sure Britain should gradually phase out its nuclear forces but not in what might appear an impetuous, self-righteous or accusatory spirit. That would only shake American opinion and NATO's morale and its negotiating position in relation to Moscow, in an especially delicate period. Partly for the same reason, the American nuclear facilities in the United Kingdom present a peculiarly awkward problem. Strictly speaking, they should soon become dispensable for technical reasons and as their (I hope changing) role is taken up by sea-based nuclear forces. Before long, American nuclear missile submarines will no longer really need Holy Loch anyway. However, the air bases are far more problematic. As I see it, the de-nuclearisation of the Central Front, including, ideally, the pulling back of its locally based nuclear-armed aircraft, is far the most urgent issue and a likely political and military price for this will be the retention for some years (and even the reinforcement) of United States nuclear strike squadrons on British airfields. Any peremptory dismissal of American bases from Britain would shock American and West European opinion far more, and rightly, than the gradual relinquishment of British nuclear weapons. (Nevertheless, the absence of a British safety catch on United States weaponries based in the United Kingdom or of clear treaty arrangements about their use is quite unacceptable and should be swiftly remedied.)

A Real Quandary

To relinquish British nuclear weapons while keeping American bases is to do things quite the most unpopular way round. Rightly or wrongly, a British majority consistently favours the British Bomb. American bombs are far less popular. Moreover, the Labour Party has learned the hard way that an unconditional 'give-away' is politically just not on. But nor can large Russian concessions be expected in exchange for so small a fraction of the Western nuclear armoury. Nor would such concessions have much meaning once Soviet and American arms were rebalanced within a further START-type agreement.

On the other hand, it is generally acknowledged that the START process could certainly not cut into the second half of the Superpowers' strategic armoury unless British (and French) missiles were included. If, meanwhile the Cold War continues to de-freeze, the Russians may become prepared to pretend to concede more than they otherwise would, provided it was in that broader context. Unfortunately however a British government undertaking a purely bilateral negotiation would always be challenged as to whether it would keep Trident if Moscow did *not* offer enough in return? Politically at least, therefore, there is a strong case for wrapping the British bomb in multilateral clothing. Moreover there would be objective value in the United Kingdom proposing exploratory 'Nuclear Stability Talks' in which the five main nuclear powers — the Superpowers plus China, France and Britain — could begin to discuss the problems of 'four against one' (the USSR) in the situation that will follow a success with START.

Politically, this is a fiendish quandary, much more to do with electoral than military realities and I wonder whether the best course might be for Britain to hand over full and sole control of its Trident force (and its other nuclear warheads) to SACEUR for the defence of Britain *within* NATO. Legally, and technically, this transfer may not be easy but its advantages would be considerable.

The essential point, after all, is that security is now regional and global, not national. At the regional level, the British weapon transfer to SACEUR would look more like a positive vote of confidence in NATO (and the United States) than a rejection — and more 'loyal' than continuing to insist on an independent capability. Nor would any unmerited or 'unilateral' concession have to be made to Moscow. At the global level, the British relinquishment could be presented as a genuine, indeed unprecedented, contribution to the international movement against proliferation and, indeed, for a comprehensive test ban. In short, this formula rides the two horses of NATO loyalty and positive globalism and seems to have much more chance of being sold to the British electorate than any other scheme I have heard suggested. The British Bomb issue is plainly a pig of a problem politically, wherever one stands. The 'sensible' Tory position is no less riddled with contradictions and humbug than Labour's, not least in relation to proliferation. And since the Tories are in danger of multiplying Britain's nuclear forces by four or more with Trident, the least they can do in the Gorbachev thaw is to restrict the number of Trident warheads to what we have had in the Polaris submarines. The time for non-negotiated unilateral *rearmament* is scarcely the present!

Next Steps in NATO

From the simplistic furies of the narrow British debate — and the near absence of a French one — we must return to the far more significant issue of where NATO should now be heading. I have agreed that there is no need to make a flat choice between the three main longer-term options and that their supporters might all see a tactical common interest in strengthening the European role in NATO and facilitating gradual Superpower disengagement.

This process would of course be entirely compatible with the overall philosophy I have commended of Co-operative Security with an ultimate minimum nuclear deterrent. If this is the aim, however, NATO cannot possibly insist on maintaining a full spectrum of (modernised!) nuclear weaponry. Nor indeed could it justify keeping a lethal range of unverifiable dual-purpose weapon systems or the 155 mm artillery with its special module for the enhanced radiation warheads ('neutron bombs') that are stored ready for air-lift to Europe at Seneca, New York. Instead, NATO must challenge President Gorbachev to move even faster than he might otherwise towards the sorts of non-provocative defence arrangements described in earlier chapters.

The owl knows this will be a long and fraught process and he cannot specify in advance what precise moves should be made or when. He has no neat kit ready to be imposed on a passive reality. Nor can the owl claim any more immunity to paradox and contradiction than can any of the existing orthodoxies — NATO's, the Kremlin's or that of the Peace Movement. He does however believe he keeps hold of the lesser idiocies and offers a real chance of shepherding the age of active nuclear confrontation towards a close.

The proposals made for the next stage concerning both conventional and nuclear weaponries would begin to make real differences at once — in testing President Gorbachev's powers to deliver on his promises, in stabilising a still treacherous Central Front and in stopping a further arms race via 'modernisation'. Their thrust is very similar to that of a recent report by a distinguished Federal Trust study group[2] which also incidentally favoured heading towards a European Security Community. If, as seems all too likely, the American, British and other hawks insist (in effect) on going slow on conventional force reductions and (in effect) refusing to delay modernisation let alone negotiate a 'third zero', then President Gorbachev would be fully entitled to ask NATO on what terms they *would* agree to these things? Indeed on what terms would NATO halve its own forces in Europe? Mr Gorbachev could fairly ask what proof, what specific verifiable proof, does NATO need before accepting his seriousness? On what grounds does the British Government, for example, apparently seem to insist on the retention of SNF weaponry — and its own full range of national nuclear delivery systems — even if conventional parity were achieved in Europe? European public opinion, not least in West

Germany, is already asking this sort of question. NATO has so far been failing to show anything like the creative thinking the circumstances demand. And this failure is, ironically enough, already weakening its political coherence.

Let us however look on the bright side. To summarise, the next decade or so could see progress in European military matters made in stages until:

▷ Following the (probable) success of the CFE talks in Vienna and consequent initiatives (not yet in view), all East–West conventional security needs are met by a reasonable parity of (considerably reduced and largely defensive) conventional forces deployed in verifiably non-provocative postures.

▷ The START process will have more than halved the immense strategic nuclear forces of both sides.

▷ All land-based short-range nuclear weapons will have been negotiated out of Europe (against much British and some American opposition) and NATO's remaining intermediate nuclear forces (missiles and aircraft of an agreed and verifiable number) are largely deployed at sea and under the sole command of SACEUR. Only a few agreed bases for nuclear-capable aircraft are now retained in Western Europe. Verifiably equivalent Soviet forces are deployed only at sea or behind the Soviet border.

▷ The increasingly symbolic role of these nuclear forces will be in process of gradual transfer to the Superpowers' still diminishing strategic nuclear forces. (The British national deterrent would be on course for dissolution: the French could well persist.)

▷ The process of general nuclear disengagement is facilitated by the progressive strengthening of the European pole of NATO although the final departure of US troops and the formal emergence of a (non-nuclear) European Security Community would depend on wider and deeper improvements in East–West relations.

Cursed by Both

Such formulae will I suppose antagonise dogmatic hawks and doves about equally. Hawks would see them as decoupling West

European security from the United States and making it a sitting duck for Soviet tank hordes. To them I would urge that such 'hordes' would no longer exist, that Western Europe would still have appropriately strong conventional defences, that nuclear defence is not 'real' defence and that the United States will not forever agree to be the prime (rather than residual) guarantor of some of its richest competitors, especially after 1992.

Meanwhile, extreme doves will see the recommended process as a compromise with nuclear evil, in so far as the American nuclear umbrella (in slighter forms) is still accepted, and hence also a compromise, worse still in some eyes, with American hegemony. To these charges I plead guilty but say that if the key criterion is the reduction of the danger of superpower conflict — as moral realism seems to require — then the suggested process is quite the most promising we could reasonably expect, starting from where we are.

15

Towards a Sustainable World Order

At the present rate of progression since 1600, it will not need
another century or half-century to tip thought upside down.
Law, in that case, would disappear as theory or *a priori*
principle and give place to force. Morality would become
police. Explosives would reach cosmic violence. Disintegration would overcome integration.

Henry Adams: a letter of 1905.

Morally it makes no difference whether a man is killed in
war or is condemned to starve to death by the indifference of
others.

Willy Brandt, United Nations General Assembly, 1973.

When we were climbing up to a Buddhist monastery in the
Szechwan hills in September 1988, my wife suddenly remarked
that there were no birds and that we had seen none anywhere in
China. This instantly focused our gathering apprehensions about
China's whole future — and this well before the 1989 massacre. In
huge areas that were not mountain, marsh or desert, every space
was a rice paddy, cornfield or vegetable patch. Every tree for miles
had been cut for fuel or charcoal: every stream was dry or
dammed: every cubic metre of water was used for irrigation.
People teemed everywhere. With immense efforts and terrible
sacrifices, the Chinese had restrained the growth of a 1950 population of 600 million, so that it had not yet quite doubled. The
people were still fed but for how much longer? The fields and
the people are beautiful. One can gaze on them for hours but
this serenity cannot last. We had seen the future and it may not
work.

It was certainly not working in Java where I lived in the mid-1960s. There the frightful pressure of numbers on material resources had further inflamed a desperate political condition that led to a civil war in which 300,000 people died. Earlier, President Sukarno's quest for *lebensraum* for Indonesia's still multiplying millions had led to his attempted absorption of Eastern Malaysia and to war. Similar environmental pressures have afflicted millions of people in India, Bangladesh, the Philippines, sub-Sahelian Africa and Latin America. At a conference in 1987 we were horrified to find that large parts of Curaçao had become a parched and often scorched dumping ground for old cars and the other detritus of consumerism. From Canton to the Caribbean, out of sight of the absurdly lavish international tourist hotels, are disturbing portents of graver problems ahead.

A New Agenda

From the all-too-familiar obsessions with the East–West conflict we have returned to the deeper crises, sketched in Chapter 2, between Rich North and Poor South and between Man and Nature. Much of history stands witness to the awful cost of obsessions whose time and relevance have passed; it puts a new perspective on great racial, national, religious and ideological conflicts that enrolled passionate loyalties and are now relegated to dusty volumes and the pompous tombs of those we called great. Vestiges smoulder or flare, from Ulster to Kashmir, but each is eventually overlaid by new perceptions of menace and yesterday's enemies often become tomorrow's friends.

For a long period after the Second World War, the United States was even more hostile to 'Red China' than to the Soviet Union. At least twice, over Korea and over the off-shore islands of Quemoy and Matsu, Washington considered using nuclear weapons against China. American imagery of 'screaming slit-eyed hordes' was met by equally noxious propaganda from Beijing about the 'the long-nosed imperialist hyenas'. And, according to Andrei Gromyko's memoirs, Mao Tse-tung once tried to involve him in a scheme for the nuclear bombing of American forces. Despite this reciprocated virulence, it took remarkably few years for Chinese–Western relations to be transformed. Agreement about a common foe encouraged active co-operation despite China's continued avowal of Communism and its large military 'capabilities'.

To nail the obvious point, somehow the West and East must similarly transcend their still substantial enmities in order to co-operate in a global struggle against a yet more fearful common foe — the threat of universal chaos and ruin. Is such a warning to indulge in doomsters' hyperbole? I fear not. We should weigh the case carefully and remember that pre-war warnings about the likely fate of the Jews under Hitler were not heard. Few believed Auschwitz was humanly possible. Likewise, warnings of scourge and famine have gone unheard from Ireland in the last century to Bengal, Ethiopia, Sudan and China in this. Yet famine is not just occasional mass tragedy: it is a terrible daily reality for millions. It is but one aspect of a converging global crisis of which we may as yet have seen only the beginnings.

A Converging Global Crisis

As we saw in Chapter 2, another billion will be added to mankind's present five billions in the 500-odd weeks between now and the arrival of the third millenium. That bald figure takes on more meaning when we realise that Bangladesh will have grown from 107 to 145 million (in a space the size of England), Indonesia from 170 to 220 million (with its oil used up) and Kenya from 22 to 36 million (with its wild life in mortal danger). Mexico will have added another 28 million to its present 85 million, adding to the pressures on the wire fences to the North. (The United States could have an Hispanic-Black-Asian majority within 50 years or so.)

The population explosion is putting an immense strain on finite mineral and energy sources, sweet ground water, the soils, the forests and the biosphere at large. By the turn of the century, we shall have lost at least 450,000 more square miles of tropical forest and degraded as much again. By then over two billion people will be dependent on fuel wood — already the focus of the world's most serious energy crisis. Sober experts also expect losses of up to half-a-million tropical species in this period with as many again lost in the wetlands and other species-rich zones. We have already extinguished thousands of insect species whose ecological roles we did not discover in time.

Awareness of the impact of industrial society's multifarious waste products has suddenly exploded. The carbon dioxide content of the atmosphere has risen by one-fifth in only 100 years. We are now realising that methane has been gathering even faster. The 'greenhouse' effects of these and other gases like the CFCs are already producing climatic effects and threatening profound disruptions of global food production, including a disastrous drying of the American grain belt. The drastic crop failures in 1988, not only there but in the Soviet Union and China, were timely warnings, whatever their cause. A melting of the Arctic ice caps would also be disastrous for low lying cities and regions.

Climatic change, soil exhaustion and soil erosion means declining food output per unit area and a lengthening list of countries unable to feed themselves. The American Mid-West is eroding as fast as in the Dust Bowl era. About four-fifths of Africa's top soil is said to be in danger. According to the Food and Agricultural Organisation (FAO), nearly 500 million (one in ten) regularly consume less than the 'minimum critical diet' to stay healthy even without much physical activity. The numbers of the hungry are still rising. Ethiopia alone has far worse trials ahead than those that so moved Bob Geldof's young armies.

A UNICEF study in 1988 showed that things have been getting worse in 32 countries — child malnutrition, levels of schooling and the absolute numbers of illiterates. There are now 25 per cent more severely malnourished children in Africa than 10 years ago. World-wide, millions of babies and young children are dying unnecessarily each year. Living standards in Africa and Latin America had fallen by from 10 – 15 per cent in the 1980s. In the developing world, only Asia had managed to maintain them. According to one United Nations official, for one-sixth of humanity, the march of progress has now become a retreat. And, as usual, it is the women who suffer most.

Economic Troubles Too

Meanwhile the huge accumulation of Third World debt, eccentric currency movements, the decline of foreign aid provision and the failure to harmonise economic policies in the broader human interest are often making things worse. They have not only crippled development programmes but led to the slashing of social services. Over 40 of the least developed countries have been forced to halve their *per capita* expenditure on health. Nor is the rich world exempt from repercussions: the same complex of factors is threatening to cause a recession, to multiply protectionist pressures and open up possibilities of a trade war or a financial crash far worse than the one in 1987. Occasional Western fantasies about casting the Poor South adrift are therefore absurd. So is the notion of Western self-sufficiency: even a 'Fortress America' would still depend for half its oil and raw materials on Third World sources. The interdependence of North and South is inescapable. Northern peace and prosperity could not long survive alongside growing poverty and instability in the Poor South.

This inevitable interdependence was one origin of the so-called Brundtland Report[1] to the United Nations of 1987 which pointed to 'a decade and a half of standstill or even deterioration in global co-operation' and articulated strategies for sustainable development. It also refused to see economic development as merely a question of making poor nations materially richer or environmental issues as separate and somehow subsidiary. It demanded an integrated and inter-disciplinary approach to global concerns and was thus the first internationally authoritative report to recognise that all three global crises, over security, development and the environment, are profoundly linked.

Collision Course?

Unfortunately, Mrs Brundtland's Report, although unanimous, made even less political impact than Brandt's[2]. The long retreat from social and humanitarian concerns has continued: the preoccupation with crude and short-term economic benefit has if anything intensified. (Yuppies are said to think of life as a meal.) Yet the conditions we have painted, this converging crisis of mass poverty, political subservience and environmental degradation, is simply not supportable, morally or practically. Within a decade or two, the aggrieved nations of the Poor South are almost bound to combine to extract from the North by pressure what they have failed to secure by persuasion. North and South could well be set on a collision course. It is impossible to predict what shape the conflict will take. Whether Southern producers of raw materials could effectively copy the OPEC oil boycott is open to doubt but they might attempt the renunciation of debts, punitive nationalisations and, eventually, covert sabotage. Certainly the occasions for civil and cross-border conflicts will multiply and perforce drag in the Northern powers.

The Rich North looks immensely strong on paper, especially in military and economic terms. Yet the United States failed to impose its will on North Vietnam as did the Soviet Union on 'feudal' Afghanistan. Moreover the great industrial powers are singularly vulnerable to selective sabotage and terrorism. Ideas of Great Power vulnerability no longer look wildly improbable and their own citizens are themselves uneasy and divided about the worldwide abuse of the Rich North's power.

The North – South division demands not only intelligent economic and political accommodation but material sacrifices, a switch of resources which the privileged have so far simply refused to make. East and West are still too obsessed with each other and the competing claims of military spending, domestic consumption and their own social welfare to take any except specific, short-term dangers really seriously. The 10- and 20-year horizon is daunting enough, yet to look further ahead — as we surely must — can be terrifying.

Towards 2100 AD

As Dr Norman Myers[3] has so vividly shown, rampant population growth (mostly of the poor), burgeoning demand (mostly amongst the rich) and environmental degradation from them both (the poor peasant can be even more destructive than the affluent consumer), are set to continue. Nigeria with a present population of about 108 million, could well reach 500 million by 2100, about three generations away. India, now 700 million-strong, could reach 1,700 million, even bigger than China's expected total, before its numbers stabilise. The political consequences of such immense changes are simply impossible to calculate: the world map is being redrawn while we sleep.

United Nations projections[4] indicate the present global population of five billion reaching eight billion by 2025 and stabilising between 2060 and 2100 (depending on when replacement-level fertility is reached) at between 7.7 and 14.2 billion. Such gargantuan yet different figures emphasise that the world has real problems but real choices. Policies bringing down fertility rates could make a difference of billions — all the more necessary considering that, of these increases, about 90 per cent would occur in the poorest countries and most of that growth in cities that are already bursting.

What then is the global response to all this? Leaving aside all the Third World families who need persuading, family planners say that there are at least 80 million women at risk of pregnancy who actually *want* contraception now but cannot get it. This alone would be enough to reduce the ultimate population by many hundreds of millions. Supply would cost about $12 per head — $1 billion, or one-third of a day's world-wide military spending. Meanwhile the Pope denounces 'unnatural' contraception and condoms are barred from American television. Are we quite mad?

A Sustainable World Population?

Some perfectly sane human ecologists like Paul Erlich put the maximum size of a permanently sustainable world population at anything like current Western standards of living at about one billion, a fifth of our current numbers. They may be rather too gloomy but we are already living off the planet's 'capital' by stripping out the effectively non-renewable fossil fuels, fossil waters, top soils, high grade minerals and the vast diversity of nature. The big question is what strategy our species should now adopt. We could reduce our birth rates below our death rates, and gradually bring about a slow decline to a population appropriate to the Earth's long-term carrying capacity. Alternatively we can allow death rates to rise, whether through starvation, disease or war. That is the ultimate choice. So far the world's governments have scarcely noticed that the choice exists.

Its gravity is best illustrated in Africa. The present population is projected to increase five-fold before stabilising at almost 2.5 billion in the 22nd century. But nothing like so many people could survive in a continent where over half the existing population is already malnourished and, indeed, getting poorer. Could a fat Europe continue to prosper unperturbed and invulnerable beside the ensuing chaos?

Looking further ahead, there are even larger questions. Is it better for, say, two or three billion people to enjoy life on this planet in comfortable perpetuity or for ten billion, locked like rats in a food store, to starve, fight and die? Is not the heart of the population and resources problem as much the greed of the rich as the numbers of the poor? Should each over-consuming yuppy be able to 'buy' his ticket to survival at the cost of a dozen 'unsuccessful' peasants? Is the same to go for the rich nations? Cannot there be enterprise without exploitation? Cannot enterprise even be harnessed to achieving sustainability?

Agenda for Global Action

What would we need to do to reach a balanced self-perpetuating ceiling? A sketch must serve:

▷ World population must be stabilised as soon as possible. This in brief requires not just the provision of contraception but the satisfaction of basic human needs — adequate nutrition, health services, education, employment, social security and the human rights that are necessary to co-operation as well as dignity. Large voluntary falls in birthrates are achieved only when more children are no longer seen as necessary to family security: lower infant death rates lead to *smaller* family size.

▷ The critical basic needs will only be met in the Poor South if the Rich North actively provides vastly more development aid and technical assistance (of the right kinds) and helps redress the desperate imbalance of world economic power. In particular the debt crisis must be resolved without further damage to the poor.

▷ The necessary economic reforms and policies for food, energy, forestry, minerals and so on must be calculated to protect and enhance the environment upon which all ultimately depend. Especially important will be the conservation of energy and raw materials, the reduction of pollution and the safe disposal of harmful wastes. All policies should become subject to environmental (and social) audit and monitoring.

▷ An international programme of world environmental controls and reform is urgently required, together with a sensible international regime for the global commons, like Antarctica and the deep seas, and for fisheries protection.

▷ Regional arrangements for trade, ecological management and Third World security need strong reinforcement. Superpower imposition of order is becoming ineffective as well as expensive and dangerous.

▷ The Communist world should be enabled (and enable itself) to join the world economic infrastructure such as the

World Bank, GATT and the International Monetary Fund, and to share in urgent processes for their reform.

▷ The United Nations also needs strengthening, especially in its capabilities for conciliation, peace-keeping and for imposing effective sanctions. Public support for the fuller use of the United Nations machinery is vital. The Security Council must begin at last to fulfil its original purposes so that 'common policies' for a common future can take on reality.

▷ The international legal apparatus needs amplification and strengthening — as does respect for law, however inconvenient, not least amongst the Great Powers. (The American record is especially bad.) Peace through domination is neither acceptable nor sustainable.

The tasks ahead of us are immense, even without those deriving from East–West conflict. In addition to the New International Economic Order sought by the Group of 77, we need a new international order for the environment, for the provision of objective news and information and for regional and global security. But better global management will best grow organically from the vigorous development of co-operation between the variously erratic sovereign states and the regional groupings and functional institutions we have now. Sovereignty cannot be 'renounced' but it can be shared. Central government powers should be devolved both upwards to the region and the world community and downwards to the locality.

Retaining the nation state as a key element in building a better world order is not the only respect in which I shall disappoint many doves. Take the not-untypical Dagomys Declaration[5] of September 1988 by the council of Pugwash, an influential body of scientists from East and West (of which I also happen to be a member). It wisely emphasised environmental dangers but it also called for 'a world free of nuclear weapons' (which is almost certainly not possible), the 'full demilitarisation of international relations' (which is totally impracticable) and 'the closing of the prosperity gap between North and South' (a *narrowing* would already be an achievement).

The building of a tolerably orderly, fair and sustainable world society is a quite sufficient challenge. To talk in terms of a sure peace and complete justice is to indulge in hyperbole, ignore human nature, invite frustration and antagonise essential allies. It would be more useful for the reformers to persuade the powerful of their own long-term interests than of the shining virtue of the poor — or of the reformers. I therefore far prefer the approach illustrated by the Safer World project, an out-crop of Freeze, with its emphasis on radical but practicable objectives.

The New Globalism

Despite my unease about idealistic hopes and universal formulae, I do think that the convergence of the three human crises requires little less than an intellectual revolution and one with a largely 'globalist' focus. Global interdependence was already becoming evident as the nuclear revolution was slowly digested. Then we realised that economic and financial stability within the North, let alone between North and South, required much more co-operation (and integration) than was once thought possible. Now the environmental issues are dramatising other limitations to the adequacy of national 'self-determination'. We are realising that if the Rich World wants a poor Brazil to save the rainforests then it must help to finance Brazil's forbearance. Likewise, if it wants a poor China to curtail a revolution in CFC-fed refrigeration to save the ozone layer, then it must find ways to compensate the Chinese. And meanwhile it must disproportionately slash its own very much higher CFC emissions.

Environmental health, like economic stability and co-operative security from military threats, will increasingly hinge on international agreement. It will also enforce much convergence of economic and hence political philosophy between East and West and beyond. So far the West has been crowing about the market-oriented devolution and individualism towards which China and the Soviet Union have been moving. Very soon it will have to recognise the relevance of their collectivist traditions. The Rich North has reached a zenith of unsustainable materials-crunching growth that simply cannot be sustained in terms of available resources, elementary fair play towards the poor or the biological sustainability of planetary life. The issues that started as military, economic and political have become philosophical and personal as well.

199

16

Politics and People

I have set before thee life and death, the blessing and the
curse; therefore choose life, that thou mayest live, thou and
thy seed.

Deuteronomy 30 v. 15

I recently talked deep into the night with a Member of Parliament
and former minister about some of 'our' immense problems like
hunger in Africa, the population explosion in Bangladesh and the
'greenhouse effect'. Such talk proved quite foreign to him; either
remote or 'speculative'. Folk in Bugsville weren't bothered about all
that, he said, with a nice grin. They didn't feel responsible for what
had gone wrong, or for putting it right. Around the same time I was
at a seminar of academic Sovietologists discussing practical responses to the Gorbachev phenomenon when a woman at the back
cried out 'Why don't we just love one another?' There was a long
embarrassed silence. Someone might have reminded her of the
Ugandan anti-Aids slogan: Love Carefully.

Defining a New Realism

Both these are familiar types of voices and both can induce despair
of constructive change. Throughout this book we have seen how
they juxtapose two false, because over-simplified, images of reality.
The super-idealism of the unqualified dove attributes a force to
virtuous example that sits ill with brutal facts, that would never
appeal to a steady democratic majority or convince any 'establishment'. The super-realism of the hawks attributes safety to a weird
mixture of narrow nationalism, military superiority and head-on
confrontation, without recognising that no one lives alone or that
fear feeds off fear.

200

As I have suggested, the owl sees a much more complex chemistry in both politics and persons, not only in the sources of international insecurity but in human nature. The political kaleidoscope is now being shaken very hard and the global agenda is shifting with it. We need to learn much more about the world and its interdependency but also about ourselves as nations, groups and individuals. Neither clever politics nor new technologies will suffice to save us. We must reappraise ourselves, our purposes, and perhaps our values.

A Kaleidoscope

Complications, ambiguities and seeming contradictions abound in a world we once thought essentially simple, indeed bipolar. At Cabinda in Angola, Cuban communist troops have for years been guarding capitalist Gulf Oil's refinery. The Soviet Union and the United Kingdom have been deliberately 'laundering' South African uranium by converting it to hexachloride to by-pass United States sanctions against South African products. Communist China, now rife with capitalist enterprise, leapt to the rescue of Hong Kong's stock exchange in the October 1987[2] crash and Britain continues to aid Marxist Mozambique.

In the Soviet Union differential birth rates mean Muslims are on the way to becoming a large proportion of the population. For similar reasons, Arabs in Israel and the Occupied Territories could well equal the Jewish population within 30 years. Meanwhile, in the *intifada*, Arab women and children with sticks and stones, are testing Israeli 'security' far more effectively than would most Arab forces of highly armed men. At the same time, new varieties of unintended violence are being inflicted on people by economic orthodoxies. Amidst a torrent of self-interested rhetoric about the virtues of a free market, the West has lent grotesque sums at outrageous interest rates to Third World countries and is now inflicting on them what has been called Financial Low Intensity Conflict (FLIC) — the erosion of living standards, social security and powers of decision-making that are implicit in the International Monetary Fund's enforced austerity programmes. (Other victims of current orthodoxy live just down the road from IMF's Washington headquarters. A 1987[3] report said 20 million Americans were going hungry and over 35 million subsisting below the US poverty line.)

Other indirect threats to security are also developing. The astronomer Sir Bernard Lovell has warned that accumulating man-made debris in space could knock out military satellites and precipitate war. The drug trade has become the world's second biggest, paying no respect to frontiers. AIDs is expected to strike 400,000 more people in the next two years and serious observers fear Africa may eventually be decimated by it. Terrorism is likewise demanding international collaboration, not least when powered by fanaticisms like that aimed at Salman Rushdie. Napoleon warned long ago that moral to material factors were as ten to one. Yet the world has yet to learn that ideas and emotions can be more powerful than tanks. Ask the Poles.

An increasingly pluralistic world no longer fits the simplistic world-picture to which most of our leaders still obstinately cling. Both Superpowers are having to draw in their horns from Afghanistan to Nicaragua. Nor is the magic of their nuclear armouries what it was. The Soviet people are demanding living standards more like Czechoslovakia's if not the West's, and the United States is lamely assembling advanced goods produced by previously 'backward' countries around the Pacific Rim. Indeed, some Americans fear the United States, now the world's biggest debtor, is still being obsessed by a quasi-military struggle with Russia while losing a more crucial economic struggle with Japan.

The Gorbachev Phenomenon

The Soviet President has shown far more alertness to the polycentricity and profound interdependence of our fast-changing world than any other national leader. His astonishing address of 7 December 1988[4] to the United Nations General Assembly may later be seen as the beginning of a new era. This is not because he announced big military cuts, nor even because he deprived Americans of their enemy. What he did, as Peter Jenkins has pointed out[5] was to deprive the Soviet peoples of *their enemy*, the wicked war-mongering capitalist imperialist West.

In doing so Mr Gorbachev also started speaking the necessary political language of the third millenium. He managed, I think, to strike most of what will be its essential notes: the 'fundamental limits of nuclear weapons'; 'the problem of mankind's survival'; the 'global nature' of most serious problems; the world economy as a 'single organism'; 'the contradictions and limits inherent in traditional-type industrialisation'; the threat of 'environmental catastrophe'; the gap between the developed and developing countries and the need for a 'universal human consensus' guided by the 'primacy of universal human values'.

He went even further. In coupling the French and Russian revolutions, (effectively consigning them equally to an heroic past) and in declaring 'closed societies' now to be impossible, he made space for a new universal revolution by consent. Freedom of choice was now 'mandatory' and 'not simply out of good intentions . . . [but] by an unbiased analysis of . . . objective trends'. The Soviet President was not asking us (or his reactionary colleagues at home) to believe in his virtue but to share his analysis.

Hostile critics said fine talk was cheap and wrote off as much as they could as propaganda. Friendlier ones remained concerned that freedom of choice did not seem to apply within the Soviet bloc. (Soon afterwards Mr Gorbachev was to say, 'A multi-party system, two parties, three parties, it is all rubbish'.) Everyone of course agrees that actions will be the test yet the words do represent a tremendous change in Soviet thinking. It is already a revolutionary act for a Marxist leader to say 'the very concept of the nature and the criteria of progress is changing'. Such recognitions would be welcome closer to home.

Persisting Dangers

When such a speech follows the INF Treaty, the withdrawals from Afghanistan and Angola, the ending of the Iran-Iraq war and the revitalisation of talks on European security, it is too easy to imagine that the real global challenge is almost over. The perturbing reality is of course that an increasingly polycentric world is not necessarily more stable. All the materials for the ignition of unintended war are still in place. The technological arms race continues as does the worldwide arms trade. About $900 billion a year is still being spent on military security. With only two weeks' worth we could pay for major United Nations programmes on contraception, clean water and sanitation, reafforestation and anti-desertification. Calculations by the Worldwatch Institute[6] suggest that expenditure of about $50 billion rising to $150 billion a year would provide sufficiently rounded programmes to achieve sub-stainable global development within a decade, including the effective retirement of Third World debt.

A Menacing Orthodoxy

Unfortunately, perhaps tragically, many of the currently dominant ideas in the West seem almost supremely ill-suited to a gathering global crisis of escalating numbers pressing on scarce resources. We have an ethic of personal success rather than general welfare; of 'loads-a'money' hedonism rather than restraint; of 'fast track' enterprise rather than prudence; of short-term profit rather than far-sighted benefit; of exploitation rather than conservation; of stimulated wants rather than essential needs; of national 'pride' rather than international responsibility; or rampant individualism ('society doesn't exist') rather than collective obligation.

In part, all our current political orthodoxies are now suspect. It is symptomatic of our condition that more than half the total expected loss of 275 billion tons of top soil over the coming decade will occur in only four countries, the United States, the Soviet Union, China and India, which respectively exemplify the world's four dominant ideologies — liberal capitalism, Soviet Communism, Chinese Communism and the mix often called social democracy. Beneath their political differences, all four share a simplistic materialism, an evangelical dediction to 'growth' and a blithe negligence towards the earth. Like virtually all present governments, they share a suspect economic orthodoxy and a ludicrous optimism about the limits of this planet. As Norman Myers has said, we behave as if we have a spare planet just parked ready in space.

A Sustainable Society

This is not, of course, to denigrate enterprise or self-help as such nor necessarily to advocate general state ownership or stifling welfare dependencies. There need be no stark choice between new-style 'blue' and old-style 'red' politics. Much depends on what we regard as real 'wealth' or 'growth'. How much social and environmental damage of kinds that are not measured by the money nexus do they allow for? What of things that have no price, like clean air or community feeling or individual meaning? What weight should we put upon the legitimate needs of so-called 'failures', whether people or nations? How far does the current economic orthodoxy take account of the needs of future generations? (This is plainly not the place to attempt answers to these riddles but on any adequate broad view of long-term security, a new 'spaceship' economics seems essential. (Might a mixture of 'red' and 'blue' with a good dash of 'green' produce khaki — an Urdu word for earth!)

Clearly, a sustainable society is one that satisfies its essential needs without diminishing the prospects of future generations. It is also one that respects the natural world in its own right, not merely as the plaything of one species. To sanctify as 'economic progress' that which leads to social and environmental disintegration through poverty, ill-health and the despairing slash-and-burn of the poor peasant is insane, not merely 'wrong'. And despoiling the earth is not just a mistake: it is a blasphemy.

A Revaluation of Values

Behind all the issues of security we find questions about values. A sustainable world society can hardly be constructed on the attitudes and values of a yuppy, nor, for that matter, on those of a wholly man-centred social engineer. The necessary revaluation of our values has to take full account not only of our social and international interdependency but of our profound biological interdependency with the natural world. Nor will the revaluation run deep enough if we do not brave some self-analysis, more, certainly, than contemporary man finds comfortable. We are none of us quite as straightforward as we sometimes imagine. Nor are our real attitudes: none of us is wholly immune to the wider world's irrationalities, hatreds and prejudices. The American psychologist I L Janis[7] has shown for example how otherwise intelligent and independently-minded American officers in Vietnam could develop a shared illusion of invulnerability and high morality. 'Group thinking' mechanisms included the reasoning away of awkward information, a shared myth of the group's unanimity and, not least, the stereotyping of the enemy as too evil for negotiation or too feeble to be a threat.

Similar processes plainly affect the individual voter, opinion-leader or policy-maker in facing, or not facing, the new global agenda. Nor do hawks have a monopoly of tunnel-vision, paranoia and self-righteousness. Doves, too, have their prejudices and not a little psychic violence — and so do owls! Any of us may be afflicted by the ancient mechanisms of reality avoidance, denial and projection. The psychoanalyst C G Jung told us that in any murder, we are all in part the judge, the victim and the murderer. We are members of one another and of one another's crimes, yet we insist on regarding ourselves as pleasantly harmless, well-meaning people. In fact, through the various groups, institutions, nations and alliances to which we actively or passively belong, we are all perforce entangled in skeins of institutionalised fear, greed, ambition and, not least, complacent inertia. There is some health in us but too much harm, for which we refuse to take responsibility. We are a little too much like the rich aristocrat walking by the river bank who, hearing a poor drowning wretch call out that he cannot swim, replies 'I can't either but I don't make such a fuss about it'.

In arguing in effect that only consciousness can rescue humankind from itself, I am not proposing some great process of moral rearmament. There is less hope in commandments than in the capacity to see the truth of what we are doing, right, wrong or mixed. Without that first requirement we merely stumble about in the dark. It may be even more important to know what we do—not least by passivity—than to do the 'right' thing. There is a wise Spanish proverb: 'Take what you can, said God: take it and pay for it.'

Take the West's largely unconscious hypocrisy over Pol Pot and the Khmer Rouge or the fearful torture and oppression in Turkey, a NATO ally. My old 'realistic' Foreign Office colleagues frown on morality being allowed to threaten the necessary compromises of power politics. But this misses the point. Consciousness does not condemn necessary compromise but it does condemn the unconscious double standard. Only by acknowledging and weighing our own dark side can we stop fooling ourselves about what we are doing. One of the most insidious and perilous vices in international (as in personal) life is 'sincerity'—our truly awful capacity to believe our own propaganda. Greater consciousness would sharpen our sense of how West and East—and many of the élites of the Poor South—are still trapped in exploitation, extravagance, self-serving humbug and profound moral confusion. This awareness might also curb our readiness to threaten or use the most appalling sorts of violence in somewhat narrow and self-interested causes and encourage our readiness to make sacrifices for broader ones.

We need to recognise how the self-righteous politics of the powerful may generate the fury of the weak; of how the rich nations' tying of trade to aid can only humiliate the poor; of how our own inaction over injustice makes others despair of gradualism. We need to see how our own passivity may turn others into terrorists.

Working With Paradoxes

Perhaps to know what we do — a deceptively simple-sounding task — is our overriding obligation. In politics, at least, it may be wrong to strive for perfection. It is not only unattainable: its Utopian exponents, East, West or elsewhere, prove insufferable at best, ruthless at worst. The 'saved' swiftly become conscienceless. Nevertheless, we have to accept that real care about human consequences always involves some compromise and paradox. In the name of peace, we have to employ the military and may sometimes have to treat with militarists. In the interests of freedom, we may have to cut (limited) deals with tyrannies. For the sake of development, we must sometimes risk subsidising the wasteful and even the partly corrupt. In the cause of a wider welfare we may sometimes even need to sacrifice the interests of the innocent. (How else, for example, can you pursue a policy of refusing to deal with terrorists?) None of these compromises should we make easily but politics is a rough old trade and sometimes unbearably cruel and approximate.

Hawks and doves alike should be more aware that we need both sensitivity and power, conciliation and main strength. International order sometimes requires an ultimate resort to sanctions in addition to moral persuasion. A conflict-free world is quite impossible and an ultimate threat of violence is not always criminal or psychotic.

Our first collective task, as I hope I have shown, is not to abolish violence but to manage it and in particular to reduce towards vanishing point the chance of another major war or of nuclear weapons ever being exploded again. Our second is to contrive a sustainable future, politically and biologically. To do these things we have to work along the grain of life, work with the mean and petty motives of men and nations as well as the generous and grand. And this is precisely to compromise with evil, in ourselves as well as others, but without tipping over backwards into mere cynicism. Once again we walk a tightrope. And we need all sorts of perspective. As Professor James O'Connell has remarked, we need not only the 'kings' who appreciate and wield power and the 'prophets' who risk odium by warning from the margins of society,

but the 'brokers' who can communicate between them and deal
with the centre.

Creative Diplomacy and the Revaluation
of the Feminine

Talk of the feminine may to some seem off the point but it may
become central now that survival depends more on co-operation
than competition, on intelligent care more than brute strength. We
must try to redress the gross imbalance not only between the
numbers of men and women involved in the machineries of policy-
making but also between the masculine and feminine aspects of our
individual thinking. Pierre Trudeau often warned against 'macho-
diplomacy' but basic policy analysis has itself been excessively
'macho', power-centred and quantitative ('How many divisions
has the Pope?') and has tended to neglect the personal, the
intuitive and the qualitative.

A holistic and nurturing approach that puts personal relations at
the centre of our thinking need not be soft, sentimental or in the
slightest bit vague. For example, the Soviet Union has great armies
but the Russians are people. We need to know them, as they need
to know us. Yet Russian language teaching, and Soviet studies,
have been sadly declining in both the United States and Britain.
Scores of schools and colleges in both countries have dropped them
altogether. Few American or British officials have visited the Soviet
Union except as Embassy staff. Obsessions with secrecy can indi-
rectly foster false images of complex realities. One Reagan adviser
dismissed the idea of visiting Moscow by saying: 'You don't need to
be hit by a locomotive to know it's dangerous'.

Too often East and West have characterised their relations with
the typically masculine models of poker, chess and the zero-sum
game: they lose, therefore we win. The deals we now need are those
from which both gain: the negotiators need to spend time together,
stand back from the problems, share common fears, define common interests. They should use role-reversal techniques to explore
each other's positions, to check their own perceptions and to find
alternative ways forward.

The slow, grave, ceremonial arts of traditional diplomacy need
both honouring and deliberate development. There is a rich,
neglected reservoir of relevant experience in industrial conciliation,
commercial arbitrage and, come to that, in marriage counselling.

New ways of settling differences should be explored, whether in the context of straight negotiation, mediation, crisis management, peace-keeping, the use of law or ultimately the application of sanctions.

Yes, the issues are complex. Yes, we must beware amateurs and exotic notions. Yes, we must prepare well, be cautious. Quite so. But we must also be bolder, more imaginative, get up some steam. As launch-on-warning technologies accelerate, the true voice of caution may be that calling for audacity. A successful START would be a good beginning, but we need proposals rivalling Sadat's descent on Jerusalem or Nixon's on Beijing. Momentum is needed, not just to achieve common security between East and West but to dramatise the new global agenda and mobilise the essential political will.

A Time for Audacity: Seven Proposals for Urgent Action

In a speech of 12 May 1989, President Bush spoke of moving beyond containment to a new policy for the 1990s with the ultimate objective of welcoming the Soviet Union back into the world order. But he also stressed the need to step carefully, for example by retaining the military might 'to convince the Soviet Union that there can be no reward in pursuing expansionism'. Some of the President's advisers are known to be warning that President Gorbachev's grip on power may be fragile and that his successors might revert to type. Other advisers argue that the reform process would anyway survive him. I strongly believe this and that the world needs both the measures and the man. To keep both, to regain some Western reputation for peacemaking and, most important of all, to deserve it, the West should now, in its various overlapping fora, prepare and present a series of measures deliberately cast in the global, not just the East – West, context. In the process, it must show it understands that arms control in Europe treats a local symptom, not the root disease. Otherwise the West is in danger of plucking defeat out of the jaws of victory. The Cold War has in a sense been won but in addition to curbing the remaining dangers of the old world order we must set about the even more fundamental challenges of creating the new.

The time is therefore ripe for audacious Western proposals generously conceived. Our task is far wider than that of integrating the Soviet Union into the community of nations. As a prelude to the much broader global programme described in the last chapter the West should decide on seven major actions. *First*, to make the sort of arms proposals suggested in Chapters 12 and 13 to test Moscow's willingness to implement a regime of common security in Central Europe. *Secondly*, directly to assist Mr Gorbachev's reform programme with economic and, especially, technical, managerial and marketing assistance in what will no doubt be dubbed a new Marshall Plan. *Thirdly*, it should encourage *glasnost* in Eastern Europe by doing the same there. *Fourthly*, it should collaborate in radical action to resolve the Third World debt crisis. *Fifthly*, not least for its symbolic value, it should help provide for a major expansion of the United Nations Disaster Relief Organisation (UNDRO) within which new habits of co-operation can be practised and dramatised. *Sixthly*, it should do the same for the United Nations Environmental Programme (UNEP) both for its own sake and again as a major exercise in public education. *Seventhly*, it should propose that eminent scientists and others be convened in a serious systematic international effort to speculate freely in a 'futures studies' spirit about a wide range of possible future developments on a 20-year (or more) time scale. The sooner this starts, the sooner we might make sensible global policies.

Some of these proposals involve a few risks but they are worth running in a world whose arsenals have over 5,000 times the explosive power used in the Second World War; in which even Brazil, crippled by debt, has 100,000 working in its arms factories; in which Washington still finds it necessary to have military exercises involving 200,000 troops in Korea, and to have over five million men under arms.

Such preliminaries to tackling the global agenda may provoke cries of 'idealism!' from hawks and 'compromise!' from doves. Yet I hope I have shown that the owl's method of purposeful, non-doctrinaire navigation lacks neither realism nor a measured sense of urgency. The 'moderate' course is not weak or tentative: in refusing extremes it can be as radical as it is fruitful. To 'plot' peace is to respect complexity and uncertainty and to refuse the siren attractions of the 'mega-answer'. It reflects the courage to face up to big problems while recognising that there may only be small answers, albeit a wide and fertile array of them.

This purposeful pragmatism has at root been this book's response to the nuclear dilemma and its cruel wider setting. The problem is strictly insoluble but it can be managed. The bomb cannot be abolished but our obsessive concern with it can be steadily reduced as our sense of other problems, especially population and consumerist pressures, grow. Psychologically, what we have desperately needed has been a greater menace than either the Russians or the Bomb. The foe from Mars did not materialise but new perils on our own planet have created superordinate goals which are crying out, perhaps just in time. for co-operation in place of the old antagonism.

If there are old and new fears, there are also new hopes dramatised by the global eradication of smallpox for the price of half-a-day's arms. But the larger hope must partly lie in a quality of vision and leadership exemplified by, say, Paul-Henri Spaak and Jean Monnet in transcending Franco-German enmity and founding the European Community. Such leadership will not emerge or flourish if we continue to project the shadow of our own individual and collective evils on to the enemy outside, whether the Soviet Union, Khomeini-type Islam or other nations, races or ideologies. Nor, for that matter, can leadership get far if we continue passively to accept the premature death of 50,000 people a day — two-thirds of them children under five — from 'readily preventable diseases'[8].

Making a Difference

Can the individual do anything? The simple answer is 'Yes, a lot'. It is a matter of applying oneself, learning the ropes, making contacts, building skills, joining others, using ingenuity, blowing the whistle, resisting the lies, spreading the facts, listening to others as well as speaking out, and trying not to be too boring! And since public apathy and ignorance is considerable (apparently one in eight Britons cannot even place their homeland on a world map), the views of the active citizen can profit from a huge (even embarrassing) 'multiplier' effect. As the anthropologist Margaret Mead once said: 'Never doubt that a small group of thoughtful committed citizens can change the world; indeed it is the only thing that ever has'.

We may, however, need encouragement from sources deeper than cheerful classes in good citizenship. In the end an entirely secular analysis of our condition may not suffice. Some say we may have been losing a necessary perspective of an eternity both behind us and before us. We are learning that if we continue to live for today there will be no tomorrow; that if we abuse Nature, we destroy ourselves.

To face reality as it is, we need to see beyond purely contemporary concerns and reach beyond a simple-minded choice between an optimism that implies that nothing *needs* to be done and a pessimism that suggests that nothing *can* be done. To keep us going, despite sometimes shallow hopes and sometimes threatening despair, we may need gifts of the spirit that some call Grace. It is sometimes suggested that we must allow a re-enchantment of the Earth. Perhaps the reverence to be detected in the flood of new documentaries on the natural world is witness to its beginning. Certainly we shall not save Creation unless we renew not just our recognition of its usefulness but our love for it — and for ourselves within it.

Whenever the Tornado aircraft scream low over the woods above our cottage, I am reminded that our governments are still in essence seeking peace by preparing for war rather than by managing conflict and reducing confrontation to secure a common future. Then I do feel despair. I did so also in December 1988 on hearing of the murder of Francisco Mendes, the Brazilian campaigner for the Amazon forests. Yet light sometimes breaks through the deepest darkness. After the Armenian earthquake in the same month there was a marvellous torrent of help from Britain as elsewhere: money, blankets, people. A team of kidney specialists returned at Christmas describing fearful horrors including three 'crush syndrome' patients lying among slime and cockroaches with one leg between them. The courage and resilience of the Armenians and Russians had been marvellous. After weeks of work, the team reckoned to have saved 15 lives but, as they were leaving, one seemingly comatose patient had suddenly risen to kiss them goodbye. Perhaps, he would be a 16th, they said. Such treasuring of individual lives is a wonder and a beacon.

A few weeks later, as the last Soviet tanks rumbled out of Kabul, Soviet *Afghantsi* and American Vietnam veterans met in Moscow to share their dreadful experiences of post-traumatic stress. The senior American veteran placed his service medal on the only Soviet memorial to the dead. Soviet and American veterans grasped each others' shoulders and shed tears for the lost lives of two continents. Packing his suitcase, one American said: 'Coming here for me was like returning to the combat zone, but without the damn guns. Like the *Afghantsi*, my own battle must continue as an internal one. It is just a shame so many people had to pay such a high price for my education.'

Epilogue

On Sunday June 4, 1989, while finishing this book, two momentous events seized the headlines. One was the vicious slaughter of the admirably non-violent student protestors in Beijing's Tiananmen Square by units of the People's Liberation Army: the other, possibly no less significant, was the Polish Solidarity Movement's crushing electoral victory against all the efforts of an entrenched regime.

A few days later the people of our tiny village had invited a charming Romanian dissenter to discuss their plan — the first in England — to 'pair' with one of his country's Hungarian-populated villages threatened by Ceaucescu's foul resettlement policy. During our conversation he asked how I saw so astonishing a conjunction of events at opposite ends of the Communist world.

Thinking about it later I concluded that the conjunction could be seen as a powerful warning alike to doves and hawks.

To doves the Beijing massacre insisted that in this world there is no inevitability to progress and that the most savage potentialities have always to be guarded against.

Yet likewise, the Polish experience insisted to hawks that there are strengths more powerful than arms, that the enduring courage of people seeking freedom, when combined with the self-interested restraint of an otherwise repressive regime (and of its foreign opponents), can still offer measured hope where there had once been measureless despair.

The absolute dove cannot readily accommodate so awful an event as the abrupt regression to savagery of a supposedly reforming (and singularly unthreatened) régime. Nor could the traditional hawk have believed only a year or two ago what we are now seeing in most of Eastern Europe and, of course, in the Soviet Union itself.

The owl, however, is surprised neither by the pitiful horror of Beijing's rape nor the staggering, if still partial, emergence of democracy within the gates of a repressive ideology. For him or her both the horror and the hope are the permanent possibilities implicit in all life and therefore in all political activity: any policies that leave either out of account, or discount either firmness or conciliation, are likely to lead to irrelevance at best, disaster at worst.

Yet way beyond that debate, the convulsive events in China and Poland both demonstrate a remarkable swelling of the appetite for freedom and individual dignity that is also to be seen from Russia to South Africa, from Central America to the Philippines. For all its highs and lows, 1989 might come to be seen as an *annus mirabilis*, as potent a symbol as 1789. And as the Chinese students and workers showed, we are seeing a rejection of capitalist corruption and privilege as well as of Communist repressions. The hunger striking signatories of the June 2 Declaration called for the birth of a new political culture.

They spoke of a democratic politics 'without enemies, without hatred . . . based on mutual respect . . . and equality.' Though they called for the Prime Minister's resignation, they declared 'Ling Peng is not our enemy — he should still enjoy the right to maintain his mistaken ideas.' There was no want of modesty or self-criticism in their own thinking: 'We protest, we appeal, we repent. We are not in search of death; we are looking for real life.' The note of anxious maturity is almost heart-breaking when we think of the ruthless old cynics whose orders were just about to violate so many young bodies.

There are lessons for everyone in this betrayal, not least that the unexpected often happens and that we know much less than we often pretend or believe. Yet just as one light died, so another, Polish, spark quickened into flame. The most remarkable good can come out of evil; astonishing hope out of the deepest darkness. Perhaps there is at least one sense in which we do need to put Jerusalem back into the centre of our mental map of the world, as it is in Richard de Bello's Mappa Mundi, further down our valley. And not just as a holy city for three great faiths but as a symbol of the spiritual heart that our world society will need if it is to become sustainable.

Yet realism insists that our mental map must likewise show the demons. Like those Americans and Russian veterans, we are learning that the evils lie not only outside us but within. Plotting peace is also an interior task.

References

Introduction

1. Ronald Higgins, *The Seventh Enemy: the Human Factor in the Global Crisis* (Hodder, 1982).

Part I Diagnosis

Chapter 1. Looking Life in the Eyes

1. *Catholics and Nuclear War: A Commentary on the Challenge of Peace* (Crossroads, New York, 1983).
2. Robert Jay Lifton, *Indefensible Weapons* (Basic Books, New York, 1982).
3. Jim Garrison, *The Darkness of God* (SCM, 1982).
4. Jonathan Schell, *The Fate of the Earth* (Picador, 1982).
5. Willis Harman, *Resurgence*, July 1985.

Chapter 2. Humanity's Triple Crisis

1. Robert McNamara, *Foreign Affairs*, Summer 1984.
2. William Gutteridge, *European Society, Nuclear Weapons and Public Confidence* (Macmillan, 1982)
3. Alvin Toffler, *Future Shock* (Pan, 1973).
4. Brandt Commission, *North-South, A Programme for Survival* (Pan, 1980).
5. World Commission on Environment and Development, *Our Common Future* (OUP, 1987).

Chapter 3. The Effects and Chances of Nuclear War

1. J. K. Galbraith, *The New Yorker*, 3 September 1984.
2. Andrew Wilson, *The Disarmers Handbook*, Penguin, 1983.
3. Ed. M. Riordan, *The Day after Midnight* (Cheshire, 1982).
4. Ed. Eric Chirian et al, *Last Aid* (Freeman, San Francisco, 1982).
5. *Ibid.*
6. R. Scheer, *With Enough Shovels* (Secker, 1983).
7. Office of Technology Assessment of the US Congress, *The Effects of Nuclear War*, Washington DC, 1979.

8. Paul R Erlich and others, *The Cold and the Dark* (Sidgwick, 1984).
9. Lord Carver, *A Policy for Peace* (Faber, 1982).
10. *The Guardian*, 9 October 1975.
11. Desmond Ball, *Can Nuclear War be Controlled?* (Adelphi Paper No. 169, IISS).
12. J. Steinbrunner, 'National Security and the Concept of Strategic Stability', *Journal of Conflict Resolution*, September 1978.
13. Desmond Ball, *op. cit.*

Chapter 4. Hawks versus Doves: A Sterile Debate

1. Ed. J. E. Dougherty, *Ethics, Deterrence and National Security* (Brassey's 1985).
2. Robert Jay Lifton and Richard Falk, *Indispensible Weapons* (Basic Books, New York, 1982).
3. *The Guardian*, 16 December 1988.
4. Oliver Ramsbotham, *Choices: Nuclear and Non-Nuclear Defence Options* (Brassey's, 1987).

Chapter 5. Politics as Process

1. Thomas Hobbes, *Leviathan* (Penguin, 1981).
2. Roger Fisher and William Ury, *Getting to YES* (Hutchinson, 1983).

Chapter 6. Six Questionable Policies

1. Cited Paul Nitze, *Foreign Policy*, Winter 1974.
2. John Ferguson, *Disarmament: The Unanswerable Case* (Heinemann, 1982).
3. American readers are warned that I use 'owl' somewhat differently than the authors of '*Hawks, Doves and Owls*' (Ed. Graham T Allison et al, W. W. Norton, New York, 1985.)

Part II Towards Treatment

Chapter 7. Peace, War and the Redefinition of Security

1. *Adelphi Paper* No. 216, 1987.
2. Wendell Berry, *Resurgence*, Jan/Feb 1987
3. K.M. von Clausewitz, *On War* (Princetown U.P., 1976).
4. Lord Carver, *A Policy for Peace*, (Faber, 1982).
5. Stan Windass, *The Rite of War*, (Brassey's, 1988).

Chapter 8. Two Troubled Giants

1. Richard Nixon, *1999: Victory without War*, (Simon and Schuster, 1988).
2. *Soviet Military Power 1988*, (Pentagon, Washington, 1988).
3. Cited in Dean Acheson, *Present at the Creation*, (Norton, 1969).
4. Barbara Tuchman, Essay in *America's Security in the 1980s* Part I, (Adelphi Paper No. 173, IISS, 1982).

References

Chapter 9. NATO's Current Policies: Pseudo-strength, Genuine Confusion

1. Desmond Ball, *Targeting for Strategic Deterrence*, (Adelphi Paper No. 185, IISS, 1983).
2. *The Guardian*, 30 November 1984.
3. Paul Bracken, *The Command and Control of Nuclear Forces*, (Yale U.P. 1983).
4. Morton Halperin, *Nuclear Fallacy*, (Ballinger, 1987).
5. *The Independent*, 6 June 1988.
6. Thomas Schelling, *The Strategy of Conflict*, (Harvard U.P. 1960).
7. Oliver Ramsbotham, *Choices: Nuclear and Non-Nuclear Defence Options*, (Brassey's, 1987).

Part III From Competitive to Co-operative Security

Chapter 10. The Philosophy of the Owl: Co-operative Security

1. McGeorge Bundy et al, 'Nuclear Weapons and the Atlantic Alliance', *Foreign Affairs*, Spring 1982.
2. Introduction, Palme Commission, *Common Security*, (Pan, 1982).
3. Hugh Hanning, *Peace: The Plain Man's Guide to War Prevention*, (Cecil Woolf, 1988).
4. *Choices*, (Brassey's, 1987) *op. cit.*
5. McGeorge Bundy et al, 'Nuclear Weapons and the Atlantic Alliance', *Foreign Affairs*, Spring 1982.
6. Cited by Freeman Dyson, *Weapons and Hope*, (Harper 1984).
7. *Choices* (Brassey's, 1987) *op. cit.*
8. Robert McNamara, *Blundering into Disaster*, (Bloomsbury, 1987).
9. Council for a Livable World, *Newsletter*, January 1989.
10. McGeorge Bundy, *Foreign Affairs*, October 1969.
11. Symposium on Global Security in the Twenty-First Century, UN, 1987.

Chapter 11. Co-operative Security in Practice

1. Paul Bracken, *The Command and Control of Nuclear Forces*, (Yale U.P., 1983).
2. *Ibid*
3. Peter Hayes et al *American Lake*, (Penguin, 1987).
4. *Bulletin of the Atomic Scientists*, September 1988.
5. Independent Commission on Disarmament and Security Issues, *Common Security*, (Pan, 1982).

Chapter 12. The Security of Western Europe

1. Jonathan Dean, *Watershed in Europe*, (Lexington, 1987).
2. Henry Kissinger, *Survival*, Sept/Oct 1982, IISS.
3. *Ibid*

4. Commission on Integrated Long-term Strategy, *Discriminate Deterrence*, US Department of Defence, 1988.
5. *The Military Balance*, 1986–7, (IISS, 1987).
6. *The Economist*, 30 August 1986.
7. Diminishing the Nuclear Threat, (British Atlantic Committee, 1984).
8. *The Guardian*, 25 November 1987.
9. *The Military Balance*, 1987–8, (IISS, 1988).
10. Robert McNamara, *Blundering into Disaster*, (Bloomsbury, 1987).
11. Cited in *Bulletin of the Atomic Scientists*, September 1988.
12. Stan Windass, *The Rite of War*, (Brassey's, 1986).
13. Frank Barnaby, *The Automated Battlefield*, (OUP, 1987).
14. *Bulletin of the Atomic Scientists*, December 1987.
15. Sir Leon Brittan, *Defence and Arms Control in a Changing Era*, (PSI, 1988).

Chapter 13. Reducing Nuclear Dependency: An Audacious Response to President Gorbachev

1. Cited in Oliver Ramsbotham, *Choices*, (Brassey's, 1987). *op. cit.*
2. *Nuclear Deterrence Post-INF*, Paper for House of Commons, Ministry of Defence, January 1988.
3. *Diminishing the Nuclear Threat*. (British Atlantic Committee, 1984).
4. Paul Rogers, *New Statesman*, 4 December 1987.
5. *Ibid.*
6. McGeorge Bundy et al, 'Nuclear Weapons and the Atlantic Alliance', *Foreign Affairs*, Spring 1982.
7. Palme Commission, *Common Security: A Programme for Security*, (Pan, 1982).
8. Leon Brittan MP, *Defence and Arms Control in a Changing Era*, (PSI, 1988).
9. Lord Carver, *Nuclear Weapons in Europe*, (Council for Arms Control, 1983).
10. Hans Binnendijk, 'NATO's nuclear modernisation dilemma', *Survival*, March/April 1989.
11. Oliver Ramsbotham, *Modernizing NATO's Nuclear Weapons*, (Macmillan/Oxford Research Group, 1989).
12. *The Independent*, 30 December 1988.

Chapter 14. Thinking Ahead: Europe's Choice of Future

1. Cited in Oliver Ramsbotham, *Choices*, (Brassey's, 1987). *op. cit.*
2. Christopher Layton, *A Step Beyond Fear*, (Federal Trust, 1989).

Chapter 15. Towards a Sustainable World Order

1. World Commission on Environment and Development, *Our Common Future* (OUP, 1987).
2. Brandt Commission, *North-South, A Programme for Survival*, (Pan, 1980).

3. Dr Norman Myers, 'Population, Environment, and Conflict', *Environmental Conservation* Vol 14, No. 1, Spring 1987.
4. Population Bulletin of the United Nations, No. 14, 1982. New York, 1983.
5. *The Independent*, 26 September 1988.

Chapter 16. Politics and People

1. *The Observer*, 11 October 1987.
2. *Financial Times*, 31 October 1987.
3. *The Guardian*, 7 December 1987.
4. Address at the United Nations, Novosti, Moscow, 1988.
5. *The Independent*, 21 December 1988.
6. Lester R Brown (Ed), *State of the World 1988* (W W Norton.)
7. I L Janis, *British Journal of Medical Psychology*, 36, 1963.
8. *The Independent*, 9 August 1988.
9. *The Guardian*, 2 February 1989.

Index

Index

223

Index

Index